Democratic Laboratories

Democratic Laboratories

Policy Diffusion among the American States

ANDREW KARCH

The University of Michigan Press   *Ann Arbor*

Published in the United States of America by
The University of Michigan Press
Manufactured in the United States of America
♾ Printed on acid-free paper

2010   2009   2008   2007   4   3   2   1

A CIP catalog record for this book is available from the British Library.

Library of Congress Cataloging-in-Publication Data

Karch, Andrew, 1975–
    Democratic laboratories : policy diffusion among the American
states / Andrew Karch.
        p.   cm.
    Includes bibliographical references and index.
    ISBN-13: 978-0-472-09968-9 (cloth : alk. paper)
    ISBN-10: 0-472-09968-X (cloth : alk. paper)
    ISBN-13: 978-0-472-06968-2 (pbk. : alk. paper)
    ISBN-10: 0-472-06968-3 (pbk. : alk. paper)
        1. Political planning—United States.   2. Diffusion of
innovations—United States.   I. Title.

JK468.P64.K37   2007
320.60973—dc22   2006020165

For my parents, Debbie and Harvey Karch

Acknowledgments

I AM EXTREMELY GRATEFUL for the generous guidance, support, and encouragement that I received from many individuals during the course of this project. I want to begin by thanking the members of my dissertation committee: Theda Skocpol, Paul Pierson, and Barry Burden. Their assistance at all stages of the project was invaluable. Their probing questions as I developed the project made sure I was headed down the right path, and their extensive feedback ensured that I never wandered too far off course as I made the seemingly endless transition from dissertation prospectus draft to completed book. I also benefited immensely from constructive suggestions and thoughtful comments provided by my fellow travelers in the subfields of state politics and public policy, my graduate school colleagues, and my departmental colleagues at the University of Texas at Austin. The following list is by no means exhaustive, but I would especially like to thank Chris Mooney, David Lowery, Craig Volden, Virginia Gray, Scott Allard, Jill Clark, Charles Lockhart, Ben Deufel, Dave Campbell, Kristin Goss, Rob Van Houweling, Rob Fannion, Orit Kedar, Alan Jacobs, Christian Brunelli, Jal Mehta, Katerina Linos, Chris Adolph, Victor Shih, Kurt Weyland, John Sides, Corrine McConnaughy, Sean Theriault, Ken Greene, and Bat Sparrow for their helpful comments and suggestions at various stages of the project. Of course, none of them should be held responsible for any shortcomings that remain in the final product.

Several individuals with an intimate knowledge of state policy-making also made valuable contributions to this book. I especially want to thank the legislators, committee staff, executive branch officials, lobbyists, and professional association staff who took time out of their busy schedules to share their thoughts with me. I am also grateful to the reference librarians in Massachusetts, Oregon, and Virginia who helped me navigate the archival materials in those three states.

Several institutions provided financial support that made this project possible. I wish to thank the National Science Foundation, the Brookings Institution, the Domestic Public Policy Program of the Smith Richardson Foundation, the College of Liberal Arts and the Department of Government at the University of Texas at Austin, and the Center for American Political Studies and the Multidisciplinary Program in Inequality and Social Policy at Harvard University for providing research funds to speed the completion of this book. Parts of chapter 2 appeared in slightly different form in "National Intervention and the Diffusion of Policy Innovations," *American Politics Research* 34, no. 4 (July 2006): 403–27. I appreciate the willingness of Sage Publications to allow the publication of a revised version here. I am also grateful for my association with the University of Michigan Press. Amy Fuller, Kevin Rennells, and especially Jim Reische made the publication process surprisingly painless even though their definition of a "fun pack" differs substantially from my own.

Most of all, I wish to express my heartfelt thanks to my family, which has been my most important source of support for as long as I can remember. My wife, Kaori, has been extremely supportive from start to finish. Our paths initially crossed in college when we became neighbors after my roommates and I won last pick in a housing lottery. It is undoubtedly the luckiest break that I have ever caught. Special thanks also go to my sister, Lisa, who taught me that no accomplishment is too small to be celebrated with a congratulatory ice cream. This book is dedicated to my parents. It is an honor and a privilege to be their son. Although my mother died very suddenly during my last year in graduate school, not a day goes by that I do not think of her warmth and her sense of humor. She and my father taught me all of life's truly important lessons and will always be my role models.

Contents

I. *Introduction: The Politics of Policy Diffusion*

How do new ideas spread? What turns a little-known product or behavior into something with widespread popularity? These straightforward questions have captured the popular imagination. Malcolm Gladwell recently wrote a national best seller devoted to the notion that "ideas and products and messages and behaviors spread just like viruses do" (2002, 7). He argued that the best way to understand the emergence of such phenomena as fashion trends and crime waves was to think of them as epidemics. Like an epidemic, modern change tends to occur in one dramatic moment. Rather than building slowly and steadily, change happens in a hurry, with small causes having large effects.

Gladwell's observations resonate with a long-standing scholarly literature on the emergence and diffusion of innovations. In fields ranging from anthropology and rural sociology to marketing and public health, analysts have examined the processes through which new ideas, practices, and objects spread.[1] These innovations need not be new in an objective sense. Instead, they need only be perceived as new by an individual or another unit of adoption. If the idea, practice, or object seems new to a potential adopter, it is an innovation. Diffusion is the process "through which an innovation is communicated through certain channels over time among the members of a social system" (Rogers 1995, 11). Spread is a critical component of this definition. Diffusion is not merely the fact of increasing usage or incidence. It implies movement from the source of an innovation to an adopter (Strang and Soule 1998).

The prototypical diffusion study occurred in the early 1940s. Rural sociologists Bryce Ryan and Neal C. Gross examined the rapid diffusion of hybrid seed corn through the American Midwest between 1936 and 1939. The authors interviewed 323 farmers in two Iowa towns about their knowledge and acceptance of this innovation. In the space of four years, two-thirds of the farmers in these two communities changed to the new seed (Ryan and Gross 1943). The research methods and substantive content of diffusion studies have changed since the publication of this seminal work, but the underlying research questions remain the same: How do innovative ideas spread? What factors facilitate the diffusion of innovative ideas and behaviors? These fundamental questions continue to resonate across many different arenas, including the world of politics.

Political Innovations and Diffusion

Heated political battles are frequently fought over innovative ideas. Politics has famously been defined as "who gets what, when, and how" (Lasswell 1936). Political innovations help determine the answers to these questions by structuring the basic rules of the political game and determining the legitimate aim and scope of governmental activity. In addition, the enactment of innovative public policies can alter the existing costs and benefits of government programs. Political innovations are particularly important because they are rarely confined to a single jurisdiction. Just as hybrid seed corn spread across the farms of the American Midwest, political innovations frequently diffuse beyond the site of their initial adoption.

A wide range of phenomena qualify as political innovations. Political innovations can be as basic as the form that a government takes, as when democracy diffused across the postcommunist world during the 1990s (Kopstein and Reilly 2000). They can be the institutions that govern a particular polity or set of polities, such as the council-manager form that diffused across the cities of the American Southwest (Bridges 1997). Political innovations can be organizational forms, such as the interest group, which spread across the United States during the early twentieth century (Clemens 1998). They can also be policy ideas designed to improve governmental performance, as when British authorities drew on American experience with crime control policy (Jones and Newburn 2002). In sum, political innovations include virtually everything that is contested and contestable about politics.

In addition to illustrating the wide range of phenomena that qualify as political innovations, the preceding examples indicate that these innovations diffuse in diverse settings. For example, new policy ideas can spread from city to city, from state to state, or from one country to another. At the city level, policies concerning the living wage diffused across American cities in the middle to late 1990s (Martin 2001). During the mid-twentieth century, no-fault divorce diffused across the American states in a pattern that resembled an Impressionist painting (Jacob 1988, 80). Policy innovations also diffuse across international boundaries. During the Progressive Era, American officials used institutional connections with the industrializing nations of Europe to learn about innovative ideas in social policy (Rodgers 1998).[2] Sometimes, diffusion is a vertical process during which officials at one level of government emulate the ideas of their colleagues at another level.

In a political setting, diffusion implies a process of learning or emulation during which decision makers look to other cities, states, or countries as models to be followed or avoided. Diffusion occurs, in other words, when the likelihood that an innovation will be adopted in jurisdiction A is significantly affected by the existence of that innovation in jurisdiction B.[3] Diffusion does not occur when officials in multiple jurisdictions adopt the same innovation completely independently, nor does it occur when later adopters are unaware of the existence of the innovation elsewhere. In contrast, diffusion implies that extant versions of an innovation affect officials' decisions to create the same political form or to enact the same policy. Diffusion occurs, in sum, when decision makers draw on others' experiences to evaluate the effectiveness of a new political form or idea. This book examines the diffusion of public policy innovations, focusing on two fundamental questions: First, what factors facilitate or hinder their spread? Second, does the impact of these factors vary across stages of the policy-making process?

Time Constraints, Electoral Considerations, and Policy Diffusion

The analytical framework of this book is organized around the policy-makers who ultimately decide whether and in what form political innovations will gain enactment. Its primary argument is that policy diffusion is profoundly affected by two major constraints that these lawmakers face. The first constraint is insufficient time to complete the many tasks for which they are responsible. People in all walks of life confront this dilemma. It forces them to prioritize certain activities over others and sometimes to neglect particular tasks entirely. In this regard, elected officials are no different from the constituents they represent. Time constraints are a crucial concept in cognitive psychology and have been used to explain legislative behavior and decision making. This book hypothesizes that time constraints are most influential during the early stages of the policy-making process, such as agenda setting and information generation. Time-pressed officials are likely to be drawn to highly visible and politically salient policy innovations and to utilize resources that provide a maximal amount of information about them for a minimal amount of effort. Time constraints, in short, affect how lawmakers become aware of and gather policy-relevant information about policy innovations.

The second constraint is lawmakers' need to retain constituent support to win reelection. If they wish to remain in office, elected officials must remain attentive to their constituents' opinions. Political scientists have long recognized the strength and importance of these electoral considerations. One need not describe officials as "single-minded seekers of reelection" (Mayhew 1974, 5) to believe that the need to win office affects their positions on various policy innovations. Officials do not necessarily need to follow every whim of the constituents they represent, but this calculation is rarely likely to stray too far from their thoughts. This book hypothesizes that electoral considerations are most influential during the later stages of the policy-making process, such as customization and enactment. Elected officials are most likely to favor policy innovations—or specific versions of these innovations—that are popular with their constituents. Electoral considerations, in short, affect which policy innovations ultimately gain enactment as well as the provisions of these policies.[4]

This book posits that the impact of time constraints and electoral considerations varies across different stages of the policy-making process. This variation explains why certain causal mechanisms are influential during specific stages but have less influence during others. This book's conceptualization of policy diffusion is therefore organized around four different political processes: agenda setting, information generation, customization, and enactment. Officials have an almost unlimited number of potential policy choices, and the agenda-setting process determines which alternatives they consider. During the information generation process, various resources explain how a policy innovation works and provide examples of existing programs. Customization is the process during which officials mold an imported policy template for political or technical reasons. Enactment occurs when officials decide to adopt or not to adopt a policy innovation. Distinguishing among these four processes allows us to examine the varying impact of time constraints and electoral considerations.

TIME CONSTRAINTS AND POLICY DIFFUSION

One of the most famous metaphors in American jurisprudential history speaks implicitly to the concept of policy diffusion. In a 1932 dissent, Supreme Court justice Louis Brandeis wrote, "It is one of the happy incidents of the federal system that a state may, if its citizens choose, serve as a laboratory; and try novel social and economic experiments without risk to the rest of the country."[5] Since this landmark dissent, the fifty states have with great regularity been referred to as "laboratories of democracy." Actors from across the political spectrum have invoked this metaphor to describe the states' innovative potential. Liberal and conservative judges have cited Brandeis's metaphor more than three dozen times, and it clearly appeals to a nation of "compulsive tinkerers" (Greve 2001).

The metaphor of laboratories of democracy implies an almost scientific process, in which the enactment of a policy innovation prompts its evaluation, then other lawmakers use this information to determine whether they, too, will put the program in place. Each new policy is assessed along a set of objective dimensions. If the evaluators agree that the policy achieves its stated goals, other states will enact an identical program once they are made aware of its achievements. For example, if Oklahoma policymakers enact a program to contain health care costs and if this policy innovation succeeds, officials in other states will endorse similar programs.[6] If the innovation is unsuccessful, it will not be adopted elsewhere. Thus, the laboratories metaphor describes a systematic and rational process of trial and error.

Few observers would agree that public policy-making operates as seamlessly or as efficiently as the preceding description implies. The laboratories metaphor falls short in a couple of ways. First, it is extraordinarily difficult, if not impossible, to evaluate policy innovations along objective dimensions that will satisfy everyone. A laboratory setting requires an uncontaminated and hygienic environment. The political world, however, is inherently messy. Important actors leave the scene, while background conditions change, making policy evaluation extremely difficult. Second and more fundamentally, political decisions are not based solely on objective criteria. In addition to meeting the standards laid out by experts, policy innovations must satisfy goals that politicians find acceptable. A decision about the desirability of a program can trump expert estimates of its ability to achieve its objectives (Rose 1993). Officials will not endorse a successful policy innovation unless they feel that it achieves desirable outcomes and is necessary.[7] Program analyses can therefore prove less influential than "ordinary knowledge," such as casual empiricism, thoughtful speculation, or political interactions (Lindblom and Cohen 1979).

Consider, for example, the notion of welfare magnets, one of the most contested issues in state welfare policy-making. The logic behind this concept is straightforward. States offering benefits that exceed those in nearby states serve as welfare magnets and spark the in-migration of welfare recipients. If welfare benefits are more generous in Wisconsin than in Illinois, a welfare recipient might be willing to move from Chicago to Milwaukee. The scholarly debate over welfare magnets has produced mixed results (Brueckner 2000; Peterson and Rom 1990; Corbett 1991; Rom, Peterson, and Scheve 1998; Allard and Danziger 2000; Figlio, Koplin, and Reid 2000; Berry, Fording, and Hanson 2003), yet the issue continually reemerges as lawmakers debate welfare policy. Even some skeptics acknowledge that the argument resonates politically because it is intuitively plausible and because it is relatively easy to find anecdotal evidence to support it. This example illustrates the difficulty of generating definitive scientific evidence about many policy issues. Despite extensive research, one would be hard-pressed to articulate a consensus scholarly view on the topic.

Faced with unclear or even conflicting information about programmatic efficacy, how will policymakers respond? We should not expect them to be paralyzed, waiting for an elusive scholarly consensus to emerge. Political imperatives do not work on the same time frame as social science research. Politicians often feel the need to act before evaluators can make definitive claims. An election or the imminent end of a legislative session can spur lawmakers to make a decision about a policy innovation before all the relevant data have been gathered and evaluated. Under those circumstances, they will often be willing to pass judgment on a policy innovation in the absence of definitive evidence about its effectiveness.

A lack of definitive evidence does not imply, however, an absence of information about policy innovations. State policymakers are generally well versed in the arguments for and against the proposals that come across their desks. A recent study of the diffusion of enterprise zones, for example, examined five states and found that lawmakers in all of them met the requirements for "informed decision making" (Mossberger 2000).[8] Officials in the five states received information from federal agencies, the White House, twenty organizations, the press, academics and consultants, members of Congress, and contacts in other states (Mossberger 2000, 193). This wide range of potential information resources is quite striking, and in the current era, other policies seem equally likely to be characterized by a "superabundance" of policy-relevant information.[9] The availability of this information should be reassuring for scholars of policy diffusion, because it implies that it is not difficult for officials to learn about policy innovations that have been adopted in other jurisdictions. However, sifting through this potentially overwhelming amount of information would seem to pose quite a challenge. Here, time constraints come into play.

Information acquisition is one of many activities that state policymakers perform. Elected officials do not have the luxury of learning everything there is to know about a policy innovation, because they face many other responsibilities. They possess limited time to carry out all of their tasks, so they must prioritize certain activities and downplay others. As a result, such activities as fund-raising and performing constituency service sometimes supersede the collection of policy-relevant information. When time-pressed officials gather information, they strive to inform themselves as efficiently as they can. Rather than performing a comprehensive, rational search for appropriate solutions, they engage in successive limited comparisons or "muddle through" (Lindblom 1959).[10] Lawmakers therefore judge information on criteria other than its quality. Timeliness and accessibility can be just as important (Sabatier and Whiteman 1985). Time-pressed officials begin with the most accessible information and then search sequentially for that which requires more effort (Mooney 1991). Officials are likely to end their information searches as soon as they feel sufficiently informed to make a particular decision. They are unlikely to strive for comprehensiveness.

Cognitive psychology recognizes the importance of time constraints and the use of shortcuts to overcome them. One important shortcut is the availability heuristic.[11] In certain instances, people will assess the frequency or probability of an event by the ease with which instances or occurrences can be brought to mind. For example, one might assess the divorce rate in a particular community by recalling the divorce rate among one's acquaintances (Tversky and Kahneman 1982, 164).[12] Similarly, officials will not search comprehensively for every bit of policy-relevant information. Rather than beginning from first principles and analyzing every possible policy solution, they are more likely to be influenced by models that grab their attention. In short, officials perform a more limited search for models and policy-relevant information. Because of the time constraints they face, they tend to rely on information that is timely, available, and salient.

The availability heuristic suggests that highly visible examples can serve as an information shortcut. When a comprehensive investigation into every alternative is not possible, lawmakers are likely to be drawn to politically salient policy solutions. In the context of policy diffusion, time-pressed lawmakers will be drawn to policy innovations that have achieved some degree of visibility. This dynamic implies that time constraints are especially likely to affect the agenda-setting process by encouraging state officials to consider specific policy innovations rather than others. As a result, political forces that are capable of raising the profile of an innovation are especially likely to serve as causal mechanisms during this process.

The key question for the analysis of agenda setting in chapter 3 of this book is which political forces possess this capability.

Time constraints also seem likely to influence the information generation process. Specifically, the political forces that are most likely to be influential during this process will be able to provide a large amount of policy-relevant information in a timely fashion. The problem for officials is generally not a lack of data. Their challenge is to sift through the massive amount of information that is available to find what is needed. Officials can receive information from a wide array of sources. One key question for the analysis of information generation in chapter 4 of this book is whether and how the information provided by these sources varies. When policy innovations emerge, are specific sources especially likely to discuss examples that exist in other jurisdictions? What types of details do they provide? This book hypothesizes that time-pressed officials will rely on information resources that consistently provide relevant information but that do not require a huge time investment. Another key question for the subsequent discussion of information generation is whether state officials use the information that is provided by these resources. An account of the information generation process must, in short, strive both to identify the political forces that provide timely and accessible information and to assess whether policymakers are especially likely to use these resources.

The concept of diffusion implies that officials are aware of the innovative policies that exist in other jurisdictions. Time constraints seem likely to affect both the models toward which officials will be drawn and the resources officials will consult to gather information about those models. The preceding discussion developed two main hypotheses that will be examined in subsequent chapters of this book. First, time-pressed officials are most likely to consider innovations that are visible and therefore politically salient. The most influential causal mechanisms during the agenda-setting process will therefore be those that can heighten the visibility of a policy innovation. Second, time-pressed officials are most likely to rely on resources that provide accessible, detailed information. During the information generation process, the most influential causal mechanisms will therefore be those that disseminate easily accessible and thorough policy-relevant information in a timely manner.

ELECTORAL CONSIDERATIONS AND POLICY DIFFUSION

Elected officials who wish to retain their posts must respond to the desires of their constituents. Political campaigns are arduous endeavors and require the investment of substantial resources. Candidates must acquire the funds and the personnel necessary to run an effective campaign. Ultimately, they must also win the electoral support of their constituents. When incumbents present themselves for reelection, voters evaluate their accomplishments. Officials whose constituents are satisfied with their performance are more likely to win reelection than are policymakers who take many stands with which their constituents disagree. This electoral calculation can affect the diffusion of policy innovations, because it implies that lawmakers are most likely to be drawn to innovative policies that voters (or organizations that can mobilize large numbers of voters) support. When constituents strongly support or strongly oppose a policy innovation, their views are likely to be taken seriously. Elected officials who must face their constituents at the ballot box are usually enthusiastic about addressing voter concerns. Ignoring their views might mobilize an opposition campaign and reduce the likelihood of winning reelection. Electoral considerations may therefore lead officials to support or not support specific policy innovations.

Given the potential importance of electoral considerations, it is tempting to posit that they will affect every stage of the policy-making process. Maybe these considerations influence how officials become aware of policy innovations, how they gather information about them, how they design them, and whether they choose to endorse them. Research on public opinion, however, suggests that such an assumption is unwarranted. Officials will keep close tabs on the opinions of their constituents, but they do not always receive clear signals about how to proceed. In fact, public demands for change are rarely specific and often grant officials significant discretion.

Consider the potential impact of electoral considerations during the agenda-setting process. Officials might avoid discussing policy innovations that their constituents find unpalatable. Due to their limited public appeal, these policies will not even be considered. The problem with such a hypothesis is that the public rarely sends clear, specific signals to their elected officials. Sometimes, voters want their representatives to address a certain topic but provide little guidance about the specific response that they favor. As American officials considered welfare reform in the 1990s, for instance, the public generally agreed that the existing welfare system was ineffective and possibly counterproductive. Public opinion, however, provided limited guidance about specific reforms or policy innovations that would address these issues (Shaw 2000). This dynamic exists in other policy areas. Aside from a general desire that elected officials "do something" about certain issues, public opinion frequently provides little specific guidance. One political scientist makes this distinction by asserting that Americans possess attitudes instead of preferences (Bartels 2003).[13]

Even studies that grant a prominent role to public opinion recognize the limits of its impact. One especially influential analysis describes public opinion as the "dominant influence" on policy-making in the American states. The authors do not argue, however, that public opinion gives officials a strict regimen to follow. Instead, they describe how it establishes the general contours within which public policy is made. Public opinion, in other words, controls the general ideological direction of policy but does not force elected officials to comply with specific demands (Erikson, Wright, and McIver 1993). This distinction implies that lawmakers are more likely to receive general guidance about broad policy issues than to receive specific, prospective signals about particular policy innovations. Voters are especially unlikely to issue specific policy demands before they are presented with one or more viable options (i.e., after the agenda-setting process has determined which options are being considered). Elected officials therefore seem to possess considerable discretion as they decide which policy innovations merit consideration and gather information about these innovations.

This book hypothesizes that electoral considerations influence the later stages of the policy-making process, such as customization and enactment. Electoral considerations may influence the content of the policy innovations that officials endorse, explaining why specific provisions are included or not included. Statutory language is developed during the customization process as general policy templates are amended. Elected officials are attentive to how the public will react to prospective changes, but not necessarily because the public carefully follows these debates. This attentiveness definitely does not result from the electorate's knowledge of every amendment. After all, "[t]he political ignorance of the American voter is one of the best-documented features of contemporary politics" (Bartels 1996, 194). There is reason to be wary of attributing too much power to public opinion, especially in the context of specific statutory provisions. Even lawmakers who are inclined to follow the dictates of their constituents as they pursue reelection will sometimes be hard-pressed to determine what exactly these voters want.

The potential relationship between electoral considerations and the customization process can be attributed to the efforts of activists who are attentive to statutory minutiae. During the policy-making process, policymakers are likely to gravitate toward versions of policy innovations that have wide support but that generate modest opposition. Interest groups and other advocacy organizations lobby officials, participate in hearings and task forces, and use other forums to voice their concerns about policy innovations. Many of these activists represent specific constituencies to whom elected officials must respond if they want to win reelection. Organizations that can mobilize their members are therefore in a good position to influence lawmakers during the give-and-take of the customization process. Threats to withhold support from or to actively oppose elected officials during future campaigns may trigger negotiations to generate support or ameliorate opposition, and statutory language can serve as a bargaining chip during these negotiations. Senior citizen groups, for example, may withhold support for a senior prescription drug program that is funded through user fees paid only by seniors, while they may endorse a similar program that is funded through general revenues. Similarly, women's groups might object to imposing a time limit on welfare benefits but relent if this limit exempts victims of domestic violence. Electoral considerations might therefore affect specific legislative provisions even though the public at large is inattentive to these details.[14]

In sum, electoral considerations seem likely to influence the specific provisions of policy innovations as well as the ultimate enactment of these programs. The preceding discussion developed two main hypotheses that will be examined in subsequent chapters of this book. First, elected officials are most likely to amend policy templates to reflect the preferences of constituencies to whom they must respond. The most influential causal mechanisms during the customization process will therefore be the individuals and organizations that represent and can mobilize these potential voting blocs. Second, elected officials are most likely to endorse policy innovations with widespread public support, because voters will look favorably on these endorsements during future electoral contests. The most influential causal mechanisms during the enactment process will therefore be individuals and organizations that can make convincing cases for the electoral benefits of supporting specific policy innovations.

Laboratories of Democracy

In an era of instantaneous communication and rapid technological shifts, the topic of diffusion seems more important than ever. The diffusion of innovative political forms and policies is not limited to the current era, but conventional wisdom speculates that individuals and countries are linked together especially tightly at the dawn of the twenty-first century. Such technological revolutions as the telephone, the automobile, the airplane, and the Internet have changed who is part of our personal communities. These communities now consist of "far-flung social networks" rather than local neighborhood solidarities (Wellman 1999). The concept of globalization refers to analogous links that connect the countries of the world both economically and culturally. One historian describes these connections as a "web of global interdependence" (Rodgers 1998, 2). Individuals and countries are closely interconnected. These connections might assist the diffusion of innovations in political and other settings. The topic of diffusion therefore possesses great contemporary significance.

This book examines five recent innovations in health care and welfare policy that diffused across the American states in the 1990s and early 2000s.[15] These "laboratories of democracy," in the words of Supreme Court justice Louis Brandeis, are an especially favorable environment in which to develop generalizations about the political processes through which policy innovations diffuse.[16] The states represent fifty units of analysis with broadly similar political structures and cultures but with significant variation across a range of politically relevant attributes

(Mooney 2001c). This combination of underlying similarity and manageable variation makes the states a good venue in which to analyze diverse political phenomena, because it is possible to assess causal relationships about policy-making in a valid way (Jewell 1982; Brace and Jewett 1995). This book uses the states in an effort to develop generalizations about how policy diffusion operates as a political process. The notion that the states are laboratories of democracy posits that innovative policies can be implemented in individual states and then disseminated if they prove successful. The remainder of this section of this chapter explains why these laboratories are currently conducting a larger number of experiments and introduces the five specific innovations that are the subject of this study.

THE RESURGENCE OF THE STATES

Recent developments have catapulted the fifty states to a more prominent place in the American political system. For the past two decades, the states have served as a main locus of policy-making. As a result, now is a timely occasion to examine diffusion in this setting. From abortion and capital punishment to education and the environment, several important policy decisions are being made in state houses across the country, in addition to in the nation's capital. Two main factors contributed to this state resurgence.[17] National political developments, especially the emergence of a Republican congressional majority, were one important factor. The second factor was a set of reforms at the state level that strengthened state political institutions.

National developments shifted significant policy-making prerogatives from the national government to the fifty states, with changes in party politics playing a critical role. Republican politicians long considered intergovernmental reform to be a central element of their domestic political agenda. In the early 1970s, President Richard Nixon advanced a proposal called the New Federalism, which emphasized an administrative rationale for devolving policy-making authority to the states. Nixon wanted to restructure the roles and responsibilities of government at all levels in an effort to make the system function more efficiently. Ronald Reagan and Newt Gingrich married these administrative concerns to a larger debate over the legitimate scope and definition of the public sector

(Conlan 1998). For Reagan, Gingrich, and other Republicans, devolution was a way to solve administrative problems and to cut back the reach of government programs.

When the 1994 midterm elections produced a Republican majority in both houses of Congress for the first time in decades, this shift sparked a fundamental rethinking of the relationship between the states and the national government. While many Republican initiatives stalled, others devolved additional policy-making prerogatives to state officials. Perhaps the most prominent example occurred in 1996, when national lawmakers endorsed landmark welfare reform legislation. The Personal Responsibility and Work Opportunity Reconciliation Act placed a time limit on welfare receipt and incorporated stringent work requirements on beneficiaries. It also granted state policymakers unprecedented discretion over the provisions of their welfare programs.[18] Since 1996, state lawmakers have used this discretion to create diverse approaches to welfare policy (Soss et al. 2001; Fellowes and Rowe 2004; Clark and Little 2002b). Welfare reform is one of many instances in which the states have taken the lead in the making of public policy in response to national legislation.

The partisan shift in Congress was crucial, but other national developments also facilitated the resurgence of the states. Sometimes congressional stalemates, caused by divided government or party polarization, prompted state lawmakers to act in the absence of a national mandate. When national lawmakers could not agree on legislation or did not address specific topics, state officials sometimes developed innovative policy solutions on their own. This dynamic was fairly common in health care policy. During the late 1980s and early 1990s, many states implemented innovative health care programs, such as MinnesotaCare (Minnesota), MassCare (Massachusetts), and the State Health Insurance Program (Hawaii) (Elliot 1993). When legislation for comprehensive national health care reform failed in 1994, state officials attempted to address this vacuum by proposing their own solutions (Leichter 1997). Over the past two decades, in health care and in other policy arenas, state officials have regularly taken independent action.

In part, state officials' ability to take action grew out of institutional changes that better equipped the states to serve as laboratories of democ-

racy. Reforms of legislatures and executive branches are the second factor that contributed to the resurgence of the states. In institutional
terms, the fifty states are stronger than they were a generation ago. In the
1960s, state governments were not professional operations, and many
reformers believed that state governments lacked the resources they
needed to be effective. Today this is a less pressing concern. James
Morone explains: "Once upon a time, good old boys ran the states with
winks and backslaps. No more" (2000, 3). The institutional capabilities
of state governments increased dramatically between the 1960s and the
1980s, thanks to a series of constitutional and institutional reforms.
These reforms made state legislatures more professional and enhanced
the administrative capacities of the executive branch. As a result, state
officials can make a credible claim that they are well equipped to design
innovative public policies.

Legislative changes illustrate the relationship between institutional
reforms and the making of public policy. These reforms proceeded along
three dimensions. First, the salaries of state legislators increased, sometimes quite significantly. Reformers argued that higher salaries would
encourage more talented persons to run for office and would reduce the
temptation to solicit bribes. Second, state legislatures began to meet in
longer and more frequent sessions. In 1960, only four states held annual
legislative sessions, but today only a few state legislatures meet every
other year. There has also been a gradual increase in the number of days
spent in session. Third, the general trend has been toward a larger legislative staff. The movement toward professionalism in state legislatures
led to large staffs that serve the needs of legislative leaders and standing
committees (Bowman and Kearney 1986, 76–106). In combination,
these changes dramatically enhanced the institutional capabilities of state
legislatures across the country.[19] Furthermore, these resources allow
legislators and their staff to perform research and to collect policy-relevant information, a key component of policy diffusion. With more time
in session and more staff to gather information, state legislators can more
easily learn about other states' experiences with policy innovations and
evaluate whether these innovative programs merit enactment (Kousser
2005, 177–202).

Executive branch reforms also increased the professionalism of state government. Governors generally gained a more extensive set of formal powers that consolidated their power and improved management of the executive branch.[20] The reforms extended the gubernatorial term of office and permitted reelection, an attempt to foster continuity. In addition, most states allowed governors to appoint executive branch officials who had previously been elected in statewide races. Finally, governors generally received greater budgetary authority and the power to reorganize and streamline the executive branch. In sum, these reforms moved state government toward a more unified executive branch that governors can use to pursue their programmatic priorities, including the design of policy innovations (Bowman and Kearney 1986, 47–75).

If the fifty states serve as laboratories, they currently are better equipped to take on this task. Institutional changes transformed them from weak backwaters into a strong counterpart to the national government. Around the same time that these state-level changes occurred, developments at the national level granted the states a more prominent place in the American political system. This combination of institutional reforms and national developments contributed to the resurgence of the states and encouraged state officials to design and enact many policy innovations. These laboratories of democracy have been particularly busy in recent years, and the range of recent state activity is quite impressive. In education policy, dozens of states followed suit after the Minnesota state legislature became the first to approve charter school legislation (Mintrom and Vergari 1997). In health care policy, at least thirty-eight states adopted each of the following policies: small business insurance reforms, high-risk insurance pools, preexisting condition legislation, certificate of need, health care commissions, guaranteed renewal legislation, portability, and guaranteed issue (Stream 1999; Carter and LaPlant 1997). These and other recent innovations illustrate why the American states are a good setting in which to examine the phenomenon of policy diffusion.

CASE SELECTION AND RESEARCH DESIGN

This book investigates the diffusion of five recent innovations in health care and welfare policy. These policies vary along several dimensions that make them appropriate for study. Table 1 summarizes these differences.[21] First, the five innovations represent different conceptualizations of the proper role and reach of government. One represents an expansive governmental role, two combine governmental efforts with private sector efforts, and two trim or retrench existing policies. This variation in the five innovations' objectives is important because comparative politics research suggests that the politics of government expansion differ considerably from the politics of retrenchment (Pierson 1994, 1996).[22] Second, the five policy innovations vary in the extent and speed with which they diffused across the states. The number of states in which these policy innovations were adopted ranges from eighteen to thirty-five. Some of these adoptions occurred in short bursts of as few as four years, while others occurred over more extended periods. Although no sample of five innovations can be considered truly representative, variation along these dimensions makes generalization a less hazardous enterprise. The following paragraphs describe the five policies that will be examined: senior prescription drug programs, medical savings accounts, individual development accounts, time limits, and family caps.

Senior pharmaceutical assistance programs, frequently called senior prescription drug programs, represent the first policy innovation. These programs provide prescription drug coverage to low-income elderly persons and to disabled persons who do not qualify for Medicaid. In other words, states subsidize the cost of these individuals' medications. Because they distribute benefits to a specific set of citizens, senior drug programs

TABLE 1.   Five Policy Innovations

Policy innovation	Conceptualization of governmental role	Dates	Number of states
Senior prescription drug programs	Expansion of government	1975–2001	27
Medical savings accounts (MSAs)	Public-private partnership	1993–97	28
Individual development accounts (IDAs)	Public-private partnership	1993–2001	35
Time limits	Retrenchment of government program	1993–96	18
Family caps	Retrenchment of government program	1992–98	23

expand the role of the state and belong to the same class of programs that typified public policy during the New Deal and Great Society eras. Individuals and organizations who support this policy argue that sharp increases in the cost of prescription drugs justify the adoption of these programs. Supporters frequently describe senior citizens who, because of the high cost of prescription drugs, need to choose between taking essential medicines and buying food or paying the rent. Individuals and organizations who oppose this policy typically argue that it is an unnecessary and overly costly governmental intervention in the private health care marketplace. In recent years, heated debates over senior prescription drug programs have occurred at both the national and state levels.

By 2001, policymakers in twenty-seven states had adopted senior pharmaceutical assistance programs. The diffusion of this policy innovation occurred over an extended period of time. Senior drug programs gained enactment in a handful of states during the 1970s. After a brief period of inactivity, officials in seven additional states adopted the policy between 1984 and 1988. Its diffusion stalled through the early 1990s, then an outburst of state-level activity began in 1996. Policymakers in sixteen states adopted this innovation over the next few years, while national officials engaged in a heated debate over whether to add a prescription drug benefit to Medicare. In sum, senior prescription drug benefits represent an expansive governmental policy that diffused across the states over an extended period of time.

Medical savings accounts (MSAs) represent the second policy innovation. They combine umbrella health insurance with a routine care account. The insurance applies only to expenses above a high deductible, and account holders spend money from their individual account until they reach this deductible. At the end of the year, any unused money remains in a tax-free individual account. MSAs permit account holders to build funds for current and future care and provide favorable tax treatment to the monies that accrue in the accounts. Supporters claim that MSAs hold down health care costs while providing patients with as much choice as fee-for-service medicine. Because they must spend money out of their own accounts, patients will be cost-conscious consumers and thereby drive down the cost of health care (Goodman and Musgrave 1992). MSA opponents argue that this innovative policy favors the healthy and the wealthy because of the high deductibles that it requires. Encouraging these individuals to acquire medical savings accounts, they argue, results in adverse selection.

By 2001, lawmakers in twenty-eight states had adopted medical savings account legislation. All of this activity occurred between 1993 and 1997, when general interest in this policy innovation peaked. In the early 1990s, the topic of health care reform topped the national agenda as lawmakers considered President Clinton's Health Security Act.[23] Its conservative opponents coalesced behind MSAs as a way to hold down health care costs while limiting government intervention in the private health care marketplace. The national debate reached a temporary impasse in 1994, but the Health Insurance Portability and Accountability Act (HIPAA) of 1996 created an MSA pilot project that proscribed the conditions under which MSAs were permissible (Nichols and Blumberg 1998). Since 1996, MSA advocates have repeatedly attempted to loosen these restrictions. Thus, medical savings accounts use the tax code to foster a specific activity. State governments do not directly provide a service or benefit but instead operate through an intermediary and play a supporting role. In addition, their rapid diffusion contrasts with the relatively slow and steady spread of senior prescription drug programs.

Individual development accounts (IDAs) represent the third policy innovation. These accounts encourage working-poor families to accumulate assets by offering funds that operate like 401(k) plans. Public and private sources match individuals' deposits, fostering a link between the governmental and nongovernmental sectors. IDA programs generally earmark savings for such objectives as attending college, business capitalization, or the purchase of a home for the first time. Individuals who open the accounts sometimes participate in classes on money management. IDA advocates argue that this asset-based policy is more effective than giving welfare grants to low-income families, because IDAs enhance feelings of personal efficacy, increase political participation, promote household stability, and foster an orientation toward the future (Sherraden 1991).

By 2001, lawmakers in thirty-five states had adopted enabling legislation for IDAs. Although this policy innovation is generally associated with welfare reform, it has never been as visible as other welfare-related reform proposals. Economist Michael Sherraden developed the idea of individual development accounts in the late 1980s. The innovation gained enactment in a handful of states through the mid-1990s, beginning with Iowa and Kansas in 1993. Its diffusion accelerated after national welfare reform legislation listed the accounts as an appropriate use of state welfare funds in 1996. IDAs gained enactment in thirty states in the five-year period following this legislation. Like MSAs, IDAs are a policy innovation that links the efforts of the public and private sectors. The widespread diffusion of IDAs took place over the course of nearly a decade.

Time limits represent the fourth policy innovation. They mandate that welfare recipients will not receive benefits after a certain period of time. Time limits represent a fundamental reformulation of American income support policy, ending the entitlement status of Aid to Families with Dependent Children (AFDC). The specific time frame and the population to which this limit is applied vary from state to state. This policy responds to the popular perception that government-funded cash benefits constitute a way of life for too many welfare recipients and entrap them in a "culture of poverty."[24] Imposing a time limit transforms welfare from an open-ended societal commitment to a temporary way for struggling individuals to maintain a basic subsistence. Opponents of time limits assert that they punish people who are struggling to make ends meet and unfairly penalize children for their parents' mistakes.

By 2001, time limits were a fundamental component of American welfare policy. The state-level diffusion of this policy innovation was relatively rapid, as policymakers in eighteen states adopted time limits between 1993 and 1996.[25] Iowa and Florida were the first states in which this policy innovation gained enactment. During the early 1990s, the implementation of time limits required a Section 1115 waiver from the U.S. Department of Health and Human Services.[26] Lawmakers in many states submitted waiver proposals incorporating time limit policies. Virtually simultaneously, national lawmakers engaged in a heated debate over the direction of welfare reform. Time limits represented one of the central elements of this debate. In August 1996, President Bill Clinton signed the Personal Responsibility and Work Opportunity Reconciliation Act (PRWORA). This statute established a nationwide five-year limit on welfare benefit receipt and effectively ended the state-level dif-fusion of time limits.[27]

Family caps represent the fifth policy innovation. States that impose family caps do not increase welfare grants when a mother who is already receiving benefits gives birth to another child. In a few states, the families affected by these caps receive only a partial increase; in others, a third party receives the additional funds. Like time limits, family caps respond to a perceived shortcoming of AFDC. Critics argue that the income sup-port program encouraged mothers to have additional children to qualify for a more generous welfare benefit. They point out that working moth-ers would not receive automatic raises from their employers upon the birth of an additional child. Family cap opponents generally respond that the caps punish children and prevent their basic needs from being met. Both family caps and time limits are sometimes characterized as ways to rein in unwarranted state spending.

By 2001, lawmakers in twenty-three states had adopted family caps.[28] All of this activity occurred between 1992 and 1998, when interest in this policy innovation peaked. New Jersey policymakers enacted the first family cap policy in 1992, and developments in that state received con-siderable attention from national officials and the mass media for the next few years. They were a lightning rod for family cap supporters and oppo-nents, due to a legal challenge and a series of academic analyses that showed mixed results. As national lawmakers discussed the merits of this innovation, lawmakers in nineteen states submitted Section 1115 waivers that incorporated family cap provisions. Ultimately, the national debate ended in a stalemate, as PRWORA was nearly silent on the topic. Family caps gained enactment in four additional states, however, in 1997 and 1998.

The five policy innovations profiled in the preceding paragraphs vary in ways that will enable me, in subsequent chapters of this book, to make broader claims about the role of time constraints and electoral consider-ations during policy diffusion. The five policies represent different con-ceptualizations of the proper role of government, and they also vary in the extent and speed with which they spread. If similar causal mecha-nisms foster or hinder the diffusion of these disparate policy innovations, we can make more confident generalizations about the political processes through which innovative policies spread. This book uses a multimethod approach that incorporates quantitative and qualitative evidence to lay the empirical foundation for these generalizations.

The quantitative component of this study examines adoption patterns across the fifty states, using national data for each policy innovation. It uses event history analysis, a statistical technique that enables scholars to trace the diffusion process over time and to incorporate state character-istics and external pressures into the same model (Berry and Berry 1990, 1992; Pavalko 1989; Box-Steffensmeier and Jones 1997). The data for this statistical analysis come from government agencies and other organi-zations that track policy developments in the states. The quantitative analysis provides a nationwide perspective on patterns of innovation adoption, evaluating conventional explanations of policy diffusion. Its results shed significant light on the enactment process. In addition, they generate several questions about the other political processes with which this study is concerned.

The qualitative component of this examination focuses on the trajec-tories of the five policy innovations in three states: Massachusetts, Ore-gon, and Virginia. These three states are located in diverse regions of the country, and they vary along the demographic and socioeconomic dimensions highlighted by previous policy diffusion research. Their scores along such dimensions as innovativeness, income, partisanship, and ideology diverge significantly.[29] In addition, their policy profiles dif-fer substantially. At times, lawmakers in these three states have been leading innovators and adopted innovations ahead of their counterparts. In other cases, they have been laggards, putting programs in place only after many of their colleagues had already done so. Sometimes these law-makers were neither leading innovators nor laggards, and sometimes they flatly rejected a policy innovation. Table 2 displays this wide range of outcomes, which permit an examination of episodes both when a pol-icy innovation diffused and when it did not. It is necessary to examine this range of outcomes to construct a compelling account of how diffu-sion works. Many scholars have criticized existing studies of policy diffu-sion for possessing insufficient variation on the dependent variable. These analyses sometimes focus only on instances where a policy innovation dif-fused successfully (Rogers 1995, 100–105; Mooney and Lee 1995;

Strang and Soule 1998). Patterns in table 2 suggest that the analysis in this book will not be subject to this potential shortcoming.

The case selection in this book corresponds to the "most different systems" design often used in the study of comparative politics (Przeworski and Teune 1970, 34–39). The three states examined here vary in ways that existing research describes as significant. If a specific causal mechanism makes a similar impact on outcomes in these three settings, this convergence suggests it is possible to make general claims about a causal relationship. The main problem with this research design is that it cannot eliminate the alternate hypothesis that unobserved factors account for this overlap.[30] To address this shortcoming, it is necessary to illustrate how specific causal mechanisms contribute to the outcomes under review. Paying careful attention to the relationships between inputs and outputs can help ensure that justified inferences are being made about the impact of particular causal forces.

The qualitative component of this analysis therefore relies on a broad range of evidentiary sources. Legislative archives trace the bills considered by state policymakers, while committee hearings illuminate the major issues associated with their consideration. The materials produced by professional associations, interest groups, and administrative agencies are important sources of information for legislators. Media coverage highlights the most visible actors in policy debates and indicates which developments receive the most press attention. Participant interviews

TABLE 2. Policy Outcomes in Three States

State	Senior prescription drug programs	Medical savings accounts (MSAs)	Individual development accounts (IDAs)	Time limits	Family caps
Massachusetts	1996 (11th of 27)	Not enacted	Not enacted	Not enacted	1995 (11th of 23)
Oregon	2001 (22nd of 27)	1997 (22nd of 28)	1999 (20th of 36)	1995 (8th of 19)	Not enacted
Virginia	Not enacted	1995 (9th of 28)	1998 (14th of 36)	1994 (3rd of 19)	1994 (4th of 23)

Note: This chart does not distinguish among the enactments in a single year, so each of the rankings in parentheses is effectively a tie. See table A1 in the appendix for a complete list of program enactments.

illuminate how various actors view these episodes, and they sometimes describe relationships between lawmakers and other actors that are not visible to outside observers.[31] The most important advantage of relying on multiple sources of evidence is the development of converging lines of inquiry. This triangulation process brings together corroboratory sources that converge on the same set of facts and findings (Yin 1989). The next section of this chapter introduces the process-oriented analytical framework that incorporates these diverse evidentiary sources and builds on existing policy diffusion research.

Examining Policy Diffusion: A Process-Oriented Approach

Since the seminal research of Jack Walker and Virginia Gray was published in the late 1960s and early 1970s (Walker 1969; Gray 1973), the study of policy diffusion has constituted a fundamental component of the subfield of state politics.[32] One especially promising recent development in diffusion research is the heightened attention that has been paid to political forces that operate in multiple states. These political forces include—but are not limited to—interstate professional associations (Balla 2001), individual policy entrepreneurs (Mintrom 1997, 2000), and national campaigns by advocacy coalitions (Haider-Markel 2001). They share a pivotal characteristic. Due to their geographic reach, these political forces are capable of transporting policy innovations across state lines. In other words, they are potential mechanisms of policy diffusion.

The analytical framework of this book builds on the recent turn toward causal mechanisms in the scholarly literature on policy diffusion. Understanding which causal mechanisms spark specific diffusion episodes promotes a better understanding of why some policy innovations spread widely and others remain confined to a smaller number of jurisdictions.[33] Rather than focusing on a single mechanism, this book is organized around the disparate effects of various causal mechanisms during different stages of the policy-making process. It argues that certain mechanisms affect how officials become aware of and gather policy-relevant information about policy innovations. As hypothesized in an earlier section of this chapter, the most influential mechanisms during these early stages of the policy-making process seem to be those political forces that respond to the time constraints faced by state officials. In contrast, a different set of mechanisms affect which policy innovations gain enactment and the provisions of these policies. As hypothesized in an earlier section, the most influential mechanisms during these stages of the policy-making process seem to be those political forces that respond to the electoral considerations of state officials.

With a few exceptions, most existing studies of policy diffusion focus exclusively on patterns of program enactment. This approach illuminates the factors associated with the early adoption of policy innovations. Identifying these correlates of policy adoption is a valuable enterprise, but it paints an incomplete portrait of the diffusion process. It says a great deal about the factors that influence the adoption decision, but it says little about the political processes through which officials become aware of policy innovations, gather information about them, and amend them. If the most influential forces vary across these stages of the policy-making process, studies that focus exclusively on enactment may underestimate the impact of certain forces while overestimating the impact of others. It is possible that the same forces affect all four processes, but such a conclusion can only be advanced after empirical analysis that examines several outcomes in addition to patterns of program adoption. Examining a wider range of outcomes will enable scholars to focus more intently on various diffusion mechanisms and to understand how their impact varies across stages of the policy-making process. In recent years, some diffusion studies have taken tentative steps in this direction.[34]

This book uses a process-oriented approach to examine how policy innovations diffuse. It builds on recent turns toward causal mechanisms and multiple outcomes that characterize the existing literature on policy diffusion, as well as broader political science literatures on the policy-making process. The process-oriented approach requires a careful analysis of how various causal mechanisms are related to specific outcomes. It stresses the causal processes and political forces that foster the diffusion of policy innovations.[35] This book divides policy diffusion into four distinct political processes: agenda setting, information generation, customization, and enactment. By examining which mechanisms affect each process, it is also possible to evaluate hypotheses about how time constraints and electoral considerations affect the diffusion of policy innovations. The remainder of this chapter describes the analytical strategy used in subsequent chapters and the major substantive findings produced by this analysis.

In many ways, enactment represents the culmination of policy diffusion. It is the most visible and easily recognizable aspect of policy diffusion. A policy innovation either gains enactment or is not adopted. Existing research on the diffusion of policy innovations across the American states generally emphasizes the adoption decision and focuses on the correlates of adoption. Important correlates include such internal state attributes as wealth (Dye 1966; Tweedie 1994), political ideology (Erikson, Wright, and McIver 1993; Berry et al. 1998), and problem severity (Nice 1994; Sapat 2004), as well as such external pressures as the existence of the innovation in a neighboring state. The enactment process is a logical place to begin a study of policy diffusion, given the voluminous literature on this topic.

Chapter 2 begins with a quantitative analysis of enactment patterns across all fifty states for the five policy innovations described in the preceding section of this chapter. Using event history analysis, it tests several conventional explanations of program enactment. Some of these hypothesized factors affect the enactment of individual policies, but their effects are generally inconsistent. These "usual suspects" are rarely a sufficient explanation of enactment. Recent diffusion research suggests that the results presented in chapter 2 are not anomalous.

This book hypothesizes that electoral considerations play an important role during the enactment process. Based on this hypothesis, the qualitative component of chapter 2 emphasizes the activities of institutionally critical actors, such as governors and chamber leaders. Principal agent theory characterizes party leaders as agents who are assigned the task of helping members attain their goals. Reelection, of course, is one such goal (Clucas 2001). In state legislatures, chamber and party leaders distribute various resources that help their colleagues win reelection. These resources include contributions from leadership political action committees, committee posts and chairmanships, and space on the legislative calendar. In their role as party leaders, governors often affect officials' reelection prospects. Treating enactment as a causal process reveals how electoral considerations equip pivotal individuals with prerogatives that facilitate the adoption of policy innovations. Most diffusion research does not address the impact of these institutionally critical actors.

Before a policy innovation is adopted, supporters must guide it through a complex lawmaking process. The enactment process is generally more complicated than making a simple yes-no decision about the merits of a policy innovation. It presents multiple hurdles that must be cleared, and institutionally critical actors, such as governors and chamber leaders, often determine whether a policy innovation overcomes these obstacles. The analysis in chapter 2 suggests that these individuals can make the adoption of a policy innovation more or less likely through their active support or opposition. Sometimes policymakers consider a policy innovation multiple times before they decide to adopt it. The correlates of adoption identified by existing research remain largely static across the debates, but the identities and positions of major actors can shift over time.[36] For example, officials in Massachusetts enacted a senior prescription drug program in 1996 after a long-running debate. The crucial change that facilitated its passage was a reversal by Thomas Finneran, Speaker of the House of Representatives. Finneran had previously blocked all attempts to establish this innovation but finally relented after ascending to the speakership. By examining these types of changes in addition to standard explanations of policy adoption, it is possible to better understand the political forces behind program enactment. Chapter 2 highlights the impact of institutionally critical actors, such as governors, chamber leaders, and committee chairs. The importance of these individuals suggests that, as expected, electoral considerations play an important role during the enactment process.

AGENDA SETTING

State lawmakers have an almost unlimited array of choices, and the agenda-setting process determines which policy alternatives they consider (Kingdon 1995, 3). Why does a specific policy innovation move onto the agenda when it represents only one of many potential ways to address a particular social condition? Achieving agenda status is an important step, but the agenda-setting process is a peripheral concern in most diffusion research. In recent years, however, some analyses have examined this process and treated the consideration of a proposal as the out-come to be explained (Glick 1992; Hays and Glick 1997; Mintrom 1997, 2000; Haider-Markel 2001). These studies suggest that the dynamics of agenda setting differ from the dynamics of enactment, a finding that is in line with the distinction I made earlier in this chapter between time con-straints and electoral considerations. When political scientists examine the agenda-setting process, they generally treat the consideration of a policy innovation as the outcome to be explained. Chapter 3 follows this precedent, using bill introduction as a proxy for consideration. In other words, a policy innovation moves onto the agenda when a state law-maker submits a bill to establish it.

This book hypothesizes that time-pressed officials will be drawn to innovations that are visible and politically salient. Political forces that can raise the profile of a new idea are therefore likely to serve as causal mech-anisms during the agenda-setting process. To assess the visibility of the five innovations analyzed in this book, chapter 3 examines the level of newspaper coverage that they received. The timing and content of this coverage are important, because they indicate what types of develop-ments lead to increased visibility. Combining this information about newspaper coverage with a systematic examination of bill submission provides a better understanding of the causal processes that move a pol-icy innovation onto the agenda. Chapter 3 does not argue that newspaper coverage or the media more generally serves as a diffusion mechanism. Examining the content and the timing of this coverage, however, high-lights which developments cause an innovation to receive a higher public profile.

Several different causal mechanisms can increase the political salience of a policy innovation. The discussion in chapter 3 emphasizes the role of national intervention. It provides empirical support for the hypothesis that national developments heighten the visibility of policy innovations and that state officials respond to this increased visibility by considering these programs. National intervention seems to affect which policies move onto state political agendas. National debates, even if they are not resolved, often receive substantial newspaper coverage and thereby raise the political profile of the policy under consideration. State lawmakers frequently respond to these national debates by submitting legislation to establish the innovation. For example, President Bill Clinton heightened the visibility of senior prescription drug programs by highlighting this issue during his State of the Union address in 1999, and this policy innovation became a defining issue of the 2000 presidential campaign. During legislative sessions in 2001–2, lawmakers in 80 percent of the states that did not have a senior prescription drug program filed bills to establish this policy innovation. National debates had similar effects on the diffusion of medical savings accounts, time limits, and family caps. All of these innovations received substantial newspaper coverage that raised their visibility, and state policymakers seemed to respond by considering the policies in their own jurisdictions.

Chapter 3 highlights three important attributes of the agenda-setting process. First, policy innovations tend to move onto state agendas virtually simultaneously. For example, officials in dozens of states filed medical savings account legislation in 1993 and 1994. These bills were filed even in many states where the policy innovation did not gain enactment. The main goal of most diffusion studies is to explain differences in the timing of program enactment, but when the agenda-setting process is examined, similarity is the prevailing pattern to be explained. A key question, then, is why state political agendas overlap so considerably.

Second, the agenda-setting process operates in both bottom-up and top-down fashion. Policy innovations are typically "invented" at the state level and then percolate upward to the national level. Although national officials rarely create policy innovations, their activities frequently affect the diffusion of these policies (Jones-Correa 2000–2001; Menzel and Feller 1977). For example, in 1992, lawmakers in New Jersey were the first to enact family caps. The national debate over the innovation began in earnest in 1994, and the publicity of this controversy seemed to spur officials in additional states to consider family caps. The second segment of this dynamic represents the top-down portion of the agenda-setting process. National debates seem to move policy innovations onto the agenda in states where they had not previously been considered.

Third, national developments and congressional controversies do not occur in a vacuum. As national officials debate policy innovations, organizations and individuals at the national and state levels also make their case for these programs. Foundations and professional associations are very important. The evidence presented in chapter 3 suggests that national activity amplifies their activities and makes it more likely that their preferred policy innovations will achieve agenda status.

INFORMATION GENERATION

One could reasonably argue that the essence of policy diffusion is officials' awareness of and interest in policy innovations that exist in other jurisdictions. The extent to which late adopters are aware of earlier experiences is what distinguishes diffusion from mere policy congruence. Thus, the generation and dissemination of policy-relevant information are crucial components of policy diffusion, and the political forces that perform these two activities are important causal mechanisms. Due to its focus on program enactment, most policy diffusion research fails to examine the content and sources of this policy-relevant information.[37] Seeking to fill this gap, chapter 4 systematically examines materials that lawmakers might consult to learn about policy innovations. It analyzes the content of media reports, legislative testimony, administrative documents, and various materials produced by such national organizations as interstate professional associations and think tanks. Participant interviews supplement this documentary analysis.

In the current information-rich policy-making environment, the challenge for time-pressed officials is to figure out which resources most efficiently provide the information they want. This book hypothesizes that time-pressed officials will be inclined to rely on information resources that provide the best returns on minimal time investments. As a result, the first task of chapter 4 is to compare the content and timing of the materials described in the previous paragraph. Its analysis suggests that media reports, testimony, and administrative documents do not respond well to officials' time constraints. A fairly small proportion of newspaper accounts refer to existing policy models, while legislative testimony and administrative documents typically appear at a late stage of policy-making. In contrast, national organizations seem to be better suited to serve the information needs of state lawmakers. Professional associations and think tanks typically provide timelier, more accessible, and more detailed information about policy innovations. Their materials frequently include examples of statutory language or model legislation on which state lawmakers can draw.

The second task for chapter 4 is to describe specific instances in which state officials relied on information made available by national organizations. Two examples from Oregon illustrate this type of evidence. Ted Abram of Jeld-Wen Inc., one of the primary proponents of welfare reform in the state, served on a welfare-related task force convened by the American Legislative Exchange Council (ALEC). ALEC is a national professional association headquartered in Washington, D.C. State representative Patti Milne, who sponsored medical savings account legislation, also coauthored a report on the policy innovation. She thanked a variety of individuals for their help with the report. Three of these individuals were affiliated with a national think tank (the National Center for Policy Analysis) and a different professional association (Council of State Governments). These examples highlight the impact of national organizations. Even though they do not estimate the frequency with which these resources are consulted or identify the political conditions that make lawmakers more or less likely to rely on specific organizations for policy-relevant information, these examples suggest that national organizations merit a prominent role in analyses of policy diffusion.

Finally, chapter 4 examines several surveys.[38] The results of these surveys suggest that state officials see national organizations as a valuable information resource. They also suggest that officials are particularly eager to obtain information about recent developments in other states when they are willing to commit their time or their staff time to a specific issue. In sum, chapter 4 describes a national search for information that is not constrained by geographic proximity or regional affinities. It provides empirical support for the hypothesis that officials are inclined to rely on information resources that generate large returns on minimal time investments. By providing detailed information in a timely manner, national organizations seem to be crucial causal mechanisms during the information generation process.

CUSTOMIZATION

Why do policy innovations take on a variety of forms in the jurisdictions in which they are enacted? These differences exist because officials tailor policy innovations to fit their states just as individuals tailor suits after buying them off the rack. Customization describes the process through which policymakers take a proposal and mold it for either political or technical reasons. The importance of program content holds in any study of public policy. Consider, for example, the details involved in a public pension program. Which individuals are eligible to receive a pension? When are citizens eligible to receive benefits? How are benefit levels calculated? How is the pension system funded? How much do employers or individuals contribute? Each of these details represents a political decision that probably provoked controversy.[39]

Policy content is especially important in the context of policy diffusion, a process through which officials learn about programs in other jurisdictions and draw lessons from them. Officials might adjust the specific provisions of a policy innovation based on early adopters' experience with it. Alternatively, the same innovation may be adapted in order to account for particularities within a state. In either case, simply answering the yes-no question of whether officials chose to adopt an innovation overlooks how they may have altered the existing template. Policy diffusion is a causal process that takes place across time and space. Ignoring the question of program content fails to address the important issue of variation across space.

Most policy diffusion research asks whether and when a policy innovation gained enactment,[40] largely ignoring the specific provisions of these policies. In recent years, a growing number of studies have begun to address the question of program content. Most of them assume, however, that programmatic differences can be attributed to the order in which states adopted the policy innovation (Glick and Hays 1991; Clark 1985; Clark and French 1984). Specifically, they assume that late adopters will enact innovations that are more expansive than the tentative approaches adopted by leading innovators. Recent studies of this process, known as reinvention, indicate that it can be affected by the amount of controversy that the policy innovation generates (Hays 1996; Mooney and Lee 1999).

This book hypothesizes that electoral considerations are especially likely to affect the customization process. It builds on the emerging reinvention literature, but it attributes differences in program content to political factors rather than to the order in which a policy innovation was adopted. Chapter 5 examines the causal processes that link specific political forces to differences in program content. It presents two main types of evidence. First, it focuses broadly on settings in which state officials are likely to amend a proposal. Second, it examines specific episodes during which state lawmakers modified an existing policy template. This combination of evidence suggests that as state officials adjust specific programmatic provisions, electoral considerations lead the officials to respond to the intrastate constituencies that they represent. Elected officials depend on intrastate constituencies to mobilize voters and for reelection resources, such as campaign contributions.

The first half of chapter 5 compares the prominence of intrastate and external forces during the customization process. It begins by examining finance data for state house campaigns in Massachusetts, Oregon, and Virginia. The data is not sufficiently fine-grained to link specific contributors to specific legislative provisions, but it suggests why elected officials respond to the entreaties of intrastate groups. State house candidates in all three states receive most of their campaign contributions from in-state sources, giving them a strong incentive to be responsive. These patterns suggest that officials motivated by electoral considerations will be particularly attentive to the preferences of intrastate groups.

Modifying legislative proposals represents a way for elected officials to illustrate their responsiveness. Policy advocates must clear a number of hurdles to enact their preferred innovation, and amending a proposal can help them generate more support or can ameliorate opposition. Chapter 5 therefore examines two settings that are likely to generate these sorts of changes—namely, lobbying registration and legislative testimony. The purpose of these analyses is to assess the balance between organizations representing intrastate constituencies and organizations representing out-of-state constituencies. This balance tilts toward intrastate groups in both settings. An analysis of national lobbying registration data suggests that the composition of interest group communities in the states remains predominantly local (Wolak et al. 2002). Thousands of organizations registered to lobby on health care and welfare issues between 1997 and 1999, and the majority of them registered in a single state. If a larger percentage of these groups had registered in multiple states, this pattern would have suggested a stronger national presence during the customization process. Similarly, witnesses who testify before legislative committees are more likely to represent intrastate constituencies than to represent national organizations. Individuals representing national organizations rarely appear before legislative committees in Oregon. Instead, most committee witnesses represent intrastate groups, state or local government agencies, and the state chapters of national organizations. These data suggest that during the customization process, intrastate forces are more influential than are national forces.

The second half of chapter 5 examines variation in program content across the three states and the causal processes that led to this variation. This analysis supplements the broad overview described in the preceding paragraph with a more systematic look at specific legislative language. It suggests that intrastate politics affect customization in a number of ways, but two findings are especially noteworthy. First, differences in the composition of the coalitions supporting a policy innovation can produce variation in program content. For example, medical savings account (MSA) legislation in Oregon reflected the technical objectives of the Oregon Society of Certified Public Accountants, while Virginia's more expansive MSA program reflected the bolder political ambitions of the Jeffersonian Health Policy Foundation. Second, variation in the strategies pursued by similar coalitions in different states is important. The provisions of welfare reform in the three states varied, in part, because of the strategic choices made by its opponents. The adversarial stance that the welfare advocacy community in Massachusetts took against welfare reform backfired and prevented that community from making changes to various proposals. The advocacy communities in Oregon and Virginia adopted more consensual stances and were able to moderate some of the strictest proposals that emerged. These episodes, in combination with the broad overview described in the preceding paragraph, suggest that lawmakers take their cues from intrastate forces during the customization process. This connection provides empirical support for the hypothesis that electoral considerations affect the provisions of the policy innovations that gain enactment.

SUMMARY

Chapters 2 through 5 of this book rely on a process-oriented analytical framework to examine the diffusion of five recent innovations in health care and welfare policy. Building on several recent developments in diffusion research, this approach examines a wide range of outcomes. In addition to asking whether and when officials enacted an innovation, it investigates how officials become aware of policy innovations, how they gather policy-relevant information about them, and the causal processes that produce variation in the specific provisions of these policies.

The analytical framework of this book suggests that time constraints and electoral considerations affect the diffusion of innovations. Their impact varies across different stages of the policy-making process. Recognizing the shifting impact of time constraints and electoral concerns enhances our understanding of the causal mechanisms that foster policy diffusion. Distinct causal mechanisms are influential during each of these stages. Chapter 2 examines the enactment process and suggests that, through active support or opposition, institutionally critical actors, such as governors and chamber leaders, affect the likelihood of program adoption. Chapter 3 examines the agenda-setting process and emphasizes the impact of national developments on state political agendas. These developments raise the visibility of new policy ideas. Chapter 4 suggests that interstate professional associations and other national organizations are influential during the information generation process. These organizations provide timely, accessible, and detailed information about new policy ideas. Chapter 5 suggests that organizations representing intrastate constituencies affect the customization process. Their efforts help explain why policy innovations take on a variety of forms in the states in which they gain enactment.

Although developments in the American states represent the substantive focus of this book, policy diffusion is not limited to this particular setting. Political scientists, in fact, have examined this phenomenon in many different contexts. Diffusion may be even more important in an era of instantaneous communication and rapid technological changes, because of the way that these forces link the citizens and countries of the world more tightly than ever. Despite its empirical focus on five innovations in health care and welfare policy, this book provides broader lessons about a political phenomenon of great contemporary significance. These broader lessons are just as important as the empirical examples that appear in the chapters that follow.

II. *Enactment as a Political Process*

W HAT FACTORS FACILITATE or hinder the diffusion of policy innovations? Political scientists tend to focus on patterns of program enactment to answer this question. For decades, scholars of state politics have attempted to explain why innovative programs gain enactment in some states but not in others and why the timing of program adoption differs across states. Given the emphasis on program enactment in the scholarly literature on policy diffusion, enactment marks a logical place to begin our inquiry. This chapter examines patterns of program adoption for five recent innovations in health care and welfare policy: senior prescription drug programs, medical savings accounts, individual development accounts, time limits, and family caps. In which states did these policy innovations gain enactment, and when were they adopted?

This chapter combines a quantitative analysis of program adoption across all fifty states with an intensive qualitative examination of developments in three states. Its quantitative analysis evaluates several conventional explanations of program enactment. It finds that these factors affect policy adoption inconsistently and are rarely a sufficient explanation of the enactment process. The qualitative component of this chapter focuses on the impact of electoral considerations. Specifically, it examines how the activities of institutionally critical actors, such as governors and chamber leaders, affect the likelihood that state lawmakers will adopt a policy innovation. These pivotal individuals distribute various resources that help their colleagues win reelection, and they make the adoption of a policy innovation more or less likely through their active support or opposition.

39

Rounding Up the Usual Suspects

Political scientists study policy diffusion in multiple ways, but the most common analytical strategy in the context of the American states is to examine nationwide patterns of enactment using a statistical technique known as event history analysis (EHA).[1] EHA is a form of pooled cross-sectional time-series analysis, and its application to the study of policy diffusion is important for two major reasons (Berry and Berry 1990). First, it enables scholars to evaluate the influence of independent variables that vary from year to year, because it incorporates longitudinal variation into the data set. Such factors as partisan control of the legislature can shift, and EHA can accommodate these changes. This is an important analytical tool because policy diffusion is a process that takes place over time, as laggards emulate early adopters. Second, EHA can simultaneously assess the relative impact of such internal factors as state characteristics and such external forces as the existence of the innovation in a neighboring state. Thus, scholars can use EHA to examine the impact of external forces—which is in many ways the essence of policy diffusion—while also controlling for the state political environment. For these and other reasons, many analyses of policy diffusion use EHA.[2] In addition, these studies have converged on a standard set of factors, or "usual suspects," that purportedly explain patterns of program enactment. The present study focuses on six potential factors: national intervention, the neighboring state effect, problem severity, state wealth, legislative professionalism, and ideology.[3]

The notion of policy diffusion assumes that the probability of program adoption in a state is affected by developments outside that jurisdiction. As a result, it is absolutely essential that analyses of policy diffusion assess the influence of external developments. In the context of the American states, this category of hypotheses includes both vertical and horizontal influences. National developments are an external influence that operates vertically, as national officials can use policy tools, such as financial incentives (Welch and Thompson 1980), to affect state policy-making (Savage 1985; Allen, Pettus, and Haider-Markel 2004; Roh and Haider-Markel 2003; Daley and Garand 2005). During the period under examination, national legislation addressed three of the policy innovations included in this study. The Health Insurance Portability and Accountability Act of 1996 (HIPAA) severely circumscribed the conditions under which medical savings accounts (MSAs) could be established, erecting several barriers to the state-level enactment of this innovation (Nichols and Blumberg 1998). The Personal Responsibility and Work Opportunity Reconciliation Act of 1996 (PRWORA) described individual development accounts (IDAs) as an acceptable use of state welfare funds and made a passing reference to the establishment of family caps. Variation in the character of national intervention in these three cases provides a good test of the vertical diffusion hypothesis.[4] Does national intervention affect the likelihood that an innovation will gain enactment in the states?

The horizontal diffusion hypothesis posits that interactions among state officials affect program enactment. Interactions among the fifty states underlie the "laboratories of democracy" metaphor, which implies that state officials pay attention to developments in other states. Most diffusion research assumes that geography plays an important role in this emulative dynamic, as policymakers pay especially close attention to developments in nearby states or in states that are considered regional leaders (Foster 1978). Tight communications networks among lawmakers in contiguous states might also promote the geographically based diffusion of innovations.[5] The significance of geographic proximity is a powerful theme in policy diffusion research, dating back to some of the earliest studies of this topic (McVoy 1940; Walker 1969). Some scholars question the assumptions behind the horizontal diffusion hypothesis (Mooney 2001a).[6] Others posit that emulation can be traced to interstate competition (Boehmke and Witmer 2004; Berry and Baybeck 2005), ideological affinities (Grossback, Nicholson-Crotty, and Peterson 2004), or the "success" of the policy innovation elsewhere (Volden 2006). The neighboring state effect nonetheless remains a foundational component of diffusion research. This book uses the most common statistical proxy used to model the impact of geography.[7] The horizontal diffusion hypothesis predicts that the existence of the innovation in a neighboring state will make officials more likely to adopt the same policy.

Another set of hypotheses emphasizes the potential impact of problem severity, positing that state officials' willingness to adopt policy innovations might reflect the existence of a certain societal condition or prob-

lem. In other words, policy innovations will be more likely to gain enactment when the conditions they seek to address are important issues in a
specific state. According to the logic of this set of hypotheses, policy
innovations that address race relations will be unlikely to gain enactment
in racially homogeneous states, such as Idaho or New Hampshire, while
agricultural policy innovations will be unlikely to gain adoption in highly
urbanized states, such as New Jersey. The cliché that necessity is the
mother of invention neatly summarizes this argument. Where a problem
is severe, change regarding that problem is likely. Where the problem is
less severe or nonexistent, change regarding that problem is less likely.
In sum, officials will be more likely to enact innovations when they agree
on the existence and source of a problem (Nice 1994; Sapat 2004). The
five policy innovations examined in this study have all been linked to
specific societal conditions, making it possible to examine the relationship between problem severity and program enactment.[8]

Existing policy diffusion research hypothesizes that internal state characteristics affect the enactment of policy innovations. For example, the
seminal research of Jack Walker (1969) described a general relationship
between wealth, urbanization, industrialization, and the early enactment
of policy innovations. Walker and other scholars hypothesized that the
existence of slack resources explained this finding. When policy innovations are developed, they argued, officials in wealthier states are better
able to risk the possibility of failure, because they know that it will not be
disastrous for their state. Officials in less wealthy states, in contrast, need
to guard their resources more carefully and may be less inclined to take a
risk on an untested policy (Rogers 1995). The models presented in this
chapter use state per capita personal income as a proxy for the availability of slack resources.

The slack resources hypothesis generally predicts that higher income
levels will be positively associated with the adoption of policy innovations. One might also expect, however, that the impact of slack
resources will vary based on the attributes of the policy innovation being
discussed. The five policies included in this study provide variation that
makes a test of this hypothesis possible. Since senior prescription drug
programs impose a heavy financial burden, the relationship between
slack resources and program adoption is likely to be especially strong.

Slack resources are likely to have a moderate impact on the adoption of policy innovations that combine governmental efforts with private sector activity, because these policies generally impose fairly modest costs on state governments. Both MSAs and IDAs fall into this category.[9] Finally, slack resources are likely to have a minimal influence on the enactment of innovations that do not involve significant governmental spending. Time limits and family caps reduce financial outlays and fall into this category.[10] In sum, the five policy innovations possess disparate goals and attributes that provide a good test of the slack resources hypothesis.

Legislative professionalism might also affect the enactment of policy innovations. Professional state legislatures are characterized by longer sessions, higher salaries, and greater staff resources (Squire 1992). Chapter 1 described how state legislatures generally became more professional during the late twentieth century, but they still vary significantly along this dimension. Members of highly professional legislatures may be more likely to possess the staff and time resources that facilitate the accumulation of knowledge about policy innovations and the adoption of these policies. The relaxation of time constraints through either longer sessions or higher salaries has been associated with the production of innovative policies (Kousser 2005, 177–202). This hypothesis predicts that legislative professionalism will be positively associated with the enactment of policy innovations.

Another hypothesis posits that political ideology influences the adoption of policy innovations. It is important to remember that conservatives and liberals embrace policy innovations with varied enthusiasm. Conservatives generally prefer policies that rely on the market or that reduce the scope of governmental activity, and liberals usually support the expansion of governmental prerogatives. This is an oversimplification, of course, but it is important to recognize these broad differences and to acknowledge that the general ideological environment in a state might influence the likelihood that a policy innovation will gain enactment. The five programs incorporated into this study provide a good test of the political ideology hypothesis, because they are supported by diverse constituencies. Liberals generally support senior prescription drug programs, and conservatives typically favor MSAs, time limits, and family caps. IDAs represent something of a middle ground and draw support from liberals as well as moderates. This variation is useful in assessing the political ideology hypothesis.

In summary, political scientists identify many factors with the potential to affect the enactment process. It is possible to test these hypotheses using event history analysis, a statistical technique that allows scholars to examine patterns of policy enactment across all fifty states. The next section of this chapter describes the results of such an analysis for five recent innovations in health care and welfare policy. It focuses on the impact of vertical and horizontal diffusion, problem severity, slack resources, legislative professionalism, and ideology.

The Verdict: Not Guilty

When the conventional hypotheses about policy innovation enactment are tested empirically, the preponderance of the evidence suggests that the usual suspects are not guilty. The usual suspects are a useful starting point for analyzing the adoption of policy innovations, and individual factors significantly affect the enactment of specific programs. However, the results presented in table 3 suggest that models relying exclusively on these conventional factors possess limited predictive power.[11] The usual suspects typically do not have a strong and consistent effect on the enactment process.

Table 3 provides strong support for the vertical diffusion hypothesis. National developments affect the state-level enactment of policy innovations in predictable ways. This impact depends on the nature of the national intervention and can be either negative or positive. The passage of HIPAA in 1996 proscribed the conditions under which MSAs could be created, by limiting eligibility to specific individuals and capping the number of taxpayers who could purchase the accounts. All else equal, this national statute reduces, by 9.96 percentage points, the probability that officials in a state will adopt MSA legislation in a given year. Its restrictive provisions seem to have helped at least some officials decide not to adopt MSAs. In contrast, the passage of national welfare reform legislation had a positive and significant effect on the state-level adoption of IDAs, after it listed the accounts as a potential use of state welfare funds. This national intervention, all else equal, increases, by 10.10 percentage points, the probability that officials in a state will adopt IDA legislation in a given

TABLE 3. Nationwide Patterns of Program Enactment

Variable	Senior prescription drug programs	Medical savings accounts (MSAs)	Individual development accounts (IDAs)	Time limits	Family caps
National intervention (+/−)		−9.96**	10.10*		3.37
		[−17.71, −4.17]	[0.45, 20.90]		[−3.83, 14.27]
Neighboring state effect (+)	−0.18	6.53**	2.00	−2.38	−5.05^
	[−0.81, 0.49]	[1.43, 13.82]	[−2.86, 7.46]	[−9.04, 4.81]	[−11.89, 0.42]
Problem severity (+)	−0.88	−1.59	2.55	−1.99	2.88
	[−2.36, 0.27]	[−6.39, 3.57]	[−3.75, 9.50]	[−11.95, 7.74]	[−1.66, 7.96]
Personal income (+)	1.07	−9.26*	−0.41	9.91^	4.94^
	[−0.76, 3.09]	[−20.31, 0.43]	[−8.26, 7.68]	[−1.58, 22.66]	[−0.36, 12.02]
Professionalism (+)	0.42	6.15*	−3.43	−0.23	−0.55
	[−0.40, 1.56]	[0.76, 13.73]	[−11.00, 3.10]	[−10.75, 9.46]	[−6.06, 4.03]
Ideology (+/−)	1.95^	2.19	2.67	−9.43^	−3.16
	[−0.33, 5.51]	[−4.64, 9.56]	[−4.53, 10.35]	[−23.04, 1.30]	[−9.15, 1.96]
Trend	−2.17**	−11.58**	−2.82	−10.06**	−9.03**
	[−4.27, −0.79]	[−18.73, −6.18]	[−11.50, 5.11]	[−18.21, −2.85]	[−15.47, −4.20]
Number of observations	1,092	273	333	167	339
Log likelihood	−104.69	−72.61	−96.58	−48.76	−71.16
χ^2	43.75	35.34	26.40	12.37	25.85
Prob. χ^2	0.0000	0.0000	0.0004	0.0543	0.0005
Pseudo R^2	0.1728	0.1957	0.1202	0.1125	0.1537
Percentage correctly predicted	97.53	89.38	89.79	89.82	93.51

Note: Expected directions are in parentheses. Confidence intervals are in brackets and represent [2.5%, 97.5%] of posterior distributions.
^ Significant at the .10 level
* Significant at the .05 level
** Significant at the .01 level

year. The same legislation also mentioned family caps, but it only included an ambiguous statement about their potential existence.[12] This statement did not affect the likelihood that state lawmakers would adopt family caps. National intervention, in sum, affects program enactment in predictable ways that support the vertical diffusion hypothesis.

The results presented in table 3 provide less support for the horizontal diffusion hypothesis. Diffusion studies generally presume that officials will be more likely to enact a policy innovation when it already exists in nearby jurisdictions. This neighboring state effect, however, is positive and significant only in the context of MSAs. All else equal, moving from a state where the policy exists in no neighboring states to a state where the policy exists in half of its neighboring states increases, by 6.53 percentage points, the probability that officials will adopt MSA legislation in a given year. The neighboring state effect is positive but not significant in the context of IDAs. In contrast to the predictions of the horizontal diffusion hypothesis, however, the effect is negative in the context of the other three innovations. It is negative and marginally significant in the context of family caps. In sum, the results presented in table 3 provide modest empirical support for the horizontal diffusion hypothesis. They suggest that scholars need to develop more subtle hypotheses about the conditions under which the neighboring state effect is most likely to affect state policy-making. A few recent diffusion studies have taken preliminary steps in this direction (Mooney 2001a; Boehmke and Witmer 2004; Berry and Baybeck 2005).

Problem severity also does not have a consistent impact on the enactment process. Table 3 shows that the hypothesized positive relationship between problem severity and enactment emerges only in the context of IDAs and family caps. In neither case does this relationship achieve conventional levels of statistical significance. The other innovations imply a negative (but not significant) relationship between problem severity and program enactment. Table 4 depicts this weak relationship by classifying the fifty states based on two criteria. The criteria separate states ranking in the top ten (high severity) from those ranking in the bottom ten (low severity) in terms of the social conditions associated with the five policies. These two subgroups are also classified according to whether the innovation gained enactment. If there is a strong relationship between problem severity and adoption, most states will cluster in the category of high severity and enactment or in the category of low severity and non-enactment. This pattern suggests that states in which a problem is severe tend to adopt the policy innovation and that states in which a problem is not severe do not.

The patterns visible in table 4 suggest a weak relationship between problem severity and enactment. The relationship between increases in prescription drug expenditures and the adoption of senior prescription drug programs is weak ($r = 0.0207$).[13] The enactment of medical savings accounts is weakly related to the percentage change in the number of citizens without health insurance ($r = 0.0929$),[14] and there is also a weak correlation ($r = 0.0692$) between problem severity and the enactment of IDAs. The enactment of time limits is weakly related to the percentage of the state welfare caseload receiving benefits for four years or more ($r = 0.0089$). Table 4 reveals that officials in an equal number of high-severity and low-severity states adopted senior prescription drug programs, MSAs, IDAs, and time limits. There is a slightly stronger correlation between the enactment of family caps and the percentage of welfare cases with four or more children ($r = 0.1106$), and officials in five high-severity states and three low-severity states enacted this policy innovation. Overall, however, tables 3 and 4 suggest that program enactment is not a function of existing social conditions. Problem severity does not seem to have a clear, consistent impact on the enactment of the five policy innovations.

The results in table 3 provide limited empirical support for the slack resources hypothesis. This hypothesis predicts a positive relationship between per capita personal income and the enactment of policy innovations, and the expected positive relationship emerges in the context of senior prescription drug programs, time limits, and family caps. The positive relationship between per capita personal income and the enactment of senior prescription drug programs supports the hypothesis that expansive policies are especially likely to be affected by the existence of slack resources. It does not achieve conventional levels of statistical significance, however. In contrast, the positive relationship between per capita personal income and the enactment of time limits and family caps is marginally statistically significant, a finding that is surprising because the two

TABLE 4. Problem Severity and Program Enactment

Problem severity	Senior prescription drug programs		Medical savings accounts (MSAs)		Individual development accounts (IDAs)		Time limits		Family caps	
	Enact	Not enact	Enact	Not enact	Enact	Not enact	Enact	Not enact	Enact	Not enact
High	OR	GA	UT	VT	AZ	MS	IL	MI	WI	HI
	AZ	NM	VA	KS	NM	LA	CT	RI	MS	LA
	NV	WA	MD	MA	TX	CA		ME	CA	SD
		UT	NV	IA	AR	AL		MS	AZ	AK
		CO	OH	ME	GA			KY	IL	MN
		ID			TN			NJ		
		AK						PA		
								CA		
Low	MA	ND	CO	AK	MN	NH	FL	ID	NC	NH
	MO	NH	NE	NH	VT	ND	TX	MT	VA	ME
	KS	IA	MT	ND	CT	MA		TN	NJ	KY
		WV	PA	SD	NJ	NE		WY		VT
		OH	WY	DE	ME			AZ		WV
		LA			IA			NV		IA
		NE						NM		OR
								UT		

policy innovations are policies of retrenchment that potentially reduce expenditures on state welfare programs. Per capita personal income is negatively related to the adoption of MSAs and IDAs, with the former relationship achieving conventional levels of statistical significance. Table 3 provides mixed support for the slack resources hypothesis and the related hypothesis that the impact of slack resources varies across different types of policy innovations.

The results in table 3 suggest that legislative professionalism provides limited explanatory leverage. Of the five policy innovations examined, the hypothesized positive and significant relationship emerges only in the context of MSAs. All else equal, moving from a less professional state legislature to a more professional state legislature increases, by 6.15 percentage points, the likelihood that officials will enact MSA legislation in a given year. The relationship between legislative professionalism and innovation enactment does not achieve conventional levels of statistical significance in the context of the other four policy innovations, and it is negative in three of these cases. These results suggest that scholars need to develop more subtle hypotheses about the conditions under which legislative professionalism is most likely to affect state policy-making. For example, one recent study posits that an especially strong relationship will emerge when state officials consider administrative reforms lacking political salience (McNeal et al. 2003). The salience of health care and welfare policy may therefore explain why the impact of legislative professionalism is so weak.

Political ideology has a modest impact on the enactment of the five innovations. With the exception of MSAs, the effect of ideology is in the expected direction. Senior prescription drug programs and IDAs are more likely to gain enactment in liberal states, whereas time limits and family caps are more likely to be adopted in conservative states. These relationships are marginally statistically significant in the context of both senior prescription drug programs and time limits. While it is important not to overestimate the influence of political ideology on the enactment process, the results in table 3 loosely conform to the discussion in chapter 1. Political ideology seems to affect the general contours within which public policy is made, but it does not force officials to comply with specific demands or give them a strict regimen to follow (Erikson,

Wright, and McIver 1993). It is a good starting point for considering the role of electoral considerations during the enactment process. It is not, however, a sufficient explanation of policy adoption.

The quantitative analysis presented in this section of this chapter provides mixed support for six conventional hypotheses about which factors affect the enactment process. An especially strong relationship between national intervention and policy adoption emerges, supporting the vertical diffusion hypothesis. Although the results provide more modest support for the ideology hypothesis, they imply a basic relationship between electoral considerations and program enactment. The four other hypotheses evaluated in this section receive less empirical support, and the analysis suggests that the neighboring state effect, problem severity, slack resources, and legislative professionalism have a limited impact on the enactment process. A recent survey of state-level diffusion research suggests that these results are not anomalous (Mooney 2001a).[15] In short, the usual suspects represent the background conditions against which state officials operate, but they seem to provide an incomplete account of the enactment process.

Consider, for example, the impact of problem severity on the enactment process. An existing social condition might stimulate officials to react by enacting an innovative public policy, but such a reaction is by no means automatic. Political dynamics transform seemingly objective conditions into policy-relevant problems, and this transformation can generate significant controversy. Before an existing social condition becomes a policy problem, officials must agree that governmental action can and should be used to address it. As a result, policy-making has been described as a "constant struggle over the criteria for classification, the boundaries of categories, and the definition of ideals that guide the way people behave" (Deborah Stone 1997a, 11). There is a perceptual, interpretive element to problem definition, and values play a substantial role (Kingdon 1995, 109–115).

In addition, it is difficult to link problem severity to specific policy innovations. If officials agree that a social condition is a problem that merits a governmental response, they can choose from an almost limitless array of policy solutions. Policy on traffic safety, for example, moved onto the national policy agenda at irregular intervals throughout the second half of the twentieth century. Officials proposed different policy solutions every time that this issue emerged. They favored highway construction during the 1950s, requirements for safer cars during the 1960s, and imprisoning drunk drivers during the 1980s and 1990s (Baumgartner and Jones 1993, 124). One can imagine an equally wide-ranging set of policy options in virtually any policy arena. Linking a social condition to the enactment of a specific policy innovation assumes that officials agree on the need for government action and that a particular solution is desirable. Treating problem severity as a correlate of program enactment therefore overlooks the equally important debates that transform an existing social condition into a problem that merits governmental action. These debates are a crucial element of the policy-making process.

Many of the "usual suspects" that have been examined in this section of this chapter are subject to similar concerns. Most diffusion studies emphasize the impact of state demographic and socioeconomic characteristics on the enactment of policy innovations. This emphasis sheds significant light on the correlates of adoption. However, it neither sheds light on institutions and decision making nor produces generalizations about the lawmakers who ultimately make the choices in which we are interested. Event history analysis implicitly conceptualizes program enactment as a set of relationships between certain inputs and a policy innovation. Such inputs as per capita income and legislative professionalism can be expected to lead or not to lead to the adoption of policy innovations. This approach does not reveal much about the causal processes that link these inputs to the enactment decision. Only by systematically assessing officials' activities can scholars appreciate the political calculations that affect the diffusion of policy innovations, but the analysis in the preceding pages says little about how officials make the decision to adopt or not to adopt a policy innovation. In contrast, the remainder of this chapter focuses on individuals who, by virtue of their positions, possess institutional perquisites that grant them substantial influence over the enactment process.

Institutionally Critical Actors and Program Enactment

Conventional accounts of policy diffusion seem not to capture the dynamism that characterizes the enactment process, which is often more complicated than a simple yes-no decision about the merits of a policy innovation. The passage of legislation frequently features multiple debates and shifting positions among key actors. It also presents many hurdles that must be cleared. Policy innovations typically need to earn the endorsements of legislative committees, two full chambers, and the governor.[16] Failure to fulfill any of these tasks means that innovations will not be enacted, and this process gives significant power to institutionally critical actors whose positions allow them to serve as veto points during the enactment process.

Chapter 1 hypothesized that electoral considerations influence the enactment process. Recent research on congressional and state legislative leadership suggests that this hypothesis resonates with the potential impact of institutionally critical actors, such as governors and chamber leaders. The power of these leaders, according to principal agent theory, represents a response to rank-and-file members' collective action problems. Party leaders possess the responsibility and the resources to help members achieve such goals as winning reelection (Cox and McCubbins 1993; Clucas 2001). Legislative leaders assign members to committees, choose chairs for these committees, distribute resources, and possess procedural powers.[17] In fulfilling their responsibilities, chamber leaders often further the reelection prospects of members of the majority party. Governors possess institutional authority that enables them to play a similar role for their fellow partisans. Governors play many critical roles in state politics, but one of the most important is that of party leader. Governors who are seen as particularly effective or ineffective can affect whether their fellow partisans achieve their electoral goals. The influence of chamber leaders and governors grows, in part, out of electoral considerations, and these individuals possess institutional perquisites that enable them to affect the enactment process.

Conventional accounts of policy diffusion rarely mention the policymakers who make the decisions in which we are interested. In his seminal work on the diffusion of innovations across the American states, Jack Walker cautions that "in order to develop explanations of these processes we must go beyond the search for demographic correlates of innovation and develop generalizations which refer to the behavior of the [individuals] who actually make the choices in which we are interested" (1969,

887). The purpose of this section of this chapter is to respond directly to Walker's admonition, by emphasizing the potential impact of the individuals who hold institutionally critical posts in state government. This discussion will emphasize the impact of governors and various legislative leaders. These individuals can make the enactment of a policy innovation more or less likely through their active support or their active opposition.

GOVERNORS AND THE ENACTMENT PROCESS

As the chief executives of their states, governors possess an impressive array of institutional perquisites. Their combination of formal and informal powers makes them extremely influential during the enactment process. Governors' formal powers include their tenure potential, budgetary power, appointment power, and veto power. In recent decades, these formal powers have generally increased (Muller 1985; Bowman and Kearney 1986), although substantial differences remain across states (Beyle 2004). Informal gubernatorial resources, meanwhile, include such factors as governors' personal popularity, personality, and objectives.[18] Despite differences across states in the reach of these prerogatives, every governor holds a prominent place in state politics. Governors initiate legislation and work for its adoption. They describe and justify their priorities in State of the State addresses and during other public appearances. The governor is generally the central political figure in a state and has been described as its "chief legislator" (Rosenthal 1990, 5–38).[19] If a policy advocate were forced to rely on the support of a single politician in their state, they would be very likely to choose the governor.

Examples from Oregon and Virginia illustrate how governors affect the enactment of policy innovations by using their formal and informal powers. One power that enables governors to serve as institutionally critical actors is the veto. A policy innovation will not become law unless either the governor signs legislation to establish it or the legislature is willing to clear the rather high hurdle of overcoming a gubernatorial veto. Veto power means that state legislatures must anticipate the gubernatorial reaction that their activities will provoke. For example, Democratic governor Barbara Roberts of Oregon was an outspoken critic of welfare reform efforts in the early 1990s. Advocates knew that they needed to accommodate the governor in order for reform legislation to gain enactment. Governor Roberts and welfare reform proponents eventually went to the bargaining table and reached a compromise. After these negotiations, Roberts cast aside her ambivalence about the measure and endorsed it, making its passage inevitable. Legislators in Oregon expanded the welfare reform program two years later, and Roberts's successor played an analogous role. A policy advisor for Democratic governor John Kitzhaber participated in negotiations and testified multiple times before legislative committees. In both cases, the implicit assent of a Democratic governor removed an important obstacle from the path of a welfare reform program and guaranteed its passage.

Governors can use other institutional prerogatives to facilitate the adoption of a specific innovation or to prevent it from gaining enactment. They can use the visibility of their posts to draw attention to specific policy innovations and away from others that they oppose. Inaugural addresses and State of the State speeches provide governors with a bully pulpit from which they can outline their priorities. Consider the trajectory of senior prescription drug programs in Virginia. In 2001, lawmakers in that state introduced a wide range of proposals on the topic. All of the proposals aimed to assist senior citizens with rising prescription drug costs.[20] Republican governor James S. Gilmore III opposed the creation of a senior prescription drug program and used his institutional prerogatives to direct attention to other health care issues. Gilmore addressed the topic of health care during his State of the Commonwealth address in January 2001 and used this speech to shift attention away from the topic of prescription drug coverage. He proposed major changes to the state Medicaid program and devoted substantial attention to the issue of mental health.[21] Proposals to create a senior prescription drug program languished after this gubernatorial address. Other factors also contributed to this outcome, but the episode shows how governors can use their institutional perquisites to block policy innovations that they oppose.

In addition to using their powers to thwart proposals, governors can also facilitate the enactment of policy innovations through their active support. Welfare reform figured prominently in Virginia's 1993 gubernatorial campaign. As the campaign progressed, the candidates' attention focused on time limits. Republican candidate George F. Allen proposed a strict, two-year time limit on welfare receipt. His proposal went well beyond the changes that had been implemented in other states, and Allen made it a centerpiece of his campaign. The Democratic candidate, Mary Sue Terry, endorsed a less stringent proposal concerning time limits. Allen won the November election, making it clear that the Virginia General Assembly would address welfare reform—specifically time limits—when it reconvened in 1994. Thus, the active support of Governor Allen facilitated the enactment of a strict time limit in Virginia. This episode illustrates the potential importance of the governor in fostering the adoption of specific innovations.

LEGISLATIVE LEADERS AND THE ENACTMENT PROCESS

Like governors, legislative leaders can have a significant impact on the enactment process. Chamber leaders, legislative party leaders, and committee chairs are especially influential, because their positions grant them institutional prerogatives that their fellow legislators do not possess. As a result, innovations are more likely to gain enactment if they have the active support of legislative leaders. For this reason, many lobbyists concentrate on earning support from presiding officers and committee chairs. This top-down strategy accounts, according to one estimate, for about half of the work of many lobbyists (Rosenthal 1993, 183). Many lobbyists cultivate support from legislative leaders because it can be more efficient than a broader lobbying campaign.

Chamber leaders, such as house Speakers and senate presidents, are particularly influential. Speakers' powers include the ability to appoint party leaders and committee chairs, to control the committee system, to provide campaign support and additional staff, to control house procedures, and to serve for an unlimited number of years (Clucas 2001; Hamm and Moncrief 2004). The extent of these powers varies across states. The ability to appoint committee chairs gives chamber leaders tremendous authority, because so much important legislative activity occurs in committee. In about half of state legislative chambers, legislators of the majority party are appointed by the top leader. In Massachusetts, for example, the ratification of committee chairs by the party caucuses is typically done pro forma. One former legislator explains,

"Because of the President's/Speaker's near-complete control over the selection process, they both hold enormous power over their respective chambers" (McDonaugh 2000, 12).[22] In addition, chamber leaders often determine which legislators will serve on the conference committees that reconcile the house and senate versions of approved legislation. These appointment powers give chamber leaders tremendous influence over legislative outputs.

The prerogatives of house Speakers and senate presidents increase as legislative sessions draw to a close. Most state legislatures meet for limited periods each year and usually do not process every measure that is introduced. As a result, legislative activity increases with the progression of a session, as time becomes a scarce resource. Committees send more legislation to the floor. Sometimes, dozens of roll-call votes occur in a single day. The close of a session frequently prompts chamber leaders to take control of the agenda, deciding which bills will come up for a vote. Controlling the legislative calendar is thus another important leadership prerogative that affects the enactment process.

Leaders' appointment powers are important because committee chairs are highly influential legislators. A former Massachusetts house member explains, "Most of the time, floor debate is only the playing out of controversies that have been sorted out and settled in the committee process" (McDonaugh 2000, 186). For example, legislative committees in Oregon can introduce bills with the committee listed as the author; offer substitute bills in place of the original; have committee amendments automatically incorporated into the bill rather than accepted or rejected on the floor; and, by requiring unanimous consent, make it very difficult to amend legislation on the floor (Hamm and Moncrief 2004).[23] Although the typical committee generally does not possess such extensive powers, many state legislators nonetheless aspire to a plum position as committee chair.[24] The active support of committee chairs helps policy innovations make it out of committee, while their active opposition can be an especially difficult hurdle for the innovation to clear.

The battle over welfare reform in Oregon demonstrates the institutionally critical role of committee chairs. In 1995, Republican Stan Bunn chaired the Senate Committee on Health and Human Services. With assistance from the Oregon Department of Human Resources and a senate colleague, Bunn authored Senate Bill 1117. The chair ensured that the committee stuck to the strict timetable necessary to guarantee the passage of this legislation. As his committee ended a work session on May 10, Bunn revealed his plan for the remainder of the session. Announcing that the committee would hold a meeting the following Monday, the chair described his "intent to bring action to bring [welfare reform legislation] out of committee at that time."[25] Within two weeks, the reform legislation had earned approval from the committee and the senate as a whole. The chairman played a critical role in the enactment of this landmark legislation.

In contrast, welfare reform proposals did not gain enactment in Oregon when they were sponsored by legislators who did not hold a leadership post. As Chair Bunn guided Senate Bill 1117 to enactment in 1995, other legislators submitted proposals to transform the state welfare system. Republican representative Jane Lokan filed a bill to impose a strict two-year time limit on welfare receipt, and Republican representative Charles Starr filed proposals concerning family caps and time limits. Democratic representative Bryan Johnston, a freshman, submitted a bill to establish an earned income tax credit at the state level. An identical fate befell all four bills. The House Committee on Children and Families held public hearings on the four proposals, but all of them remained bottled up in committee when the session adjourned. The limited progress on these measures was due, in part, to the fact that their sponsors could not draw on a leadership position or on the support of fellow legislators who held leadership posts.

Developments in Virginia also illustrate how policy innovations are more likely to gain enactment when they have the active support of committee chairs. Two Democratic committee chairs in the House of Delegates actively supported welfare reform and played important roles in the passage of legislation. Delegate Richard Cranwell chaired or cochaired the House Finance Committee between 1994 and 2001. A forceful advocate for welfare reform in Virginia, Cranwell served on the Commission to Stimulate Personal Initiative to Overcome Poverty, which developed many proposals that formed the backbone of the state's reform program.[26] From 1994 to 1997, Delegate David Brickey chaired the House Committee on Health, Welfare, and Institutions. Brickey also headed a legislative task force on welfare reform.[27] The support of these two committee chairs and influential Democrats helped welfare reform sail to easy passage in the Virginia General Assembly.

While welfare reform gained enactment in Virginia, multiple proposals to create a senior prescription drug program in the state languished. These outcomes varied, in part, because the chief patrons of the health care bills did not hold committee chairs. In 2000, a proposal submitted by Democratic delegate R. Creigh Deeds went nowhere. Delegate Harvey Morgan, a Republican, filed similar legislation in 2001. His proposal would have forced state policymakers to choose between enacting a senior prescription drug program and lowering the state car tax. Delegate Morgan was a "senior member in the majority caucus" and an "influential player on the Appropriations Committee," yet his bill did not gain enactment.[28] The contrasting fates of senior prescription drug programs and welfare reform in Virginia suggest that committee chairs serve as institutionally critical actors.[29] Policy innovations are more likely to gain enactment when they have the active support of these legislative leaders.

Institutionally Critical Actors and Program Enactment in Massachusetts

The examples in the preceding section of this chapter suggest that governors and legislative leaders possess institutional powers that enable them to wield significant influence over the enactment process. Ultimately, however, these examples are more suggestive than definitive. The impact of executive and legislative leadership depends on the political context. In both Oregon and Virginia, however, this context fluctuated throughout the period under study in this book, making it difficult to develop generalizations about the influence of these institutionally critical actors. In Virginia, the governorship shifted between Republicans and Democrats, while the Democrats had and then lost a majority in the Virginia General Assembly. Throughout the period, Democratic governors held office in Oregon, but control of the state legislature shifted. Republicans controlled the state house for the entire 1990s and seized control of the senate after the 1994 elections. These changes and the periodic existence of divided government might have affected the impact of these institutionally critical actors (Mayhew 1991; Binder 2003).

Of the three states examined in this book, partisan control remained most stable in Massachusetts. Throughout the 1990s, a Republican governor faced an overwhelmingly Democratic state legislature. Massachusetts therefore represents an especially favorable context in which to examine the effects of governors and legislative leaders on program enactment. Its partisan alignment was stable, but Republican governors and Democratic legislative leaders took varied stances on senior prescription drug programs, MSAs, IDAs, time limits, and family caps. Furthermore, these institutionally critical actors pursued a range of activities to further their objectives. Under these stable background conditions, it is easier to isolate the impact of these individuals. This section of this chapter therefore examines the causal processes that led to the adoption or nonadoption of the five policy innovations.

During the 1990s, policymakers in Massachusetts enacted a senior prescription drug program and a landmark welfare reform program but did not establish either MSAs or IDAs. The most important debates occurred during the tenure of Governor William Weld, a fiscal conservative and social libertarian who won elections in 1990 and 1994.[30] The governor successfully maneuvered a conservative welfare reform program through the state legislature, but the legislature rejected his MSA proposal and overrode his veto of a senior prescription drug program. The most powerful legislative figure during this period was Democratic representative Thomas Finneran, who served as chair of the House Ways and Means Committee before becoming Speaker of the House. Finneran and other Democratic committee chairs exercised a tremendous influence on the enactment process, sometimes working in tandem with Governor Weld and sometimes working in opposition to him. Developments in Massachusetts suggest that a compelling account of enactment must describe the impact of institutionally critical actors in the executive and legislative branches.

The establishment of a senior pharmaceutical assistance program in Massachusetts demonstrates the limits of gubernatorial prerogatives. The senior drug program was one element of a larger health care bill that gained enactment in 1996, and the legislature overrode a veto by Governor Weld to enact it. The statute increased the state cigarette tax and imposed new taxes on cigars and smoking tobacco, and the governor specifically cited these tax provisions as grounds for his veto. Weld proposed an assessment on insurers instead, but he realized that he was fighting a losing battle. As soon as the governor issued his veto, he conceded that it was likely to be overridden and joked that he had about three votes in the state senate.[31] Sure enough, the legislature overrode the veto, and the measure gained enactment, suggesting that gubernatorial authority decreases when the opposition controls the legislature by a comfortable, or veto-proof, margin.

The passage and subsequent expansion of a senior prescription drug program in Massachusetts testifies to the importance of institutionally critical actors in the legislature. The impact of Speaker Finneran was especially important. While he led the House Ways and Means Committee, Finneran had beaten aside numerous attempts to create a senior drug program. After he became Speaker of the House in early 1996, however, the health care access bill that included this policy innovation became an important symbolic battle. Finneran improved his tense relationship with traditional Democratic constituencies by maneuvering the bill through the state house. He also demonstrated his ability to stand up to Governor Weld. The Speaker was aided in this task by the two Democratic authors of the bill, Senator Mark Montigny and Representative John McDonaugh. These two legislators headed the Joint Committee on Health Care and helped Speaker Finneran assemble a coalition that was large enough to override the gubernatorial veto (McDonaugh 2000, 237–84).

The subsequent evolution of the Massachusetts senior prescription drug program is also a tribute to legislative leadership. Senator Montigny eventually became chair of the Senate Committee on Ways and Means and played a critical role in the expansion of the program.[32] In 1999, policymakers transformed the existing program into one known as Prescription Advantage. Speaker Finneran played a key role in facilitating this change. For the purposes of this discussion, his most important contribution was to place a timeline on the passage of the proposal.[33] When Speaker Finneran announced plans to include the program in the 1999 budget, his pledge convinced observers that its passage was inevitable. One lobbyist explained: "If he tells you that he wants to run a marathon in three hours, you better be at the finish line at 2:59 because he'll be there. If he says that he'll do it, then he'll do it."[34] This illustrative example lays bare the legendary control that Speaker Finneran exercised over his chamber.[35] Powerful chamber leaders possess important institutional prerogatives and can sometimes overcome gubernatorial resistance during the enactment process.

The limited progress of MSAs in Massachusetts illustrates that a gubernatorial endorsement is insufficient to prompt the adoption of a policy innovation. Inactive gubernatorial support has a limited effect on the enactment process. Governor Weld submitted legislation to establish an MSA program, but many factors prevented its adoption. Gubernatorial disengagement ranked among the most important. Submitting a bill is a low-cost activity, and the governor essentially filed his proposal and then turned his attention elsewhere.[36] Weld supported MSAs, but the accounts were not a very high priority for him. He did not utilize either his formal or his informal powers to lobby for his own MSA bill, and the proposal languished. This episode suggests that gubernatorial support alone is insufficient to spur the enactment of a policy innovation.

The opposition of a powerful legislator also contributed to the limited progress of MSAs in Massachusetts. The governor submitted MSA legislation in 1994. Democratic representative Carmen Buell, cochair of the Joint Committee on Health Care, responded with a health care reform proposal of her own. The bills overlapped in significant ways. Both proposals shied away from universal coverage and favored an incremental approach to health care reform. The bill that Representative Buell filed, however, did not include MSAs.[37] Opposition from an important committee chair was one of the many factors that militated against the adoption of MSA legislation. Governor Weld submitted a proposal but did not pursue it energetically. His bill might have faced better legislative prospects had he actively used his gubernatorial powers to pursue the support of Representative Buell. However, inactive gubernatorial support and the opposition of a committee chair combined to prevent the enactment of MSA legislation.

Individual development accounts did not gain enactment in Massachusetts. IDAs were adopted in many states in the late 1990s, but this policy innovation retained a very low political profile in Massachusetts. No institutionally critical actor in the state took a strong stance on the issue. Neither Governor Weld nor his successors actively promoted or opposed this policy innovation, while the chamber leaders and committee chairs in the legislature were similarly silent. This gubernatorial and legislative inactivity contributed to the limited state action on IDAs. The first legislative proposal to establish this policy in Massachusetts was not even filed until 2001.

Omnibus welfare reform legislation gained enactment in Massachusetts in 1995, and Governor Weld played a key role in its passage. The governor introduced the main elements of this reform package and lobbied extensively and successfully for its adoption. His proposals to establish time limits, a strict family cap, and stringent work requirements set the tone for the legislative debate that occurred in 1994 and 1995.[38] While this debate occurred, the governor used virtually every weapon in his arsenal to ensure the passage of a restrictive welfare reform bill. The state legislature passed a compromise measure in 1994, but Governor Weld vetoed it. He argued that it incorporated too many exemptions to be effective. Weld raised the stakes even further when he included in his budget only eight months of funding for Aid to Families with Dependent Children (AFDC).[39] This was an extremely risky strategy: Democrats dominated the legislature, and many observers suspected that the legislature would override the veto. Governor Weld sprung into action to defend his veto, convincing two liberal state senators to vote to uphold it.[40] This active defense of his veto stands in stark contrast with his tone of resignation when the legislature overrode his veto of a senior prescription drug program.

Governor Weld used both his formal and his informal powers during the enactment process, and his veto gamble paid off. After using the veto, a formal power, the governor used his negotiating skills, an informal power, to uphold it. During his 1994 reelection campaign, Governor Weld prominently featured his advocacy of a tough welfare reform program. The governor won a resounding reelection victory. In combination, this result and the governor's budgetary tactics from the previous session forced the legislature to act in early 1995. The governor had allocated only eight months of funding for AFDC in his previous budget, so the legislature needed to act before the funds expired in February. By the

end of that month, a conference committee had endorsed a more stringent welfare reform package than the one that Weld had vetoed in 1994.
The final measure included strict provisions on time limits and family
caps, and the governor signed it into law.

In summary, developments in Massachusetts suggest that the active
support of institutionally critical actors makes program enactment more
likely. On the one hand, Speaker Finneran, with an assist from powerful
committee chairs, was important to the passage of a senior pharmaceutical assistance program. On the other hand, MSAs did not gain enactment, because the governor did not prioritize their adoption, while a
significant committee chair opposed that policy innovation. Institutionally critical actors largely ignored IDAs, and that policy innovation made
little headway in Massachusetts. Finally, Governor Weld played an indis-
pensable role in the passage of a welfare reform program, using both his
formal and his informal powers to advocate a proposal that included
strict provisions on time limits and family caps.

It is often possible to trace the adoption or rejection of a policy innovation to the active support or opposition of institutionally critical actors,
such as governors and chamber leaders. Governors affect the enactment
process due to their institutional perquisites and their informal powers.
Proposals that the chief executive endorses are more likely to gain enactment than are measures that the governor opposes. Not all endorsements
are equal, however. A governor might endorse several policy innovations but devote his or her time and energy to only a handful of them. For
example, Governor Weld devoted much more energy to his welfare
reform proposal than to his health care legislation that incorporated MSA
provisions. The amount of energy that governors devote to a policy innovation is likely to affect the probability that it will gain enactment. Governors can invest energy in a policy innovation by endorsing it during
their electoral campaigns, by mentioning it in an inaugural or State of the
State address, and by sending representatives to testify on its behalf
before legislative committees.

Legislative leaders have a similar effect on the enactment process.
Legislatures are complex amalgamations of elected officials who work in
two separate chambers and belong to different political parties. Innovations must navigate a complicated legislative process before gaining

enactment. At every step along the way, specific legislators serve as gate-keepers. Institutionally critical actors, such as chamber leaders and committee chairs, possess specific powers by virtue of their leadership posts. Their active support makes program enactment more likely, while their active opposition makes it less likely. The impact of Speaker Finneran and committee chairs on the enactment and expansion of a senior prescription drug program illustrates the significant role of institutionally critical actors during the enactment process.

Evaluating the impact of institutionally critical actors should be a high priority for policy diffusion research. However, most existing studies fall short in this regard. These analyses sometimes include proxies for partisan control of state governmental institutions, but party affiliations do not adequately capture the impact of these individuals. Members of the same party might share an interest in specific policy innovations yet differ in how much energy they are willing to invest in promoting them. The episodes described in the preceding pages suggest that such differences are critical. Party affiliation might affect the likelihood that a governor will endorse a policy, but it says little about the enthusiasm of this endorsement and even less about the activities that a governor pursues to influence the enactment process.

This section of this chapter suggests several constructive avenues for research on the enactment process. One way to extend its analysis is to construct an index that compares gubernatorial activities. The preceding analysis suggests that policy innovations are more likely to gain enactment when a governor undertakes a wide range of activities in support of them. It also suggests that a governor is more likely to achieve his or her goals when he or she works energetically on behalf of a policy. One can test these hypotheses by adding the variable of gubernatorial activity to a nationwide study of program enactment[41] or through intensive case studies of individual governors' activities and their relationship to the enactment process. In addition, one could assess the relative impact of these activities by analyzing them separately. This type of analysis might shed light on which gubernatorial activities are most likely to lead to the enactment of policy innovations. It would resonate with a long-standing literature (among scholars of state politics) on gubernatorial "success" in the legislative arena (Bernick 1979; Ferguson 2003). It would be possible to devise a similar set of actions by chamber leaders and to assess their impact on the adoption of policy innovations. Developments in Massachusetts, in combination with examples from Oregon and Virginia, suggest that the activities of these institutionally critical actors play an important role during the enactment process. Their virtual absence from conventional accounts of policy diffusion is a troubling oversight.

From Enactment to Diffusion

When scholars of state politics analyze the adoption of policy innovations, they tend to emphasize precipitating factors within a state but to neglect the causal mechanisms that are capable of transporting a policy innovation from one state to another. Their analyses therefore blur the distinction between diffusion and enactment. Policy diffusion is about the transfer of new policies across jurisdictional boundaries, but enactment is the decision to enact a program in an individual jurisdiction. The enactment of policy innovations is clearly an important phenomenon, but focusing exclusively on this process neglects other equally significant components of policy diffusion. Failing to present a complete picture of policy diffusion may mean that political scientists are overstating the impact of certain political forces while understating the impact of others.

Most policy diffusion studies assess which factors affect whether and when state officials enact policy innovations. Political scientists typically use event history analysis to examine the impact of several internal and external forces. The evidence presented in this chapter suggests that, despite its considerable merits, this approach is not sufficient. An analysis of national enactment patterns for five recent innovations in health care and welfare policy provides mixed support for several conventional hypotheses. It provides especially strong support for the vertical diffusion hypothesis, yet even this result raises important additional questions. National policymakers debated senior prescription drug programs but did not pass legislation during the period under study in this book. Did these unsettled debates affect the making of public policy in the states? If they did, what sort of impact did they have? One could ask similar questions about each policy innovation included in this study, and the impact of congressional debates might extend beyond the enactment process. Whether resolved or unresolved, these discussions might also affect the models to which state officials are drawn, the information that they bring to bear on their decisions, and the specific provisions of the policy innovations that gain enactment. Focusing exclusively on the enactment decision does not address these equally important questions.

In his seminal work on the diffusion of policy innovations, Jack Walker cautioned scholars against devoting so much energy to discovering the correlates of innovation that they neglected to consider the impact of individual officials. This chapter took Walker's admonition seriously by examining the impact of institutionally critical actors during the enactment process. Its analysis of developments in Massachusetts, Oregon, and Virginia suggests that powerful officeholders—such as governors, chamber leaders, and committee chairs—are highly influential. Their impact suggests that, as hypothesized in chapter 1, electoral considerations influence the enactment process. They possess the responsibility and the resources to help their fellow partisans achieve such goals as winning reelection.

Highlighting the potential impact of institutionally critical actors, however, raises almost as many questions about policy diffusion as it answers. Why did state lawmakers decide to consider a particular policy innovation? How did they become aware of the policy innovation? Were they inspired by developments in other jurisdictions, and if so, from what sources did they acquire information about these examples? Once again, these questions imply that political scientists need to examine outcomes in addition to patterns of program enactment. The remaining chapters of this book expand the standard scope of scholarly inquiry by examining multiple stages of the policy-making process—starting, in chapter 3, with an intensive examination of the agenda-setting process.

III. *National Activity and State Political Agendas*

W HEN AN EXISTING SOCIAL CONDITION becomes a political issue, elected officials can respond in virtually unlimited ways. For example, they can address dissatisfaction with the education system by creating charter schools, establishing school choice programs, implementing standardized testing, raising teacher salaries and requirements, or taking other steps. Similarly, lawmakers can respond to rising crime rates by hiring additional law enforcement personnel, imposing tougher sentencing guidelines, or pursuing another policy solution. This chapter examines the agenda-setting process, a process that narrows the complete set of possible alternatives to the subset that actually becomes the focus of officials' attention. Agenda setting determines whether officials will consider a policy innovation and is therefore a crucial stage of policy-making. An innovation cannot gain enactment without first moving onto the agenda.

Most research on policy diffusion focuses on the enactment of specific programs and largely ignores the agenda-setting process. Recently, however, several scholars have expanded the scope of their studies and analyzed the consideration of a policy innovation in addition to enactment patterns (Haider-Markel 2001; Mintrom 1997). This is a significant shift, because it begins to address the political processes through which a policy innovation becomes an option to be taken seriously. Furthermore, their analyses suggest that the forces that influence the agenda-setting process differ from those that influence enactment. These results resonate with the process-oriented approach used in this book and suggest that diffusion studies remain incomplete unless they examine the factors that place a policy innovation on the decision-making agenda. Careful examination of the agenda-setting process will therefore allow political scientists to develop a better understanding of how various political forces affect the diffusion of policy innovations.

This chapter examines the emergence of five recent innovations in health care and welfare policy, focusing on when these innovations achieved agenda status. Its analysis suggests that time-pressed officials are drawn to visible and salient policy options. As a result, political forces that can increase the visibility of a new policy idea serve as causal mechanisms during the agenda-setting process. This chapter emphasizes the impact of national activity. Developments at the national level, such as congressional debates, raise the political profile of specific innovations and foster their widespread consideration. The agenda-setting process seems to operate in both bottom-up and top-down fashion. Policy innovations are typically developed at the state level and then percolate upward to the national level, while national debates over these policies seem to spark lawmakers in additional states to consider their merits. National activity, in short, is an important causal mechanism that can foster the widespread consideration of a policy innovation by increasing its political salience.

Agenda Setting: General Patterns and the Impact of Federalism

The remainder of this chapter examines the emergence of senior prescription drug programs, medical savings accounts (MSAs), individual development accounts (IDAs), time limits, and family caps. It focuses on developments in Massachusetts, Oregon, and Virginia. Prevailing accounts of policy diffusion suggest two reasons why these policies might achieve agenda status at different times in these three states. First, the states vary in terms of region, demographic characteristics, partisan alignments, and other attributes that are sometimes associated with the diffusion of innovations. If this variation affects the agenda-setting process, the five innovations will be likely to emerge at different times in the three states. Second, the three states differ in terms of program enactment. Given the intuitive connection between agenda setting and program enactment, one might expect that the five innovations achieved agenda status first in early adopting states, later in other adopting states, and even later or not at all in nonadopting states. The diverse policy profiles of these three states might lead us to expect significant differences in terms of agenda status.

Systematically assessing the agenda-setting process requires the development of a proxy that indicates that a policy innovation has moved onto the agenda. This chapter uses bill introduction as a proxy for achieving agenda status.[1] In other words, a policy innovation has moved onto the political agenda when a state lawmaker introduces a bill to establish it. Bill introduction is a good proxy for agenda status because it suggests that officials are paying attention to, aware of, and interested in the new policy idea. It may also imply that interest groups and other "outsiders" who work closely with policymakers possess similarly high levels of awareness and interest. For these reasons, this chapter examines both the extent and the timing of bill introduction in the states. Patterns of bill introduction have also been used to assess the agenda-setting impact of such factors as the increased presence of women and minorities in state legislatures (Saint-Germain 1989; Thomas and Welch 1991; Bratton and Haynie 1999).[2]

Before examining the emergence of individual innovations in particular states, let us begin with an overview of bill introduction patterns. Table 5 displays these patterns. Its most striking feature is the overlap among Massachusetts, Oregon, and Virginia. The initial bills to establish the policy innovations in these three states were introduced nearly simultaneously, suggesting that the policy innovations moved onto the political agendas of these very different states at approximately the same time. For example, officials in all three states first introduced MSA bills in 1993 and 1994 and first considered family cap proposals between 1993 and 1995. This overlap is puzzling in light of current theorizing about policy diffusion. Examining a new dependent variable seems to introduce a new set of puzzles for policy diffusion research. The main objective of most diffusion studies is to explain differences in the timing of program enactment, but when the agenda-setting process is examined, similarity is the most important pattern to be explained. Why do innovative programs seem to achieve agenda status in one fell swoop? This striking overlap is not limited to the five policy innovations examined in this book. For example, officials in at least forty-one states considered term limits for state legislators in 1991 (Moncrief et al. 1992, 37). The debate over embryonic stem cells burst onto the state level in similar fashion in 2004, with thirty states considering seventy-eight bills related to the stem cell issue.[3]

Internal forces represent one possible explanation for the overlap in state political agendas. This argument implies that individual bill submissions are driven by groups and actors operating within states. For example, a policy entrepreneur in Oregon might work feverishly to convince a state lawmaker to submit MSA legislation at the same time that an interest group in Virginia convinces a state legislator to submit a similar proposal. In this case, the overlap in the two states' political agendas would be a largely coincidental by-product of independent lobbying efforts. This explanation is plausible, but the patterns in table 5 suggest its potential limitations. They indicate that proposals to create five disparate policy innovations emerged in three very different states at approximately the same time. When lawmakers in states as diverse as Massachusetts, Oregon, and Virginia are filing similar bills virtually simultaneously across a range of policy innovations, it is difficult to believe that independent forces are responsible for this wide-ranging overlap.

A second possible explanation—and the one on which this chapter will focus—is that officials take cues from similar sources. This hypothesis implies that the overlap in state political agendas is the by-product of an external source that affects multiple states at approximately the same time. Chapter 1 hypothesized that time constraints affect the agenda-setting process, and the patterns in table 5 resonate with this earlier discussion. Time-pressed officials are likely to be drawn to highly visible policy

TABLE 5.   Patterns of Bill Introduction in Three States

State	Senior prescription drug programs	Medical savings accounts (MSAs)	Individual development accounts (IDAs)	Time limits	Family caps
Massachusetts	1996	1994	2001	1993	1993
Oregon	2001	1993	1999	1993	1995
Virginia	2000	1994	1998	1994	1994

innovations. The most influential causal mechanisms during the agenda-setting process will therefore be political forces that increase the salience of policy innovations. If state officials face largely similar constraints on their time, it is possible that they will rely on similar cues or examples. This dynamic potentially explains why state political agendas overlap to such a considerable extent.

The same political force may drive the agenda process in multiple states because it responds to officials' time constraints. Its impact may cause certain policy innovations to move onto the agenda, transforming them into a topic of debate in state houses across the country. In prompting the consideration of a new policy, the political force does not necessarily have to invent or develop the innovation.[4] Instead, its main contribution is to raise the political profile of this program through its actions and thus to make it more likely that time-pressed state officials will consider that specific policy alternative. Consideration does not guarantee that the policy in question will ultimately gain enactment, but it is a critical component of policy diffusion. Once it becomes an option that is taken seriously in many different settings, an innovation has already diffused to a certain extent.

Various political forces can raise the visibility of a policy innovation. A crisis, a disaster, or some other "focusing event" can cause an issue to become an active agenda item (Kingdon 1995, 94–100). A policy innovation that is seen as a response to these developments may become more prominent as a result. Interest groups and advocacy coalitions can also increase the visibility of a particular policy, such as when the National Campaign to Protect Marriage urged state policymakers to consider (and to adopt) legislation banning same-sex marriage (Haider-Markel 2001). Finally, policy professionals can heighten interest in both an issue and an accompanying policy reform. This dynamic occurred in the 1960s when an article titled "The Battered-Child Syndrome" appeared in the *Journal of the American Medical Association*. This article, mushrooming media coverage, and competing model statutes combined to place laws on reporting child abuse on the political agenda in every single state between 1963 and 1967 (Nelson 1984). Each of these political forces is capable of raising the visibility of an innovation and thereby spurring lawmakers to consider it.[5]

The national government is another external force capable of producing overlap in state political agendas. National politics, whether they are political campaigns or policy debates, generally receive great attention from the mass media and rank among the most visible elements of American politics. As a result, time-pressed officials who are looking for cues about "hot" political issues might be inclined to use developments in the nation's capital as a measure of what is on the agenda. Many scholars have examined the impact of national activity on the diffusion of policy innovations. A common theme emerges. It is rare that the national government invents a policy innovation or imposes a mandate that requires states to adopt it. Even so, national developments can have an important impact. They can narrow the choice set considerably (Menzel and Feller 1977). Through intergovernmental grants, the national government can encourage policies to diffuse more widely and more rapidly (Welch and Thompson 1980; Allen, Pettus, and Haider-Markel 2004; Bingham 1976). By adopting an innovative idea that has been developed by state or local actors, the national government can spur additional states to act (Jones-Correa 2000–2001). Similarly, the quantitative analysis in chapter 2 suggests that national intervention influences the adoption of policy innovations. The remainder of this chapter extends that discussion by examining the relationship between national developments and the agenda-setting process, although it is important to remember that national developments represent a class of political forces. During the 1990s and early 2000s, national officials debated the futures of health care and welfare policy. It is possible that these debates, regardless of whether they were resolved, affected the trajectories of the five policy innovations under consideration in this book.

The objective of this chapter is to examine the causal processes that link national developments to state political agendas. Assessing this relationship requires two steps. The first step is to demonstrate that national developments increased the visibility of the policy innovations. After all, the theoretical argument in favor of external forces is that state officials who want to inform themselves as efficiently as possible will turn to visible and politically salient cues. To serve as such a cue, national developments must be visible. Although it is difficult to give a precise assessment of a policy innovation's visibility, newspaper coverage is a reasonably good proxy. Media accounts rarely change public attitudes on a specific issue, but they affect perceptions of issue salience among both government officials (Cook et al. 1983) and the general public (Mutz and Soss 1997). This coverage can enhance the visibility and salience of specific programs and broader policy issues (Winter and Eyal 1981), and it has also been linked to the diffusion of policy innovations (Hays and Glick 1997). Thus, newspaper coverage can raise the political profile of an innovative program. It is important to reiterate that newspaper coverage is a proxy for the visibility of a policy innovation, not a causal mechanism that facilitates its spread. This chapter does not argue that mass media coverage causes the diffusion of policy innovations. National intervention is the key causal mechanism that increases the visibility of a program, with media coverage representing a proxy for visibility.

The second step in assessing the linkage between national developments and state political agendas is to examine the timing of national debates and newspaper coverage and to compare them to trends in state policy-making. For national activity to influence state policy-making, it must satisfy two criteria. First, national activity must be visible and politically salient. Second, national developments must precede state-level activity. Only by demonstrating that visible national developments preceded movement at the state level is it possible to illustrate the national impact on state political agendas. The primary focus of the subsequent discussion is on developments in Massachusetts, Oregon, and Virginia. The case studies cannot provide a comprehensive nationwide overview, but they facilitate a careful assessment of agenda status over time.

This chapter uses the number of newspaper articles appearing on an innovation in a given year as a measure of that innovation's visibility. It relies on a unique data set of 1,938 articles from a variety of sources, on senior prescription drug programs, MSAs, IDAs, time limits, and family caps. It includes coverage from the *Washington Post,* because such leading news organizations as the *Post* and the *New York Times* "set the news agenda that everyone else follows."[6] In addition, the data set includes local coverage in Massachusetts (*Boston Globe*) and Virginia (*Richmond Times-Dispatch, Norfolk Virginian-Pilot, Newport News Daily Press,* and *Roanoke Times*).[7] These articles were gathered based on policy-relevant keyword searches performed on databases available in state capitals.[8] The searches generated a set of articles that provide both a rough measure of the policies' visibility and substantive information about their political trajectories.

The articles fall into two distinct categories. "National" articles feature politicians holding national offices, describe national legislation or existing national programs, or provide a general perspective on a social condition, such as the increasing cost of prescription drugs. "State" or "local" articles feature governors or other state lawmakers, describe state legislation or existing state programs, or describe a private or local attempt to provide a service or benefit.[9] Because this chapter focuses on the impact of national intervention, it emphasizes the number of articles that fall into the "national" category in a given year.[10]

In interpreting trends in newspaper coverage, the discussion that follows focuses on the early iterations of national debates. Early discussions and controversies may not draw the most extensive media coverage, but they may garner enough attention to cause an innovation to be taken seriously as a policy option. This initial burst of publicity may capture the attention of time-pressed state officials who are drawn to policy innovations that are politically salient. Therefore, the key questions in this analysis concern when newspapers first devote significant attention to an innovation and how state officials respond to this coverage. As a result, the subsequent discussions will emphasize the earliest episodes during which policy innovations received extensive coverage. These episodes are not necessarily those during which the largest number of articles was published.

The Emergence of Senior Prescription Drug Programs: State Activity amid National Indecision

National involvement in prescription drug coverage for seniors is characterized by a series of fits and starts. Medicare, the national health program for senior citizens, did not include a prescription drug benefit until the recent passage of the Medicare Prescription Drug, Improvement, and Modernization Act of 2003. When Medicare was established in 1965, this omission was not an issue, because outpatient medications did not make up a substantial portion of seniors' health care costs.[11] The increasing use, effectiveness, and cost of prescription drugs, however, led many people to argue that Medicare should include such a benefit. Senior citizens increasingly rely on outpatient medications that are not covered by Medicare but whose cost has risen significantly. Senior prescription drug programs subsidize the cost of these medications.

This chapter focuses on the most recent national debate over adding prescription drug coverage to Medicare. This debate, which began in the late 1990s, was not the first time that the issue moved onto the congressional agenda. In 1988, a limited and budget-neutral expansion of Medicare included an outpatient drug benefit, but Congress repealed the legislation when it sparked a virulent backlash among the very same constituency that it hoped to assist (Himelfarb 1995). Another effort to provide prescription drug coverage for Medicare enrollees took place in the early 1990s. Bill Clinton pledged to add a prescription drug benefit to Medicare during the 1992 presidential campaign, and his Health Security Act attempted to make good on this pledge by funding the benefit through an indirect tax on employers. The Health Security Act died a quiet death compared to the pomp and fanfare that accompanied its introduction (Skocpol 1997; Johnson and Broder 1996). None of the congressional committees that worked on the bill was able to forge a compromise that had majority support in the House or in the Senate. Eventually, the president was forced to admit defeat. As a result, the issue of prescription drug coverage for Medicare enrollees remained unresolved.

During the late 1990s, national policymakers discussed the future of Medicare, and President Clinton appointed a commission to recommend changes. The national debate over senior prescription drug programs resumed and became more politically salient. By March 1999, adding a prescription drug benefit to Medicare was considered the "most divisive issue" facing the commission.[12] President Clinton endorsed the idea in his 1999 State of the Union address, incorporated it into his Medicare modernization plan, and continued to lobby unsuccessfully for its enactment. Republicans expressed reservations about the potential cost of the prescription drug benefit and worried about its impact on the private market. Interest in the topic remained high as Clinton's second term ended, and the topic became a "defining issue" of the 2000 presidential campaign.[13] Although the candidates differed sharply on the best way to provide this coverage, both George W. Bush and Al Gore endorsed adding a prescription drug benefit to Medicare. This policy innovation received substantial newspaper coverage in 1999 and 2000, suggesting that its visibility increased substantially. Table 6 indicates that fifty-four articles were published on the policy in 1999 and that 152 articles appeared in 2000. This visible national activity in 1999 and 2000 represents the phenomenon of interest for purposes of our discussion. Did it affect state political agendas?

Trends in bill introduction at the state level suggest that the national discussion of senior prescription drug programs, particularly during the presidential campaign, had a profound impact on state political agendas. There was a dramatic surge of interest in this policy innovation, as officials in fourteen states adopted it between 1999 and 2001. By the end of 2001, senior prescription drug programs existed in twenty-seven states. Focusing exclusively on patterns of program enactment, how-ever, overlooks the nearly nationwide consideration of this policy inno-

TABLE 6. Newspaper Coverage of Five Policy Innovations

Year	Senior prescription drug programs	Medical savings accounts (MSAs)	Individual development accounts (IDAs)	Time limits	Family caps
1990	1	—	4	—	—
1991	3	—	0	3	—
1992	3	1	3	2	—
1993	23	*13*	1	*11*	0
1994	24	24	1	41	*24*
1995	20	70	1	57	56.5
1996	7	164	*1*	85	15
1997	6	59	3	30	6
1998	12	58	3	17	5
1999	*54*	47	3	19	0
2000	152	30	6	10	1
2001	35	15	3	20	0

Note: Cell values are the number of "national" articles published on a policy innovation in a given year. Values in italics represent the beginning of the relevant national debate or action. Years preceding the initial appearance of any articles on the policy innovation are indicated by a dash. Although the first "national" article on family caps did not appear until 1994, the first "state" or "local" article was published in 1993. Consequently, "0" appears in the family cap column for 1993. Disaggregated information about the number of articles appearing in individual newspapers is available from the author on request.

vation. During 2001–2 legislative sessions, bills were introduced in at least twenty-four (80 percent) of the thirty states in which no senior prescription drug program existed.[14] Furthermore, lawmakers in nine states passed legislation that affected the operation of existing programs. Clearly, this policy innovation achieved national agenda status following the 2000 presidential campaign.[15] The trajectories of this innovation in Massachusetts, Oregon, and Virginia suggest that national developments affected bill introductions in the states.

MASSACHUSETTS

The enactment of a senior prescription drug program in Massachusetts preceded the 2000 presidential campaign. Senior citizen groups in the state began their campaign for such a program in the late 1980s. Although they ranked a prescription drug subsidy program among their top priorities, they did not experience any success until 1996. The chairman of the House Ways and Means Committee, Democrat Thomas Finneran, personally brushed aside all attempts to establish this program. Chapter 2 of the present study described how, once Finneran ascended to the speakership, he used his institutional prerogatives and the assistance of two committee chairs to assemble a coalition that was large enough to overcome a veto by Governor William Weld. Finneran dropped his opposition to the senior prescription drug program when supporters linked it to a twenty-five-cent increase in the cigarette tax. The program was part of omnibus health care legislation to expand health care access to uninsured children (McDonaugh 2000, 237–84). Intrastate events and politicians were the driving forces behind the establishment of a senior drug program.

The earliest iterations of the Massachusetts debate over senior prescription drug programs suggest independence from national developments. Officials in Massachusetts revisited and amended their state program as national controversy increased the visibility of senior prescription drug programs in 1999 and 2000. Although these national and state developments coincided, it would not be appropriate to draw a causal connection between them. The 1999 revisions raised the annual benefit to $1,250 and also expanded program eligibility to younger persons with qualified disabilities. State policymakers made more dramatic changes in 2000. They removed restrictions on enrollment and remodeled the program as an insurance plan. Under the revised plan, enrollees paid monthly premiums, an annual deductible, and copayments at the point of drug purchase. The new program, called Prescription Advantage, was the first state program to be modeled on insurance principles.

OREGON

Developments in Oregon suggest that national controversy influences the agenda-setting process. The first serious discussions about creating a senior prescription drug program in the state did not take place until after the 2000 presidential election. In 2001, Oregon lawmakers considered various proposals with different copayments and different eligibility requirements. In addition to these proposals, lawmakers also filed five bills on purchasing prescription drugs in bulk and three bills on prescription drug prices.[16] Clearly, the rising cost of prescription drugs was a prominent concern among state officials, and the creation of a senior prescription drug program was one of the policy solutions proposed to address this concern. In fact, Oregon lawmakers created the Senior Prescription Drug Program during their 2001 session. Administered by the Department of Human Services and funded in part by cigarette tax revenues, it created an annual drug benefit capped at two thousand dollars for seniors whose income did not exceed 185 percent of the federal poverty level.

Importantly, the topic of prescription drug prices had received significantly less attention during the previous, 1999 legislative session, when Oregon lawmakers did not hold any legislative hearings on the general topic of prescription drugs or file any proposals to create a senior prescription drug program. In 2001, many bills on these topics received serious consideration from state legislators. Legislators filed bills and convened hearings on these proposals. The timing of this sharp increase suggests that it grew out of this policy innovation's prominence during the 2000 presidential campaign.

VIRGINIA

In Virginia, senior prescription drug programs moved onto the political agenda in 2000, as national developments raised the visibility of this policy innovation. Delegate R. Creigh Deeds, a Democrat, proposed a bill to establish a senior prescription drug program, but his bill went nowhere. Its demise, however, did not signal the end of this issue. State lawmakers submitted at least five additional bills in 2001, some of which were described briefly in chapter 2 of the present study. Patterns of bill submission in Virginia look remarkably similar to those in Oregon. Wide interest in senior prescription drug programs characterized the 2001 legislative session in both states. This interest followed a prominent national debate over this policy innovation in 1999 and 2000. In contrast to their counterparts in Oregon, Virginia policymakers ultimately decided not to adopt any of the bills that were proposed in 2001.

Developments in Virginia illustrate the limitations of looking solely at program enactment in studying policy diffusion. Lawmakers in Virginia decided not to endorse a senior prescription drug program, but they were certainly aware of this innovation and considered adopting it. Democrats and Republicans introduced proposals to establish this policy innovation, suggesting that it had moved firmly onto the state's political agenda. As an alternative that was taken seriously, one could argue that senior prescription drug programs had, to a certain extent, diffused. Furthermore, the timing of these proposals suggests that state officials took their cues from national debates.

SUMMARY

Senior prescription drug programs generated a heated national debate in the late 1990s. This debate sparked significant newspaper coverage, suggesting that it raised the political profile of the policy innovation. The episodes described in the previous pages suggest that officials in Oregon and Virginia reacted by considering their own versions of this innovation. Lawmakers in both states had shown limited interest in the policy before the national debate, but senior prescription drug programs received serious consideration in both states in 2000 and 2001. National intervention seems to have had a weaker impact in Massachusetts. The trajectory of the policy in that state suggests that national officials rarely invent innovations but sometimes debate policy ideas that have been developed at the state level.[17]

The Emergence of Medical Savings Accounts:
State Activity following National Controversy

As the cost of medical care rose dramatically in the late 1980s and early 1990s, officials at all levels of government looked for ways to hold down health care costs. The supporters of medical savings accounts portrayed them as a market-oriented solution to the problem. A coalition of national organizations promoted the accounts at the national level. The Golden Rule Insurance Company of Indianapolis, Indiana, doggedly pursued MSA legislation for many years. In addition to making hundreds of thousands of dollars in campaign contributions to the Republican Party, the insurance company worked with such think tanks as the National Center for Policy Analysis (NCPA) and the Council for Affordable Health Insurance (CAHI). MSA advocates formed a policy network that released various publications extolling the virtues of the accounts. Despite their efforts, however, medical savings accounts were not a very visible public policy option. Table 6 reveals that MSAs received minimal newspaper coverage through 1992, appearing in a single *Washington Post* article.

The national debate over health care policy in 1993 and 1994 dramatically raised the visibility of medical savings accounts. President Bill Clinton introduced his Health Security Act to the American public in a well-received speech in September 1993, and the political firestorm surrounding his proposal marked a key moment for supporters of the policy innovation. As national officials debated the proper governmental role in health care policy, conservative Republicans promoted MSAs as a free-market alternative to the Clinton plan. An ad hoc coalition called Citizens against Rationing Health endorsed the accounts,[18] and House Republicans introduced bills to establish them. In the U.S. Senate, Republicans Phil Gramm of Texas and Don Nickles of Oklahoma supported this policy innovation. Senate majority leader Robert Dole of Kansas, during his response to the 1994 State of the Union address, referred to medical savings accounts as one of several "common-sense solutions" to health care problems.[19] Conservative opponents of the Clinton plan thus coalesced around MSAs as their preferred alternative. As a result, the national health care debate raised the visibility of this policy innovation. Increased newspaper coverage, displayed in table 6, testifies to this heightened visibility. MSAs received moderate publicity in 1993 (thirteen articles) and in 1994 (twenty-four articles), suggesting that they became a visible and politically salient policy alternative.

The increased prominence of medical savings accounts at the national level led to a flurry of state-level activity in terms of bill introduction. As the national debate began in earnest in late 1993, Missouri was the only state in which lawmakers had endorsed MSA legislation. In 1994 and 1995, MSAs gained enactment in sixteen states. Looking only at patterns of program enactment, however, ignores how medical savings accounts moved onto the political agenda elsewhere. In 1995, for example, lawmakers introduced MSA proposals in twenty-nine (67 percent) of the forty-three states in which the accounts had not already gained enactment. Another summary of state-level MSA activity noted that at least thirty-nine states had considered MSA legislation and characterized this activity as "an epilogue to the 1993–94 health care debate" (Bordonaro 1995).[20] The widespread consideration of MSAs occurred after this policy had assumed a prominent place on the national political agenda. Developments in Massachusetts, Oregon, and Virginia illustrate this dynamic and suggest that the publicity generated by the national debate encouraged state lawmakers to introduce MSA proposals.

MASSACHUSETTS

In Massachusetts, medical savings accounts first appeared on the political agenda in 1994. The consideration of such a conservative policy innovation in Massachusetts, a relatively liberal state, is somewhat surprising.[21] This ideological mismatch did not prevent the accounts from moving onto the state political agenda after the national debate over health care policy increased their political salience. Like other state officials, Massachusetts politicians seemed to respond to the heightened visibility of MSAs by considering their merits. The liberal state was not immune from the national forces that placed MSAs on the political agenda.

Limited movement occurred on MSAs in Massachusetts, but it took place after conservatives in Washington coalesced behind MSAs as their preferred alternative to the Health Security Act. In 1994, Republican governor William Weld submitted omnibus health care legislation that incorporated MSAs. The accounts represented a fairly minor component of the proposal, however, and a *Boston Globe* article describing the plan did not even mention MSAs in the body of the text.[22] By the time the governor submitted his bill, the national health care debate was well underway, and prominent Republican officials, such as Senator Dole, had already endorsed medical savings accounts. Leading Democrats in Massachusetts had pledged to cooperate with Governor Weld on health care reform, but his proposal did not make much progress, and its MSA provisions were never seriously considered. Despite this inaction, high-profile Republicans in Massachusetts continued to voice their support for the accounts. Both Governor Weld and U.S. Senate candidate Mitt Romney endorsed MSAs during their 1994 election campaigns, and an editorial in the *Boston Globe* took their stances seriously enough to declare that the two candidates were "careless in their solutions to the national [health care] problem."[23]

The debate over MSAs in Massachusetts was not a central element of health care discussions in that state. This policy innovation never came close to gaining enactment. Even in this liberal state, however, medical savings accounts moved onto the agenda and received the endorsement of prominent state politicians. The timing of this activity suggests that it was influenced by developments at the national level. Such politicians as Governor Weld seemed to take their cues from their national counterparts. In fact, critics of the policy innovation suggested that Weld included MSAs in his health care plan due to his national political ambitions. Some observers speculated that the governor had supported the accounts to buttress his conservative credentials for a possible senatorial, vice presidential, or even presidential candidacy.

OREGON

The national debate over the Health Security Act spurred medical savings accounts to a more prominent place on the political agenda in Oregon. The earliest MSA debate in that state occurred in 1993, when lawmakers endorsed Senate Bill 5530. The legislation required that the Oregon health plan administrator prepare a report on the policy before the 1995 legislative session. Published in 1994, the report examined various state MSA programs and bills that had been proposed in the U.S. Congress

(Gates 1994). Administrative reports do not always spark legislative activity. In fact, opponents of a specific policy innovation sometimes use these reports as a way to slow down the momentum of a new idea. This dynamic did not occur in Oregon, however. MSAs possessed heightened salience when the legislature reconvened in 1995. Although national intervention did not cause the initial consideration of MSAs in the state, it helped ensure that the policy innovation stayed on the political agenda.

Developments both outside and within the Oregon state legislature illustrate the prominence of medical savings accounts during the 1995 session. The Cascade Policy Institute, a conservative think tank based in the state, hosted a one-day conference on the accounts in February. The conference was geared toward state officials and the business community and sought to raise awareness of the policy innovation.[24] Legislative activity also took place in 1995, as state legislators introduced multiple MSA measures. In March and April, both the House Committee on State and School Finance and the Senate Committee on Health and Human Services held hearings on MSA legislation. The conference and the committee hearings did not result in the passage of legislation. Ultimately, neither committee produced a bill that was presented to the entire chamber for a vote. Even so, these developments indicate that medical savings accounts were firmly entrenched on the political agenda in 1995. As an innovation that received serious consideration, one could reasonably argue that MSAs had, to a certain extent, diffused to the state.

VIRGINIA

The congressional debate over the Health Security Act in 1993–94 profoundly affected the trajectory of medical savings accounts in Virginia. The debate inspired state-level discussions that eventually led to the enactment of MSA legislation. In March 1994, the Jeffersonian Health Policy Foundation presented an MSA proposal at a conference in Williamsburg, Virginia. Developments at the national level inspired the organizers of the conference, and the foundation and conference attendees hoped to influence the national health care debate. However, the foundation lacked sufficient clout to be a player on the national scene, and the general contours of the national debate were well established by the time of the March 1994 conference. Fifteen reform plans had already been submitted to Congress. Similarly, it would be a mistake to overestimate the short-term impact of this conference in Virginia, as conference organizers admitted their disappointment with the sparse attendance.[25]

Despite its poor timing and limited popular appeal, however, the conference laid the groundwork for later MSA legislation in Virginia. The Jeffersonian Health Policy Foundation continued to press for the adoption of MSAs in the state, and the Virginia General Assembly turned to this issue in 1995. Foundation leaders distributed model legislation—called the American Health Care Plan—that proved very influential. Drawing heavily on the foundation's work, officials drafted an MSA statute that gained enactment in 1995. The statute was based largely on the American Health Care Plan and used the language that was originally developed by the Jeffersonian Health Policy Foundation (Joint Commission on Health Care 2002).[26] The national health care debate, in sum, inspired the foundation that ultimately played a crucial role in the emergence and the enactment of MSA legislation in Virginia.

SUMMARY

Medical savings accounts moved onto state political agendas after the national debate over the Health Security Act. Opponents of this presidential initiative coalesced around MSAs as their preferred alternative, generating moderate newspaper coverage of the policy innovation and raising its political salience. Of the three states profiled in this chapter, MSAs immediately gained enactment only in Virginia. Oregon officials adopted the policy in 1997, and MSAs did not gain enactment in Massachusetts. Focusing solely on adoption patterns, however, overlooks how lawmakers in all three states considered MSA legislation in 1994 or 1995. This overlap resonates with the proposition that state lawmakers will be drawn to visible and politically salient programs during the agenda-setting process.[27] The trajectory of MSAs in the three states also illustrates that national debates do not occur in a vacuum. Various interest groups worked to enact the accounts in the states, and the preceding cases suggest that national activity amplified these efforts. Such organizations as the Jeffersonian Health Policy Foundation were more likely to succeed—at least in terms of moving their preferred policies onto the political agenda—after national intervention heightened the visibility of MSAs.

The Emergence of Individual Development Accounts: National Legislation and State Activity

Individual development accounts (IDAs) were one of many policy innovations to emerge during the late 1980s and early 1990s in response to dissatisfaction with income support policy in the United States. Individuals across the political spectrum felt that the existing program, Aid to Families with Dependent Children (AFDC), was not functioning effectively. Some critics even suggested that the welfare system was counterproductive, harming the very constituency it intended to assist. In reforming their welfare programs, state officials could draw on an almost limitless array of possibilities. IDAs were one of many potential policy responses.

Economist Michael Sherraden devised the IDA concept during the late 1980s. He argued that welfare policy should encourage low-income individuals to accumulate assets. The accumulation of assets, he argued, would provide them with a sense of stability and would help them focus on the future. Sherraden felt that AFDC was counterproductive because it disqualified any recipients whose assets increased, deliberately discouraging savings. He devised IDAs as a way to correct these perverse incentives, modeling them on individual retirement accounts. Low-income individuals would deposit money into accounts earmarked for such purposes as home ownership or secondary education, then public and private sources would match these deposits. This arrangement, Sherraden argued, would give low-income individuals an incentive to save their money for long-term objectives (Sherraden 1991).

Individual development accounts received limited publicity. Table 6 describes the modest number of newspaper articles that appeared on the policy innovation between 1990 and 2001. Three favorable profiles appeared in the *Washington Post* in 1990, and the Democratic Leadership Council included IDAs in its proposed G.I. Bill for America's Workers a few years later. Throughout the 1990s, however, this policy innovation possessed limited visibility. The trajectory of IDAs suggests that the mid-1990s marked a key turning point in the diffusion of this policy innovation. By the end of 1995, policymakers in only four states had endorsed IDA legislation. Within two years, that number had more than tripled, and the accounts had a nationwide presence. The low numbers in table 6 suggest that the sudden emergence of IDAs cannot be explained by visible national debates over this policy. In contrast to the highly public battles that characterized senior prescription drug programs and medical savings accounts, IDAs generally flew under the radar during the national debate over welfare reform in the mid-1990s. National developments nonetheless had a tremendous impact on the emergence of this policy innovation.

The sudden emergence of individual development accounts can be traced to three developments at the national level. The first and most important development occurred in 1996, when Congress and President Clinton agreed on welfare reform legislation. This legislation, the Personal Responsibility and Work Opportunity Reconciliation Act (PRWORA), was a watershed moment in American income support policy. IDAs were not a central element of the legislation or of the heated debates that produced it. In fact, the accounts received only two pages of attention in a law that spanned over 250 pages. Yet these passages were critical. Section 404 stated, "A state to which a grant is made . . . may use the grant to carry out a program to fund individual development accounts . . . established by individuals eligible for assistance under the State program funded under this part."[28] Officials in a few states had already established IDA programs, but this legislative language marked the first time that a national statute recognized the accounts as a legitimate public policy option for state welfare programs. PRWORA explicitly listed IDAs as an appropriate use of state welfare funds and legitimated the accounts as a potential policy alternative.

Two well-funded national initiatives to study and expand the use of IDAs were established in the aftermath of PRWORA and also fostered nationwide interest in IDAs. The first initiative emerged in April 1997. The Ford Foundation pledged fifteen million dollars to study and to expand savings accounts programs in poor American communities, and the foundation wanted its grantees to analyze how effectively IDAs lifted poor families out of poverty.[29] The second initiative emerged five months later. A coalition of foundations established a twelve-million-dollar program allowing two thousand individuals in twelve cities to establish IDAs. Coordinated by the Corporation for Enterprise Development, the program was described as "the first well-funded, large-scale effort to encourage people who have little money in the first place to put some of it away."[30] Both initiatives sought to expand the use of IDAs and evaluate their effectiveness. They indicate the increased visibility of the accounts in public policy circles. They also illustrate the mobilizing or amplifying role of the national government, as the adoption of PRWORA spurred foundation activity that helped place the accounts on the decision-making agenda.

Developments in the states suggest that national legislation and the pilot projects played a pivotal role in the emergence of IDAs as a legitimate policy alternative, even though they did not raise the accounts' media profile. Officials in thirteen states adopted IDA legislation in 1997 and 1998, suggesting that 1996 was a crucial turning point in the diffusion of the accounts. Enactment patterns were just the tip of the iceberg, however, as IDA-related activity commenced in fifteen additional states. In many states, lawmakers introduced bills or included IDA provisions in their state welfare plans.[31] The diffusion of individual development accounts continued in 1999: IDA legislation was enacted in three additional states, and an IDA task force formed in a fourth state. Three years after the passage of federal welfare reform, IDA legislation had been introduced or IDA activity had begun in nearly 70 percent of the states in which no legislation had been passed as of 1996. IDA-related activity had occurred in forty-seven states by March 2000.[32] The specific provisions of some of these proposals illuminate the importance of the national legislation.[33] The emergence of IDAs in Massachusetts, Oregon, and Virginia illustrates the impact of national developments on state political agendas.

MASSACHUSETTS

National developments did not spur immediate IDA activity in Massachusetts. The state was something of a laggard in this policy arena. The national welfare reform statute did not spark an immediate reaction by lawmakers or interest groups in the state. Only in 1999 did IDA-related activity begin in earnest, and this activity occurred outside the halls of the state capitol. A number of private sector IDA programs were operating in the state, and in 1999, five of the programs formed a coalition called MIDAS (Massachusetts IDA Solutions). One of the coalition's major objectives was to encourage the state legislature to consider and to adopt IDA legislation, but they made limited progress on those fronts. The coalition held roundtable discussions in early 2001. Later that year, a state legislator submitted the first proposal to establish a public IDA program in Massachusetts. In sum, the accounts did not achieve agenda status until nearly five years after their inclusion in national welfare reform legislation.[34]

Massachusetts was one of the last states in which IDAs moved onto the political agenda. The first legislative proposal to establish individual development accounts was not submitted until 2001. This submission came after national legislation had bestowed an element of legitimacy on this policy innovation, but it certainly did not come on the heels of the national statute. The Massachusetts case, then, suggests that national developments will not spur activity in every state. State lawmakers seem inclined to rely on the national government as a source of cues about political salience, but not all of them will respond by introducing bills in their own state. After national developments raise the profile of an innovation, bill introduction appears to be widespread but not uniform.

OREGON

The trajectory of individual development accounts in Oregon reveals a tighter link between national activity and state political agendas. Encouraging low-income individuals to save money had been discussed in the early 1990s, and these discussions fostered the creation of IDA-like accounts. In 1993, for example, state lawmakers enacted legislation that created Children's Development Accounts. However, the statute did not appropriate any money for their administration or implementation. The state welfare reform program incorporated a different type of account that resonates with IDAs. It permitted employers to contribute funds to special savings accounts that their employees could use for higher education or for job training. Both of these examples suggest that Oregon officials were concerned with the same types of issues that motivated IDA advocates, but their policy solutions differed slightly from

IDAs. The welfare program's employer-based accounts, for instance, did not incorporate the matched savings that are a key component of IDAs.

National developments shifted the contours of the Oregon debate and contributed to the submission of an IDA bill in the state. One of the national IDA pilot projects was particularly influential. The Corporation for Enterprise Development named its program the American Dream Demonstration Project. The program began in 1997, and it established program sites in thirteen American cities. Portland, Oregon, was one site, and the existence of a program site within the state helped facilitate the serious consideration of IDAs as a policy option. The Oregon state legislature meets every other year. There was no regular session in 1998, but IDA legislation was introduced when the legislature reconvened in 1999. The timing of this bill introduction is suggestive evidence of the impact of national intervention, and the specifics of this debate provide additional support for such a claim. During a public hearing on the proposal, one witness represented the organization that administered the Portland IDA program site and talked about its experiences.[35] When the cosponsor of the bill, Representative Jeff Merkeley, explained it to his colleagues on the House Revenue Committee, he mentioned his discussions with the "national network."[36] This legislative testimony suggests that national developments affected the trajectory of IDAs in Oregon, promoting their emergence as an item on the political agenda.

VIRGINIA

The timing of IDA-related activity in Virginia also illustrates the impact of national developments on state political agendas. Individual development accounts moved onto the agenda in Virginia in 1998, when the state budget bill created an IDA demonstration project. The specific provisions of this bill suggest that the national reform legislation was a motivating factor. It used five hundred thousand dollars from the welfare block grant that had been created by PRWORA to fund the state-level IDA demonstration project. The creation of the pilot project followed the administrative strategy that the national welfare reform legislation set forth. That same year, state officials also addressed the topic of IDAs in a separate joint resolution. They adopted the resolution, which created a committee to study strategies to promote self-sufficiency among welfare recipients and the working poor. IDAs were one of the policy options that the study examined. This state-level activity occurred after the national developments that have been the focus of this section of this chapter. Its timing and the specific provisions of the budget bill suggest that these national developments helped spur IDAs to a more prominent place on the state political agenda.

SUMMARY

The national debate over welfare reform did not generate significant publicity for individual development accounts, but it established the policy innovation as a legitimate policy alternative. Perhaps more important, PRWORA explicitly listed the accounts as an appropriate use of state welfare funds and therefore provided resources that facilitate innovation. After IDAs were included within the national legislation, a pair of foundations launched demonstration projects, and IDA-related activity commenced in virtually all fifty states. Legislation was not submitted in Massachusetts until 2001, but IDAs moved onto the political agenda and gained enactment in both Oregon and Virginia. Virginia lawmakers drew especially heavily on the national statute. Thus, national activity promoted the emergence of a policy innovation that had previously received minimal attention from state officials.

The Emergence of Time Limits and Family Caps: National Debates and State-Level Activity

Time limits and family caps, like IDAs, responded to the perceived shortcomings of American welfare policy. Critics asserted that the existing welfare system fostered long-term dependency, and they argued that time limits would eliminate the pathologies associated with long-term receipt of welfare benefits. They also claimed that the extant system encouraged welfare recipients to have additional children to qualify for more generous welfare benefits. Family caps, they argued, would eliminate this incentive. In the early 1990s, national officials debated the establishment of these innovations and the specific provisions that would guide their implementation. The evidence presented in this section of this chapter, which examines time limits and family caps in tandem due to the impact of similar national developments, suggests that the high visibility of the national debate led to the introduction of bills to establish the policies in state houses across the country.

During the 1992 presidential campaign, Bill Clinton pledged to "end welfare as we know it."[37] Time limits became a central element of his reform plan. The innovation appealed to politicians across the political spectrum. Such New Democrats as Clinton were joined by such liberals as New York governor Mario Cuomo and by Republicans who wanted to enact more stringent requirements on welfare recipients.[38] Turning his campaign pledge into legislation proved to be a challenge once Clinton took office in January 1993. The administration appointed an interagency task force (with three cochairs and thirty-two members) to develop a welfare reform proposal. In May 1993, observers speculated that time limits would be one of the four central components of this proposal, which was still being formulated.[39] The task force, hamstrung by philosophical disagreements among its membership and by a multilayered decision-making process with unclear lines of authority, struggled to come up with a proposal. In December, it listed a two-year time limit as a programmatic option. Republican supporters of time limits questioned whether the president was sincerely committed to this policy.[40] As a result, the policy innovation became a centerpiece of the national battle over welfare reform. Increased newspaper coverage resulted from its centrality.

Table 6 displays the increasing number of newspaper articles published on time limits during the early 1990s. The formulation of Clinton's reform proposal received moderate publicity in 1993, and coverage increased as the national debate continued into 1994 and 1995. The tone of this debate spurred an outbreak of "just plain toughness in state [welfare] programs,"[41] and time limits were a crucial component of this state-level activity. Time limits existed in only two states as of December 1993, but the innovation received considerable attention in the following two years. Twenty-four states grappled with welfare reform legislation in 1994, and many of these legislative programs included time limits.[42] Lawmakers in fourteen states adopted time limits in 1994 and 1995. The timing of this state-level activity, coming on the heels of the 1992 presidential campaign and of the Clinton administration's discussions of how to carry out the president's pledge to "end welfare as we know it," suggests that the visibility and salience of time limits contributed to their emergence.

Family caps also emerged as a central issue during national discussions of welfare reform. This policy innovation figured prominently in the discussions of the interagency task force that had been appointed to develop a reform proposal. It split the task force and caused "the most divisive debate" in the administration's effort to develop a reform proposal.[43] Unwilling to cede control of the political agenda, congressional Republicans introduced multiple welfare reform proposals before the task force completed its work. The main Republican bill, House Resolution 3500, sought to impose a range of stringent requirements on the recipients of welfare grants. It required state officials to impose family caps and to deny benefits to minor parents unless the officials passed legislation explicitly overriding these requirements. Several Republicans, including Senator Lauch Faircloth of North Carolina and Representative James Talent of Missouri, argued that family caps should be a central component of any national welfare reform legislation.[44] Table 6 indicates that national developments increased the visibility of the policy innovation. The initial surge of publicity occurred in 1994, as the administration debated the merits of family caps and as congressional Republicans made a strong push for their enactment.

The national controversy surrounding family caps seemed to aid their diffusion as a topic of debate. Rather than shying away from the controversy, state officials introduced and debated legislation to establish family caps in many states. The extent and the timing of these bill introductions are difficult to ascertain, because officials often included family caps within more comprehensive reform legislation. According to one source, however, family cap proposals had been considered in nearly two dozen states by May 1994.[45] By 1995, the policy had moved solidly onto the political agenda in Massachusetts, Oregon, and Virginia. Developments in these three states suggest that the national welfare reform debate contributed to the state-level emergence of family caps.

In addition, the emergence of family caps suggests that the agenda-setting process operates in both bottom-up and top-down fashion. The policy innovation appeared in a few states before becoming a controversial topic of discussion at the national level. In 1992, New Jersey officials enacted the first family cap. The New Jersey program became a lightning rod for both supporters and opponents of family caps. Policy analysts studied the state's family cap program and reached divergent conclusions about its impact.[46] The program also sparked a legal battle that pitted the National Organization for Women, the American Civil Liberties Union, and the Legal Services Corporation against the Institute for Justice, the Empowerment Network, and the American Legislative Exchange Council. The program catalyzed interest in family caps. Developments in New Jersey were "closely watched by other states that are considering similar welfare-reform measures."[47] Another press account asserted, "[New Jersey] has put its finger on the hot button that Massachusetts and a half-dozen states are itching to push."[48] In sum, after being invented in New Jersey, family caps percolated upward to the national level. National developments then seemed to spur officials in additional states to consider this innovative policy.

MASSACHUSETTS

The debate over imposing a time limit and family cap on benefit recipients was a key element of welfare policy-making in Massachusetts. Republican governor William Weld faced an overwhelmingly Democratic state legislature in a two-year struggle over welfare reform, and a key area of disagreement was the stringency with which both of these policy innovations would be applied to welfare recipients. The timing and tone of the Massachusetts debate suggests that the national discussions of welfare reform had an important impact. The emergence of time limits occurred after the 1992 presidential race brought heightened attention to that policy innovation. Family caps initially received a chilly reception in Massachusetts, but politicians came to view them more favorably as they took on a more central role at the national level.

Imposing a time limit on the receipt of welfare benefits was an important element of the Massachusetts welfare reform debate. After the 1992 presidential campaign, time limits possessed relatively high visibility as a policy alternative. This political salience rose as a national task force debated welfare reform options, and a comparable debate occurred in Massachusetts beginning in 1993. That year, Governor Weld called for a strict two-year time limit on welfare benefit receipt. The stringency of this proposal generated immense controversy. In February 1994, the state senate passed a moderate bill on time limits. This compromise measure provided a middle ground between Weld and the relatively liberal state house. One month later, however, the Joint Committee on Human Services and Elderly Affairs removed the two-year time limit from the bill. Time limit supporters, including Republicans and moderate Democrats, bristled at this committee action.[49] Their reaction reflected an emerging consensus on the merits of time limits. Lawmakers disagreed only on specific elements of the legislation, such as the existence of exemptions. The timing of these state-level developments suggests that welfare reform discussions in Massachusetts, like those elsewhere, reflected the increased national visibility of time limits.

Family caps experienced a dramatic transformation during the early 1990s. In a few short years, the policy innovation went from one that was roundly rejected to one that was a key component of the state's welfare reform program. Family caps first appeared in the state during the 1990 gubernatorial campaign between Weld and his Democratic opponent, John Silber. When Silber mentioned his support for a family cap, his proposal was "roundly hooted."[50] Officials across the political spectrum reacted negatively to this idea, and Silber lost the election.[51] Like other officeholders in Massachusetts, Governor Weld was initially skeptical about the idea of imposing a family cap on welfare recipients in the state. When the New Jersey family cap program gained enactment in 1992, Weld publicly criticized the policy innovation. Family caps played a marginal role during early iterations of the Massachusetts welfare reform debate.

As the national prominence of family caps grew, however, the policy innovation received a warmer reception in Massachusetts. In March 1993, the Joint Committee on Human Services and the Elderly held a hearing on family cap legislation introduced by Democratic representative Evelyn Chesky. Chesky's proposal drew heavy criticism at the hearing and was not enacted,[52] but it illustrated the mounting bipartisan interest in the policy innovation. Family caps, in short, moved onto the state political agenda less than three years after being roundly dismissed in the heat of a gubernatorial campaign. As the national debate over family caps became more contentious, state officials continued to discuss the policy innovation. Governor Weld submitted omnibus welfare reform legislation in 1994, and a strict family cap was a key component of this proposal.[53] In four years, the Republican governor had completely reversed his position on the policy. A critic of family caps during his 1990 campaign, Weld endorsed the policy in 1994 and insisted on strict enforcement provisions.[54] The governor's transformation was symbolic of a larger sea change in Massachusetts politics. Family caps were a non-starter in 1990, but they were a central component of the state welfare reform debate in 1994 and 1995.[55] This transformation occurred as the national debate over welfare reform heightened the visibility of this policy innovation.

OREGON

In Oregon, the initial welfare reform debate focused on job training rather than on such policy innovations as time limits and family caps. In 1990, a coalition led by local business executives submitted Ballot Measure 7. This ballot initiative was known as the Full Employment Program. Its primary objective was to reduce welfare dependency by replacing public assistance benefits with wages for transitional jobs leading to regular employment. Ballot Measure 7 attempted to provide new employment opportunities for welfare recipients rather than imposing new requirements on them. As a result, it did not include a time limit or a family cap. Ballot Measure 7 passed easily, receiving 58 percent support from the state electorate. Importantly, the passage of this ballot proposition took place before the national welfare reform debate began in earnest.

As state officials continued to discuss welfare policy, time limits and family caps moved onto the agenda. In 1993, legislative negotiations transformed the ballot measure into omnibus welfare reform legislation. The omnibus bill retained the ballot initiative's original focus on on-the-job training and skill enhancement. National activity on this topic, however, seemed to affect the negotiations. The 1992 presidential campaign had raised the visibility of time limits, and the policy innovation made its first appearance in Oregon in 1993. The negotiations over the implementation of Ballot Measure 7 produced House Bill 2459, omnibus welfare reform legislation that included a time limit. Republicans in the state legislature added this provision to the original ballot initiative, and their proposal passed as a pilot program. Thus, time limits moved onto the political agenda in Oregon after national developments raised their political profile.

When the Oregon state legislature reconvened in 1995, time limits again played a major role in welfare policy-making. The legislation that passed in 1993 created a pilot program that did not apply to the entire state, and many legislators wanted to impose a statewide time limit. Republicans Charles Starr and Jane Lokan submitted separate bills that proposed a strict, two-year time limit on welfare receipt. These bills illustrate the continued interest in time limits that existed among conservative Oregon legislators. In March 1995, the House Committee on Children and Families held a public hearing on both bills. Neither proposal gained enactment. In sum, time limits were not a significant component of the early debates over welfare in Oregon, but national developments seemed to move the policy innovation onto the state political agenda.

Similarly, family caps also received heightened attention in Oregon after national developments increased their visibility. State officials discussed welfare reform in the early 1990s without considering family caps. By 1994, however, a presidential task force had debated the policy innovation, and congressional Republicans had pressed strongly for its adoption. These developments raised the political profile of the policy, and family caps subsequently achieved agenda status in Oregon. Republican representative Charles Starr submitted House Bill 3155 in 1995. It prohibited payment increases for additional children born to families who were already receiving AFDC benefits. Starr clearly took cues from his counterparts in the nation's capital. When he testified on behalf of his bill before the House Committee on Children and Families, he introduced an amendment that drew on language that had been advanced in Congress.[56] Starr's proposal stalled after the public hearing, and it did not gain enactment. Its existence suggests, however, that national debates can affect state political agendas. Early iterations of the welfare reform debate in Oregon did not address family caps, but lawmakers considered a family cap proposal after national developments heightened the visibility of this policy innovation.

VIRGINIA

In terms of welfare reform, the 1993 gubernatorial campaign in Virginia echoed some of the main themes that had occupied the presidential candidates in 1992. Welfare reform was a central element of this campaign, and both candidates endorsed time limits. The policy innovation had already been discussed in several states when the Republican gubernatorial candidate, George F. Allen, proposed a strict two-year time limit that went "far beyond any of the changes that have been implemented in other states."[57] Allen made the time limit proposal a centerpiece of his gubernatorial campaign, trumpeting his welfare plan during a campaign appearance at the state capitol and in one of his television advertisements. Democrat Mary Sue Terry endorsed a less stringent time limit proposal. Although the two candidates disagreed on the specific provisions of the time limit, their underlying agreement on the desirability of this policy innovation indicated its bipartisan appeal in Virginia.

Allen won the November election, and the Republican's victory made clear that the Virginia General Assembly would address welfare reform when it convened in 1994. The state Commission to Stimulate Personal Initiative to Overcome Poverty proposed a pilot program in early 1994 that included time limits. The state legislature, meanwhile, considered omnibus welfare reform legislation later that year. This reform package was known as the Virginia Independence Program. This omnibus legislation included a strict, two-year time limit along the lines suggested by Allen during the gubernatorial campaign. The topic of family caps also emerged, even though they had not played a central role during Allen's campaign. Many liberal constituencies objected to this policy innovation. Women's groups and the state's Black Caucus were particularly vocal opponents. In fact, the passage of the Virginia Independence Program was held up by disagreement over its family cap provisions. State officials eventually brokered a compromise, agreeing to limit the family cap to the first two years of the pilot program. The family cap was the only part of the omnibus legislation that could be described as a pilot project.[58] The timing of these developments in Virginia suggests that national activity had an important impact. The prominence of time limits during the governor's race in 1993 came on the heels of the 1992 presidential cam-

paign, and the highly contentious family cap debate occurred as that policy innovation occupied a more prominent place in national discussions
of welfare reform.

SUMMARY

Time limits and family caps were two of the most controversial elements
of the national debate over welfare reform in the mid-1990s. The
episodes described in this section of this chapter suggest, however, that
state lawmakers did not shy away from these controversies. Instead, the
heightened visibility of these two policy innovations seemed to facilitate
their diffusion as topics of debate and changed the content of state-level
discussions of welfare reform. For example, family caps moved onto the
agenda in Massachusetts and Oregon even though early discussions of
welfare reform in these states either viewed this innovation as a non-
starter or did not at all address it as a topic. The trajectories of time limits and family caps suggest that by raising the visibility of specific policy
innovations, national controversies can make state officials more inclined
to consider those innovations.

National Activity, Agenda Setting, and Policy Diffusion

The consideration of a policy innovation marks an important step in its
diffusion. It indicates that policymakers are aware of and interested in the
new policy idea. One could reasonably argue that, to a certain extent, a
policy innovation has already diffused once it has moved onto the political agenda. This chapter examined the politics of the agenda-setting
process, focusing on bill introduction patterns for five recent innovations
in health care and welfare policy. Bill introduction indicates that a policy
is viewed as a legitimate policy option by at least a subset of decision
makers. Whereas most diffusion research emphasizes differences across
jurisdictions in the timing of program enactment, the main pattern found
in the analysis in this chapter is one of overlap. Officials in states as
diverse as Massachusetts, Oregon, and Virginia tended to introduce legislation at approximately the same time, even though the three states differed markedly in terms of program enactment. The preceding analysis
attempted to isolate the sources of this overlap. It suggests that we can
draw three tentative conclusions about the agenda-setting process.

First, the preceding analysis suggests that national activity has a profound impact on state political agendas. The emergence of a policy innovation in the states frequently follows national activity on the same program. National debates can affect state political agendas before these controversies are resolved. In fact, national activity often influences state political agendas before members of Congress reach a definitive conclusion on the merits of a policy. For example, even before the passage of the Personal Responsibility and Work Opportunity Reconciliation Act (PRWORA) of 1996, national welfare reform discussions seemed to spur time limits and family caps to move onto many state political agendas. Similarly, the national debate over the Health Security Act seemed to encourage state officials to introduce MSA legislation in 1994 and 1995, even though Congress did not endorse an MSA pilot program until 1996.[59] Thus, the emergence of medical savings accounts in the states was an "epilogue" to the national debate during which Republican legislators coalesced around MSAs as their preferred alternative for health care reform. Table 7 illustrates this pattern for the five policy innovations reviewed in the preceding sections of this chapter. It constitutes an addition to table 5, in that it lists the year during which national activity began for each of the five policy innovations. Table 7 suggests that the consideration of the five policy innovations at the state level frequently followed national developments.

Chapter 1 hypothesized that time-pressed lawmakers will be drawn to highly visible policy innovations and that, as a result, political forces capable of raising the political profile of an innovation are likely to serve as causal mechanisms during the agenda-setting process. The analysis in the present chapter provides tentative empirical support for this hypothesis. Rather than undertaking a comprehensive search and reviewing every possible policy alternative, officials strive to inform themselves as efficiently as they can. Officials who want to inform themselves about politically salient or "hot" policy issues will therefore be drawn to highly visible policy ideas. This chapter examined newspaper coverage of the five innovations as a proxy for their visibility. These data suggest that national developments frequently raise the political profile of specific policy innovations and that state activity frequently follows this heightened visibility. In sum, state political agendas seem to overlap because time-pressed state officials are drawn to highly visible policy ideas. Policy innovations are more likely to appear on state political agendas after a national debate because these debates increase their visibility. When a national debate ends in stalemate or when Congress rejects a controversial proposal, the fight is not necessarily over. The battle can continue to rage at the state level. The states frequently fill the vacuum left by inaction on a particular initiative. This dynamic was relatively common among the episodes examined in this chapter. Senior prescription drug programs, MSAs, time limits, and family caps all received heightened publicity as national officials debated their merits. The visible national debates raiséd the political profile of these innovations, which then moved onto state political agendas.

Federalism seems to affect the diffusion of innovations across the American states, especially during the agenda-setting process. In other words, national developments seem to be an important diffusion mechanism that can transport policy innovations across state lines and contribute to the emergence of specific programs. Time-pressed state officials appear to take policy cues from their national counterparts. Innovations that are debated at the national level provide a visible, salient example on which state lawmakers can draw. In terms of setting state political agendas, national debates have a similar impact across the country. This national impact seems to explain why states as disparate as Massachusetts, Oregon, and Virginia consider specific policy innovations almost simultaneously.

Second, the preceding analysis suggests that the agenda-setting

TABLE 7. National Intervention and Patterns of Bill Introduction in Three States

	Senior prescription drug programs	Medical savings accounts (MSAs)	Individual development accounts (IDAs)	Time limits	Family caps
National government	1999	1993	1996	1993	1994
Massachusetts	1996	1994	2001	1993	1993
Oregon	2001	1993	1999	1993	1995
Virginia	2000	1994	1998	1994	1994

process operates in both bottom-up and top-down fashion. National officials did not invent any of the policy innovations profiled in this book. In other words, national officials are usually not the source of a new idea. Instead, national activity focuses attention on an innovation that has been developed at the state level. The policy innovation percolates upward from an individual state or small number of states to the national level. It then spreads outward to a larger number of states after national discussions or actions. For example, New Jersey officials were the first to impose a family cap on welfare recipients, and Missouri was the first state in which MSA legislation gained enactment. Both innovations were the subject of heated national debates. Introduction of bills on family caps and MSAs rose dramatically after this national activity. In sum, national officials generally become aware of an innovative program after it has already been invented at the state level. After national officials debate the policy innovation, it moves onto the political agenda in additional states where it had not previously been considered.

Third, the preceding analysis suggests that congressional controversies and other national developments do not occur in a vacuum. As national officials debate the merits of policy innovations, advocates at the state level also make their case for these programs. National activity can amplify the activities of interest groups and other organizations that are working on behalf of specific innovations. For example, congressional discussions of MSAs helped think tanks like the Cascade Policy Institute in Oregon and the Jeffersonian Health Policy Foundation in Virginia move their favored policy onto the political agenda. These types of policy advocates are more likely to experience success—at least in terms of achieving agenda status for their preferred programs—after national debates increase the visibility of these policy innovations.

Directions for Future Research

Given the importance of the agenda-setting process, it is somewhat puzzling that it has received limited attention from political scientists interested in policy diffusion. The preceding analysis, however, suggests several productive avenues for future research on this topic. For example, the relationship between national intervention and state political agendas certainly merits additional examination. The episodes described in this chapter suggest that national intervention raises the visibility of policy innovations and that time-pressed state officials are consequently drawn to these policies even if the national debates are not resolved. One could extend the analysis presented in this chapter by examining nationwide patterns of bill introduction to assess the amount of overlap among the fifty states, although this would be a laborious and extremely time-consuming endeavor. An alternative approach would be to perform intensive case studies of individual policies to examine how national developments affected their emergence in a small number of states. Before drawing definitive conclusions about the impact of national intervention, it is also necessary to compare these episodes to others in which the national government did not intervene. Such a comparison would allow scholars to isolate the national impact.[60]

Another potential line of inquiry concerns variation across states in responding to national intervention. The preceding analysis suggests that the impact of national debates is not uniform. State political agendas do overlap considerably, but the consideration of a policy innovation is rarely unanimous. In all cases examined in this chapter, there were holdout states in which the policy did not move onto the agenda. For example, IDA legislation was not introduced in Massachusetts until well after it had moved onto the agenda elsewhere. Similarly, the introduction of MSA legislation was widespread but not uniform after the congressional controversy over the Health Security Act. As a result, a logical question for future research is why some states are unaffected by the national controversies. Are there particular state attributes that account for this resistance to national trends?

It is also important to remember that national intervention represents a broader set of causal mechanisms with the potential to increase the visibility of a policy innovation and thereby affect state political agendas. Focusing events, interest groups and advocacy coalitions, and professional associations might have a similar impact. Future research on the agenda-setting process should examine the impact of these forces. Although several analyses suggest that these political forces affect the diffusion of policy innovations, they generally neither analyze their impact on state political agendas nor assess the conditions under which they are most likely to be influential.

Finally, the episodes profiled in this chapter point to distinctions among the type of consideration that the policies received. Lawmakers introduced MSA legislation in Massachusetts, Oregon, and Virginia in the mid-1990s, but the proposals received more serious consideration in some states than in others. Republican officials in Massachusetts praised the accounts, but MSA legislation did not come close to gaining enactment in that state. Oregon officials did not enact the MSA proposal that was introduced in 1995, but they held committee hearings on the bill. Noting whether officials introduced legislation cannot distinguish among these differences, and developing a subtler measure of agenda status will facilitate a more nuanced analysis of the agenda-setting process. This measure might incorporate bill introductions, committee hearings, committee votes, floor votes, and other steps in the policy-making process.

Although many important questions about the agenda-setting process remain open, this chapter provides two broad lessons about the analysis of policy diffusion. The first lesson is that examining new dependent variables can help scholars assess the impact of heretofore underappreciated causal mechanisms. The evidence presented in this chapter suggests that existing research understates the impact of the national government, because most studies do not examine the agenda-setting process. The second lesson is that it is easier to understand the impact of these causal mechanisms by considering their impact on the individuals who ultimately make the political decisions in which we are interested. The evidence presented in this chapter suggests that during the agenda-setting process, state officials are apt to depend on political forces that help them overcome the restrictive time constraints that they face. Chapter 4 examines whether the influence of time constraints extends to the information resources that these officials consult.

IV. *National Organizations and the Information Generation Process*

STATE OFFICIALS TYPICALLY HAVE access to libraries and other reference centers whose main job is to collect and distribute information that will be useful during the formulation of public policy. In Virginia, for example, the Legislative Reference Center in Richmond serves the information needs of the Virginia General Assembly. Its collection includes state legislation, legal publications, and topical information to support the research needs of representatives and legislative staff. A shelf near the entrance of the reference center provides introductory materials that describe the information available in the collection. These materials include a bookmark that describes the functions of the center. It states: "We compile state comparative data on a variety of issues. One of our most frequently asked questions is: 'What are other states doing in the area of . . . ?'" The notion of policy diffusion presumes that lawmakers have access to and are sometimes influenced by this type of comparative information. One could reasonably argue that an awareness of and interest in developments elsewhere is the essence of policy diffusion, and this bookmark suggests that such a dynamic is at least a semiregular occurrence.

It is crucial to distinguish enactment from diffusion. When state lawmakers adopt a policy innovation that was previously enacted in another state, this convergence does not necessarily demonstrate that diffusion has occurred. Late adopters can enact a policy that exists elsewhere without possessing any knowledge about existing programs. Under such circumstances, it would be inappropriate to characterize later adoptions as evidence of policy diffusion. Diffusion is not the fact of increasing inci-

105

dence; it is a causal process that implies movement from the source of an innovation to an adopter (Strang and Soule 1998). This process can take on many different forms, such as face-to-face interactions between early adopters and those who follow suit. Early adopters possess firsthand experience with innovative programs and can testify to their merits or demerits. Their perspective would presumably be useful to policymakers in states where the innovation is being considered but does not yet exist. Even when a definitive evaluation is not possible, however, diffusion implies that late adopters are at least aware of the developments that preceded their own decision to implement a new policy idea.

Information generation and dissemination are crucial components of policy diffusion. Policy congruence is distinct from policy diffusion, and these two phenomena can be distinguished by the extent to which late adopters are aware of earlier experiences with a policy innovation. With its emphasis on program enactment, most policy diffusion research does not consider this distinction or examine the resources from which officials might acquire policy-relevant information. Developments in neighboring states are often described as a logical information source, but diffusion studies rarely test this hypothesis systematically.[1] This chapter examines the information that is available to state officials. Its examination of legislative testimony, media accounts, administrative reports, and other documentary resources suggests that state lawmakers have access to an impressively broad perspective on policy innovations. These sources provide a national—and sometimes international—frame of reference. They contain information that overlaps in significant ways but diverges in others.

In an era of instantaneous communication, finding information is less likely to challenge lawmakers than is the process of sifting through a glut of information. The latter challenge is especially relevant for time-pressed state lawmakers who must perform a wide variety of activities in addition to information acquisition. The availability of information does not guarantee that state officials consult it. Through its close reading of various documentary sources, this chapter suggests that national organizations, such as professional associations, are well situated to serve the needs of state lawmakers. It also provides illustrative examples that suggest that state officials do rely on national organizations as a source of policy-relevant information.

The Current Information Environment

Public officials currently operate in an information-rich environment. Compared to their predecessors, they generally have more resources at their disposal. These varied resources provide access to a wider range of policy-relevant information. Several recent institutional, technological, and organizational changes facilitate the generation and the collection of policy-relevant information. This section of this chapter briefly reviews some of the most important changes and describes their potential impact.

In recent decades, institutional changes augmented state officials' ability to gather policy-relevant information. These changes, described briefly in chapter 1, made an especially profound impact on the legislative branch. As late as the mid-1960s, reformers argued that these bodies were ill equipped to process information and to study emerging policy problems. One response to the reformers' complaints was a dramatic increase in the number and the quality of legislative staff (Bowman and Kearney 1986, 76–106). Today, a larger and more qualified staff can gather information for state legislators, although there remain important disparities across states (Squire 1992; King 2000). Legislative staffers are now such an important part of state government, in fact, that a common complaint about the recent imposition of term limits in some states has been that term limits increase the power of unelected legislative staffers (Moncrief and Thompson 2001). Larger and more professional staffs also serve the executive branch of many state governments.

Technological advancements seem to make more information resources available for state officials. The emergence of new information technologies, such as the Internet, increased the ease and speed with which many organizations can provide policy-relevant information. The representative of one professional association explains: "The advances are enormous. Compared with what is going on now, we were asleep fifteen years ago."[2] Technological shifts also increased the ease and speed with which state officials can consult policy-relevant information. State officials can examine model legislation and statutory language online without contacting an organization directly. In addition, they can mark up legislation and send it to a professional association for comment. This electronic exchange is significantly easier than relying on a telephone, a fax machine, or snail mail. In the past, finding information sometimes involved phone calls and waiting for the mail. Today, similar information is often only a click of the mouse away.

Additional technological changes also make it easier for officials to consult their colleagues in other states. Travel is less onerous than it was in the past, facilitating attendance at regional and national meetings of professional organizations that bring together lawmakers and staff from across the country. Alan Rosenthal argues that "legislation tends to spread like wildfire" because of these conferences (1993, 67–68). Public officials frequently discuss new programs with one another at these meetings, learning about the substantive impact and political feasibility of policy innovations. When state lawmakers and their staff travel to these out-of-state meetings, they often look for bills to introduce when they return to their own states. Attendees also forge long-lasting bonds at these meetings, and they can use these connections to develop legislation once they return to their own states. A legislative staffer in Massachusetts explains the significance of such connections: "If someone called me and asked me to send information on our laws on managed care or HMOs I would know exactly what chapter to go to whereas someone from another state wouldn't. People do the same thing for me when I know exactly what I'm looking for."[3] Communications technologies, such as e-mail and relatively inexpensive long-distance phone calls, facilitate quick correspondence. It is not much of a stretch to imagine that these connections facilitate the dissemination of policy-relevant information. In sum, technological changes suggest that state officials are more closely connected than they were in the past and are therefore better able to exchange ideas and information.

Finally, organizational changes also altered the information environment in which public officials operate. Writing in 1969, Jack Walker noted the increased prominence of professional associations and the emergence of interstate and national government agencies devoted to facilitating communication between state officials. He argued that these organizations had begun to replace older modes of communication based on regional and cultural ties, explaining, "Decision-makers in the states seem to be adopting a broader, national focus based on new lines of communication which extend beyond regional boundaries" (Walker 1969, 896). Some scholars built on this insight by examining the impact of professional associations. The abundance of professional associations involved in health care policy, for example, can facilitate the diffusion of policy innovations and supersede the impacts of conventional factors, such as state innovativeness, regional ties, and federal incentives (Gray 1999). The committee system of the National Association of Insurance Commissioners facilitated the diffusion of the HMO Model Act in the early 1990s (Balla 2001). Professional associations exist in other policy domains, although the universe of such groups is especially dense in health care. These organizations can be a valuable information resource for state officials.

Other organizations rely on similar tools to disseminate information about policy innovations. Policy research institutes or think tanks host conferences and distribute publications that potentially introduce state lawmakers to innovative public policy ideas. Like professional associations, the influence of think tanks extends across state and even international boundaries (Diane Stone 2000; Jones and Newburn 2002). Even think tanks that focus most of their activities on a single state sometimes possess connections with organizations located all over the country. The potential impact of think tanks, like that of professional associations, might supersede ties based on regional affinities or cultural similarities.

Even a fairly brief overview of the current information environment suggests that public officials have easy access to a wide range of information resources. They work in better-staffed institutions that are situated in a denser organizational environment, while several technological changes facilitate the generation and the dissemination of policy-relevant information. As a result, it seems that acquiring information is not nearly as difficult as sorting through everything that is available. This sorting process might be an especially vexing challenge for time-pressed state officials.

Time Constraints and Information Acquisition

When policy innovations emerge, officials generally find two different types of information useful. First, lawmakers frequently want to learn about the programmatic effectiveness of an innovative program. Does the innovation achieve the objectives that it sets out to achieve, or does it fall short of these goals? Due to its emphasis on program evaluation, this substantive information is an important element of the "laboratories of democracy" metaphor. It implies officials' interest in the information that policy analysts produce. Social scientific research and other policy analyses amplify issues, elucidate the available options, and emphasize the nuts and bolts of how to design specific programs (Nathan 2000, 10). Officials want to duplicate the successes of their counterparts while avoiding the pitfalls faced by early adopters. Even though it is usually difficult to reach a definitive consensus on the success or failure of a policy, substantive evaluations are an important resource for state lawmakers.

In addition to acquiring substantive information, elected officials also assess the political impact of policy innovations. The political experiences of early adopters can be just as important as an innovation's substantive impact. A policy innovation might prove beneficial to its primary sponsor, or it might spark an electoral backlash. Either of these outcomes would be noteworthy from the perspective of an elected official. It is important to realize that politicians are interested in both substantive and political information. In the mid-1990s, for example, Wisconsin's innovative welfare reform programs garnered significant attention from officials in other states. These officials noticed the precipitous declines in welfare caseloads in Wisconsin, a substantive impact, as well as the sustained political popularity of Governor Tommy Thompson, a political impact. State lawmakers typically use a comparable blend of substantive and political information. It is tempting to think of this blended information as a weakness, but it is actually an important resource. This variety of information gives state officials an expertise that is not available to those who either perform detailed studies or work on the "operational firing line" (Kingdon 1995, 37).

Advocates of specific policies sometimes blur the distinction between substantive and political information. They frequently claim that the existence of a policy innovation in another jurisdiction legitimates it as a reform alternative. Sometimes, proponents and opponents will use the same example to bolster their arguments. Supporters will describe an existing program as an indisputable success, while opponents will emphasize its main shortcomings. This type of rhetoric provides both substantive information about the reach of a policy innovation and political information about how a vote for or against its enactment can be justified.

Learning about policy innovations that exist elsewhere can sometimes provide officials with valuable knowledge. In the current information environment, officials can gather such information from several different sources. Where are they most likely to look for the substantive and political information that they crave? It is important to remember that acquiring information represents one of the many tasks that public officials must perform simultaneously. These officials face severe time constraints, and the many demands on their time influence how their information search proceeds. When policymakers must solicit campaign contributions, perform constituency service, attend committee hearings, and undertake a variety of additional tasks, they will try to acquire information about policy innovations as efficiently as possible. Officials do not possess the time to undertake a comprehensive search, so they begin with the most accessible information and search sequentially for that which requires more effort. Once they feel sufficiently informed to make a given decision, the search ends (Mooney 1991). Due to time constraints, the timeliness and accessibility of this information can be just as important as its quality (Sabatier and Whiteman 1985). Chapter 1 hypothesized that officials will rely on information resources that consistently provide relevant information but do not require a huge time investment. The most important information producers are therefore likely to be the organizations and individuals who provide detailed, timely, and accessible information.

With its emphasis on developments in neighboring or nearby states, most policy diffusion research examines whether geographical proximity affects program enactment, but little research addresses the acquisition of information. Occasionally, scholars describe the neighboring state effect as an outgrowth of the tight communications networks that state officials share with their counterparts in nearby states. These potential connections have rarely been examined empirically, and the neighboring state hypothesis seems to possess two major shortcomings. First, it understates the importance of the time constraints that officials face.

Information about developments in neighboring states may not always be the most accessible. Second, the neighboring state hypothesis seems to overlook the largely pragmatic attitude of most state officials and their staffs. A committee staffer in Massachusetts explains, "It isn't necessarily limited to who borders [our state] but rather who has taken the lead or who has really shown initiative and done a better job with a type of program than we have."[4] Representatives of professional associations recognize that state officials tend to be open to new ideas from all over the country. One such representative explains: "If there is a problem that their state is facing, they don't care which state came up with the idea . . . Policymakers are very open to any ideas that will help them solve problems in their state."[5] The preceding quotations suggest that the availability of information about an innovative program matters more than that policy's geographic locale.

Given the time constraints faced by state legislators, the accessibility of policy-relevant information is a crucial component of the information generation process. State officials undertake a highly focused information search rather than a comprehensive one. State officials currently operate in an information-rich environment in which disparate sources provide policy-relevant information from around the country and even the globe, and their biggest challenge is sifting through this massive amount of information to find what they need. As a result, a key question for any study of the information generation process is whether and how the information provided by these disparate sources varies. Subsequent sections of this chapter examine several potential sources of policy-relevant information, paying particular attention to the frequency with which they cite existing policy models and the level of detail that they provide. The primary goal of this analysis is to assess which resources provide the timely and detailed information that officials presumably find useful.

Media Reports, Legislative Testimony, and Administrative Documents

A variety of sources provide state policymakers with policy-relevant information about innovative programs. This section of this chapter focuses on the five policy innovations analyzed throughout this book: senior prescription drug programs, medical savings accounts, individual development accounts, time limits, and family caps. It examines the information on these innovations that is featured in media reports, legislative testimony, and administrative documents. It focuses on the models cited as relevant in these documentary resources, emphasizing their geographic reach and the level of detail contained in these references.

INFORMATION GENERATION AND MEDIA COVERAGE

Media coverage magnifies movements that have started elsewhere and serves as a "communicator" within a policy community (Kingdon 1995, 58–60). This is an especially important task in the decentralized American constitutional system, where important policy-making decisions take place in many distinct venues. The media enable otherwise disjointed actors to keep tabs on each other (and on what they consider the public mood) by linking these different venues together and serving as a "privileged means of communication" (Baumgartner and Jones 1993, 107). State officials, given their interest in politics, are likely to be the sorts of individuals who actively follow the news through such activities as regularly reading newspapers and consulting other media outlets. These resources consequently represent a potential source of information about policy innovations. This subsection of this chapter examines newspaper coverage of the five innovations in Massachusetts and Virginia.[6] How often does this coverage include detailed discussions of programs that exist in other states?

Coverage in the *Boston Globe* is national in scope. Once policy innovations move onto the Massachusetts political agenda, articles in the *Globe* sometimes mention similar programs that exist elsewhere. In general, these references serve as illustrative examples and are not very detailed. References that appeared in the *Boston Globe* constitute the "Massachusetts coverage" identified in table 8. When Massachusetts officials considered whether to reform the state's senior prescription drug program in 1999, one *Globe* article reviewed their policy options and mentioned programs in New Jersey, Pennsylvania, and New York.[7] An opponent of this policy innovation, meanwhile, cited the cost of the New Jersey program as a development that should give legislators pause.[8] Coverage of MSAs in the *Boston Globe* mentioned a similar program in Singapore and described an MSA program administered by the Golden Rule Insurance

Company in Indianapolis, Indiana.[9] Coverage of IDAs, in contrast, did not include out-of-state examples. Instead, it described various private sector examples that were already operational within the state of Massachusetts. Coverage of time limits in Massachusetts mentioned the Family Transition Program in Florida, the Family Investment Plan in Iowa, and the JOBS Plus Program in Oregon.[10] Finally, family cap coverage was also national in scope. Early accounts profiled developments in New Jersey, the first state in which the policy innovation gained enactment, and other articles described how the Massachusetts program compared to those in Wisconsin and Virginia.[11]

Newspaper articles in Virginia similarly provide a national perspective on the five policy innovations under examination in this book. Table 8 identifies the Virginia coverage's references to programs in other states. During the 2001 gubernatorial campaign, Republican candidate Mark Early announced his support of a senior prescription drug program, and one article noted that Early's proposal fell "far short of a direct government subsidy for prescription purchases, something done in at least 21 states."[12] Out-of-state examples also appeared periodically during coverage of MSAs. Newspaper accounts described how the policy innovation

TABLE 8.   National Examples in Local Media Coverage

Policy innovation	Massachusetts coverage	Virginia coverage
Senior prescription drug programs	New Jersey Pennsylvania New York	"21 states"
Medical savings accounts (MSAs)	Singapore Golden Rule Insurance Company, Indiana	*Forbes* magazine, New York
Individual development accounts (IDAs)	Intrastate examples only	South Shore Bank, Chicago
Time limits	Florida Iowa Oregon	Wisconsin Iowa
Family caps	New Jersey Wisconsin Virginia	New Jersey Georgia

worked in the private sector, mentioning MSA programs at *Forbes* magazine in New York.[13] Coverage of IDAs was limited in general, but one opinion column mentioned the policy innovation as it profiled the South Shore Bank in Chicago and other community development institutes.[14] Newspaper coverage of time limits cited examples from Wisconsin and Iowa, with one editorial concluding that officials in "Virginia should be watching [the Wisconsin] experiment closely."[15] Lastly, coverage of family caps mentioned existing programs in New Jersey and Georgia.[16] The information in table 8 suggests that newspaper coverage in Massachusetts and Virginia referred to existing programs across the country.

The broad geographic reach of the references in table 8 is noteworthy, but it is important not to overstate their importance to the information generation process. Public officials who want to learn more about programs that exist elsewhere certainly could rely on newspaper coverage for very general information, but this would not be an especially efficient approach. Most articles do not mention these examples, and those that do often make only brief references to existing programs. For instance, they will mention that lawmakers in a certain state or in certain states enacted a policy innovation. These references tend to describe general developments across the country. They tend not to describe the specific provisions of existing programs or to provide hard evidence about their effectiveness. It is rare for an article to focus exclusively on developments in another state. Media coverage seems to be a good source of background knowledge and a decent way to become knowledgeable about emerging trends, but it does not seem to be an effective way of acquiring specific policy-relevant information. It rarely mentions statutory language or the details of program implementation.

INFORMATION GENERATION AND LEGISLATIVE TESTIMONY

When legislators hold hearings, these forums represent opportunities for witnesses to express their support of or opposition to a policy innovation. In addition, hearings also enable lawmakers to learn more about the mechanics, advantages, and disadvantages of a new program. Legislative testimony can therefore potentially provide the combination of substantive and political information that lawmakers crave. Occasionally, witnesses cite examples in other states during their testimony. For the most part, these references are a rhetorical device. Proponents use them to contend that the policy innovation is legitimate and feasible, while opponents use them to point out the innovation's shortcomings and disadvantages. The use of these examples is thus simply an extension of the larger debate over the enactment of the policy innovation.

Committee witnesses testifying on behalf of policy innovations sometimes refer to examples in other states. In Massachusetts, for instance, the Joint Committee on Health Care held a hearing on senior prescription drug legislation on March 30, 1999. Most of the witnesses made general arguments in support of the policy innovation, but a Harvard University professor referred to existing programs in other states. He argued that senior citizens in the state faced challenges that were "compounded by the fact that the current Massachusetts pharmacy assistance program for the elderly is tiny in comparison to well-funded programs in New Jersey and Pennsylvania."[17] This witness used existing state programs to criticize the policy in his home state, rather than using them to justify the enactment of a new program. Witnesses at various hearings in Oregon highlighted existing programs in other states as they attempted to convince policymakers to enact an innovation. During a hearing on MSA legislation in Oregon in 1995, one MSA supporter sought to legitimate this policy innovation by noting that seven states had had two to four years of experience with MSAs and that twenty additional states were considering MSA legislation.[18] At a hearing on IDA legislation in Oregon in 1999, one supporter described other state programs: "[We] believe IDAs have great promise. A lot of people around the country feel [the] same way. Other states including Pennsylvania, Indiana, and North Carolina have passed supportive legislation *and* allocated state funding."[19] These brief examples illustrate how the supporters of policy innovations sometimes use models from other states to bolster their cases.

Similarly, state legislators sometimes mention the existence of policy innovations in other states when they testify on behalf of legislation that they have submitted. During the 1993 welfare reform debate in Oregon, for example, Representative Cynthia Wooten sought to draw attention to a bill that would help employers fund worker retraining. She modeled her proposal after "successful" programs in California and Rhode Island

and also noted that a similar measure recently gained enactment in Washington State.[20] Two years later, Representative Frank Shields submitted a proposal that would have created a hotline for reporting welfare fraud. While testifying on behalf of the bill, Shields briefly traced the history of a similar hotline in Washington State and distributed information from the Washington State Support Services Office of Special Investigation.[21] Thus, bill sponsors sometimes use examples from other states to try to convince their colleagues to support a policy innovation.

In terms of information generation, the preceding examples are noteworthy for at least three reasons. First, interest group representatives and bill sponsors alike relied on policy models that were national in scope. In Oregon, for example, witnesses referred to existing policies in Pennsylvania, Indiana, North Carolina, Rhode Island, and neighboring Washington State. The geographic range of these examples suggests that proximity alone does not determine the relevance of an existing program. Second, most of the references are best characterized as political rhetoric. They generally incorporate a rather superficial description of an existing policy, with little mention of programmatic details—though there are some exceptions to this pattern. Like the references that appear in newspaper articles, these brief citations may be an effective way to acquire background information but may be less effective in other respects. Third, witnesses provide testimony at a relatively late stage of the policy-making process. By the time witnesses testify, officials may already be well versed in the arguments for and against policy innovations. This testimony may therefore be more important as a measure of the support that a bill possesses and the opposition that it faces.

INFORMATION GENERATION AND

ADMINISTRATIVE DOCUMENTS

Legislative staff and executive branch personnel sometimes produce reports about policy innovations. Sometimes, legislators solicit these reports by mandating a study of a particular topic or establishing a task force. These analyses may incorporate policy recommendations that lead to legislative proposals in a subsequent session. In addition, administrative documents may report on the evolution of a policy innovation after it has been enacted. Both types of documents may describe developments in òther states and at the national level, even though such analysis is rarely the primary objective of these administrative reports.

In 2000, officials in Massachusetts created Prescription Advantage, a senior prescription drug program. An administrative report later reviewed the program's first nine months of operations. The document provides a brief history of Massachusetts programs for senior prescription drug assistance. It then examines early enrollment trends, member demographics, utilization and costs, and many other features of the new program. Twice, it touches on developments outside the state. First, it notes that in the absence of national action, "many states" have devised interim measures to help senior citizens gain access to medically necessary prescription drugs (Glickman 2002, i).[22] Later, the report describes how policymakers in Illinois were the first to receive a federal waiver to offer prescription drug coverage to low-income individuals through the Medicaid program (Glickman 2002, 29). These references to programs or initiatives in other states do not constitute a major focus of the report, as most of the text emphasizes developments in the nascent Massachusetts program. Such a focus is to be expected when the primary objective of an administrative document is to analyze the evolution of an existing state program.

The Oregon state legislature held several hearings on the creation of "individual medical accounts" in 1993. MSA legislation did not gain enactment, but the legislature eventually passed a statute requiring the Oregon health plan administrator to prepare a report on medical savings accounts by January 1, 1995. When MSA legislation received a hearing from the House Committee on State and School Finance in 1995, the report was submitted as an exhibit. Published in December 1994, it illustrates how an administrative document can generate information about a policy innovation as lawmakers consider its merits. The report begins with a brief history of MSAs and then describes various private sector programs, including the ones offered by the Golden Rule Insurance Company of Indianapolis, Indiana; Dominion Resources of Richmond, Virginia; and Forbes magazine of New York, New York.[23] A section on MSA legislation compares—along a number of dimensions—seven existing state programs and two of the best-known MSA bills considered in Congress in 1994 (Gates 1994).[24] The Oregon report also describes how officials in other states had dealt with the implementation of the accounts. It highlights how programs in Colorado, Idaho, and Illinois define eligible expenditures, and it describes sunset provisions in Idaho, Michigan, Illinois, and Mississippi. In sum, the report is noteworthy both for the national content of the examples it cites and for the fairly detailed treatment it gives to these examples.

Similar administrative documents were published during the debate over welfare reform in Oregon. A 1991 statute created the Oregon Family Support Council to review family support plans and services within the Oregon Department of Human Resources (DHR). Consisting of DHR division administrators, other executive branch officials, and family members representing the target populations, the council issued a comprehensive report in 1994. The report focuses almost exclusively on existing Oregon programs. It refers to a wide array of supports and services provided by "more progressive states," but it otherwise does not reference any external models (Oregon Family Support Council 1994, 19).[25] Another administrative document on welfare policy maintains a similar intrastate focus. House Bill 3309, enacted in 1993, directed the Oregon Progress Board and Workforce Quality Council to develop a plan to replace the public assistance system with a system for family support and workforce development. The work group's report argues that a Job Opportunities and Basic Skills (JOBS) training program for noncustodial parents should be developed, and it points specifically to a model called Parents Fair Share (Oregon Welfare Reform Work Group 1995, 14). The report also notes that "unlike most states," Oregon has not separated its JOBS programs from the rest of the welfare agency since 1982 (Oregon Welfare Reform Work Group 1995, 38). These two passing references are the only two times that the report cites developments in other states.

The Virginia Independence Program, a landmark welfare reform initiative, gained enactment in 1994. The state secretary of health and human resources issued a report on the program in March 1995. The study describes the main features of the welfare plan and argues that a national waiver would allow the state "to implement its comprehensive, statewide welfare reform program and provide a model for other states interested in similar reforms" (Commonwealth of Virginia 1995, iii). In addition, the study describes other state welfare reform programs whose provisions are relevant to the Virginia Independence Program. The appendix of the report describes time limit provisions in Massachusetts, Nebraska, Wisconsin, and Vermont and family cap provisions in Arkansas, Georgia, and New Jersey (Commonwealth of Virginia 1995, 26–27). In terms of information generation, two features of the report are noteworthy. First, in making a case for a national waiver, the authors note that officials in other states might use Virginia as a model. This is an implicit reference to the possibility of policy diffusion. Second, the examples that they cite are national in scope. The report refers to existing innovations in states all over the country. It does not emphasize developments in neighboring states or in a specific region of the country.

In 2002, the Virginia Joint Commission on Health Care issued a study of the state MSA program. This document examines the limited implementation of the Virginia program and the challenges facing the state agencies charged with this task. Two models appear prominently during this discussion. The first model is the American Health Care Plan developed by the Jeffersonian Health Policy Foundation, and the second model is the demonstration program established by national legislation in 1996. One figure in the report, prepared by the Virginia Department of Taxation, compares the provisions of the Virginia and national statutes along a number of dimensions (Joint Commission on Health Care 2002, 21–22). This comparison is logical because the Virginia MSA program is conditional on the authorization of MSAs by Congress. As a result, the figure focuses on how the national program and the conditional state law overlap and diverge.

The administrative documents cited in preceding paragraphs examine a range of policy innovations and were published in three different states. Even though this is not a representative sample of documents, it is appropriate to draw a few tentative conclusions. First, relatively few of these documents perform a comprehensive search for relevant models in other states. This pattern makes sense for the evaluative reports that examine the operation of an existing program. Yet even some of the prescriptive reports, such as the ones on welfare reform in Oregon, feature few, if any, external examples. This pattern suggests that these documents are not an especially efficient way through which to gather information about developments elsewhere. Since state policymakers requested some of these reports, this pattern might suggest that they are not interested in gathering such information. Before drawing that conclusion, however, it is necessary to consider the reports' timeliness. There is often a substantial lag time between a legislative request and publication. Years sometimes pass before the reports are published.[26] For legislators who are pressed for time and want to move quickly, it seems to make little sense to rely on these administrative documents for policy-relevant information about innovations in other states.

The most important characteristics of administrative documents overlap with those of media reports and legislative testimony. In terms of content, all of these sources suggest that the conventional emphasis on neighboring states is overstated, at least during the information generation process. These sources sometimes refer to developments in neighboring states, but it is just as common for them to incorporate a national frame of reference. In addition, their discussions rarely provide much information about statutory language or programmatic detail. It is far more common for the information conveyed in these resources to refer simply to the existence of a specific program. In sum, the content of these documentary resources suggests their limited usefulness during the information generation process. A similar conclusion seems warranted when their timing is taken into consideration. A relatively small proportion of newspaper accounts contain references to existing policy models, while legislative testimony and administrative documents appear at a relatively late stage of debate. In combination, then, the content and timing of these resources suggest that time-pressed policymakers will look elsewhere for the substantive and political information that they find useful.

National Organizations and Information Generation

National organizations, including professional associations and think tanks, seem especially well suited to serving the information needs of state lawmakers. They sponsor conferences that bring together state officials, publish reports on policy innovations, and frequently view the dissemination of policy-relevant information as a key component of their organizational missions. In addition, many of these national organizations possess ties with intrastate actors who play a crucial role in promoting policy innovations within their states. This section of this chapter reviews documents published by professional associations and think tanks and the ties between these organizations and state-level officials. Its analysis suggests that the information provided by these organizations is more comprehensive and timelier than the information contained in media reports, legislative testimony, and administrative documents. It also suggests that policymakers and other important figures sometimes approach these groups for information. Professional associations and various other national organizations seem to play a critical role during the information generation process.

PROFESSIONAL ASSOCIATIONS, THINK TANKS, AND INFORMATION GENERATION

A wide array of professional associations, sometimes called "government interest groups," represent individuals who work in the public sector. The increased prominence of these organizations has contributed to the information-rich environment in which state officials operate. Professional associations include highly specialized organizations, such as the Association of State Drinking Water Administrators and the National Association of State and Provincial Lotteries, as well as broader associations of elected state officials. This subsection focuses on professional associations whose primary constituencies include institutionally critical actors, such as governors and legislators, because these groups are typically active on a wide array of policy issues. It also examines the impact of national think tanks on the information generation process.

Professional associations often possess organizational features that suggest their interest in disseminating information. For example, information dissemination has long been a paramount objective for the Council of State Governments (CSG). CSG produces *The Book of the States,* a wide-ranging compilation of comparative state data. An early volume of this resource lists the organization's objectives, and the very first task listed is to serve as a "clearing house for information and research, serving all the states" (Council of State Governments 1950, 3). CSG produces research and reference publications that profile policy innovations and describe suggested state legislation. The national office also manages a loan library and operates a States Information Center, which provides comparative information for all fifty U.S. states. These varied activities suggest that information dissemination is a crucial element of the organization's mission.

Like CSG, the National Conference of State Legislatures (NCSL) is a professional association that views the dissemination of policy-relevant information as important. The membership structure of this organization testifies to the significance of this task. The state legislatures constitute its membership. Once a legislature pays its membership dues, its elected officials and staff gain access to the voluminous databases maintained by NCSL and the Health Policy Tracking Service. NCSL also serves as a policy information bureau by hosting conferences, sponsoring task forces that cover individual policy areas, encouraging the transfer of personnel, and publishing documents that are frequently made available online.

The National Governors Association (NGA) relies on many of the same tools to generate and disseminate policy-relevant information. Like CSG and NCSL, it publishes short reports on policy innovations and hosts networking seminars for executive branch officials. The professional association grew out of a 1908 meeting about interstate water problems. Today, it meets twice a year, and the NGA meetings provide governors with an opportunity to share problems and policy solutions with their colleagues. One history of the organization describes the "political, social, and substantive need for officials facing like situations to share information" (Weissert 1983, 51), and NGA responds to this need in multiple ways. In addition to the association's three standing committees on economic development and commerce, human resources, and natural resources, NGA operates a Center for Best Practices, which focuses on policy innovations and other innovative state programs. These resources illustrate the organization's interest in disseminating policy-relevant information.

Founded in 1973 by a group of conservative state legislators and policy advocates, the American Legislative Exchange Council (ALEC) differs from the other professional associations that have been profiled so far in this analysis. Other organizations attempt to preserve a reputation for nonpartisanship and objectivity, but ALEC promotes a conservative political agenda. It promotes "Jeffersonian principles," such as free markets, limited government, federalism, and individual liberty. This conservative political agenda distinguishes ALEC from CSG, NCSL, and NGA, but ALEC relies on many of the same strategies to disseminate policy-relevant information. The association holds a national conference and an annual meeting every year, and it hosts December policy summits geared primarily toward freshman and sophomore legislators. ALEC publishes newsletters and journals for its members, and its representatives perform legislative briefings. Due to its political agenda, ALEC places an especially high premium on producing model legislation.

Think tanks share many characteristics with the professional associations profiled in the preceding paragraphs. Like organizations of public officials, think tanks attempt to disseminate policy-relevant information about policy innovations, and they rely on the same set of tools to accomplish this objective. Their publications range from scholarly books to one-page policy briefs that summarize pressing policy issues. In addition, they host conferences and disseminate information at conferences hosted by other groups. In general, what distinguishes think tanks from professional associations is their willingness to take strong stances on innovative public policies. For example, such national think tanks as the National Center for Policy Analysis argued forcefully for the enactment of MSAs. In addition, think tanks usually emphasize their technical expertise and produce model legislation. The policy-relevant information that they publish tends to be fairly detailed.

Professional associations and think tanks have produced a wide range of documents on senior prescription drug programs, MSAs, IDAs, time limits, and family caps. The next few subsections of this chapter examine some of these documents, paying careful attention to their content. More specifically, they focus on their level of technical detail and on the extent to which they cite existing policy models from around the country. These two attributes appear to distinguish the documents produced by professional associations and think tanks from the documents produced by other sources. In general, national organizations are more likely to produce documents that refer to existing programs and that provide detailed information about those programs. As a result, these documents seem well suited to meet the information needs of time-pressed officials.

TECHNICAL DETAIL AND POLICY MODELS:

SENIOR PRESCRIPTION DRUG PROGRAMS

As the political profile of senior prescription drug programs rose in the late 1990s and remained high in the early 2000s, national organizations, such as NCSL, produced many reports and other documents on this policy innovation. NCSL published a wide range of documents and made many of these resources available on its Web site. During the 2001–2 legislative sessions, for example, the organization tracked proposals to establish a senior prescription drug program. One document features proposals that did and did not pass, describing their eligibility requirements and the benefits they would provide.[27] In addition, another document compares existing state programs along various dimensions. A chart in this document examines forty programs in twenty-six states, providing brief details about each of the state programs. The chart includes "web links to state laws where available, year of creation, basic eligibility requirements, and contact telephone numbers within each state for further details."[28] NCSL periodically updated this online document, and two sections focused exclusively on recent activity and recent major actions.

Two characteristics of the NCSL documents stand out as especially noteworthy. First, the documents contain an impressive level of detail compared to the other resources featured in this chapter, and they display this information systematically. By presenting information in this manner, these documents make it easy for state lawmakers to understand the range of activity being pursued by their colleagues across the country. Through a single source (NCSL), they can easily acquire information on eligibility requirements, benefit levels, and statutory language. Second, it is important to recognize the national reach of the information provided in the NCSL documents. Lawmakers who use them are not confined to learning about developments in nearby states or states in their region. The ease with which this national information can be acquired is important, although its existence does not guarantee that lawmakers use it as a guide to action. Even so, the accessibility and timeliness of such detailed policy profiles suggests that they are a valuable resource for time-pressed state lawmakers who wish to gather policy-relevant information as efficiently as possible.

In addition to documents that profiled national developments, NCSL published a variety of magazine articles, newsletter features, and press releases on senior prescription drug programs. The professional association made some of these publications available on its Web site. For example, NCSL publishes *State Legislatures* magazine, a periodical that features commentary and analysis on significant current, past, and future legislation. In December 1999, as the national debate over the policy innovation was heating up, the magazine featured an article that examined existing state programs. The article reviews various characteristics of these programs, including differences in their size, their use of earmarked funds, their spending caps, and their cost-sharing features (Cauchi 1999). Another article, published a few months later, focuses on regional discussions among lawmakers in New England about creating a program for bulk purchasing (Cauchi 2000). NCSL also publishes *State Health Notes,* a biweekly newsletter that focuses on developments in health care policy in the fifty states. In June 2000, an article in this newsletter describes a meeting during which New England state legislators compared their experiences in dealing with rising prescription drug costs. It characterizes this policy issue as the "most vigorously debated health care problem in the land" (Kemkovich 2000).[29] It is important to note that all three of these articles were featured on a section of the NCSL Web site dealing exclusively with the issue of prescription drug costs. Lawmakers did not need to thumb through these publications to acquire this policy-relevant information. They needed simply to visit the appropriate section of the professional association's Web site, where they would also find a news release with a general overview of state-level activity.[30] The accessibility of this information seems to facilitate its use by time-pressed state lawmakers.

Other national associations provided similar information. The National Academy for State Health Policy, for example, published a comprehensive report on state initiatives to contain costs and improve access to prescription drugs. A table in this report profiles thirty-one programs in twenty-six states, incorporating five different categories of information: program, lead agency, access initiative, cost-containment features, and status. Although its level of detail varies across states, the chart includes age and income eligibility requirements, the sources of state funding, upper limits on benefits received, enrollment fees, copayments, drugs covered by the program, and (in a few cases) current budget and enrollment (Kaye 2002). This level of detail distinguishes the document from many of the other resources that have been profiled in this chapter. The American Association of Retired Persons (AARP) published a similar report in April 1999, as the topic of prescription drug coverage gained increasing prominence. This report provides basic information on the structure, enrollment, and administration of state pharmacy assistance programs. Its fourteen state profiles contain extremely detailed information about the provisions of existing policies (Gross and Bee 1999).[31] Like NCSL, these organizations generated a great deal of policy-relevant information about senior prescription drug programs. This information included programmatic details that presumably would be useful for officials considering whether to enact this policy innovation.[32]

TECHNICAL DETAIL AND POLICY MODELS:
MEDICAL SAVINGS ACCOUNTS (MSAs)

National organizations generated numerous policy briefs and reports on medical savings accounts. During the mid-1990s, many of them were published by think tanks and professional associations that favored the enactment of this policy innovation. Among the organizations producing background reports were think tanks located in Washington, D.C.—such as the Cato Institute (Ferrara 1995; Goodman and Musgrave 1992), the Urban Institute (Moon, Nichols, and Wall 1996),[33] and the Economic and Social Research Institute (Wicks and Meyer 1998)—and such organizations as the National Center for Policy Analysis in Dallas, Texas (Scandlen 1998b). These reports usually describe the theory behind MSAs, explaining why supporters believe that the accounts will hold down health care costs and increase access to health care insurance. They often review the economic research on MSAs, describe state legislation, and, after 1996, discuss the national MSA pilot program and general use of the accounts. Most of their references to other state programs contain more specific information than appeared in newspaper articles, legislative testimony, and administrative documents.

Several other organizations published reports that took a strong stance in favor of medical savings accounts. One of the most prominent organizations was the Council for Affordable Health Insurance (CAHI). CAHI is a research and advocacy association of insurance carriers active in the insurance markets for individuals, small groups, MSAs, and seniors. Since 1992, the association has been an active advocate for market-oriented solutions to the problems in America's health care system. Despite its advocacy of the policy innovation, however, CAHI produced documents that contained similar information to NCSL reports on senior prescription drug programs. For example, in 1998, the organization issued a policy brief that examined the spread of MSA legislation across the states. This report notes that at least thirty-nine states had considered MSA proposals over the "last several years" and that several others were developing proposals for their state employees or Medicaid populations. The report also includes general information about a variety of approaches to the policy innovation (Bunce 2000). The author of this report published a trade journal article on MSAs that focuses on the mechanics of the accounts and describes how national legislation restricts their use. Importantly, the article profiles various private sector MSA programs, such as the ones operated by Dominion Resources, the American Dental Association, the Association for Family Finances, and a Maryland-based benefit service firm called Plan3 (Bunce 1998). Like many of the other examples cited in other documents, these references are national in scope.

CAHI provided more detailed information about existing state MSA programs on its Web site. Its "State MSA Synopsis" profiles all fifty states, asking whether lawmakers had adopted MSA legislation or a memorial, study, or Medicaid pilot project. For states in which such legislation had passed, the synopsis provides the bill number and its date of passage. In addition, it summarizes the relevant legislation. Although the content of the summaries varies across states, they generally discuss legislative provisions on annual contributions, policy deductibles, and tax treatment.[34] This detailed information would presumably be of great interest to time-pressed state policymakers interested in gathering information about the innovation. A single source provides both a national perspective on the reach of this innovation and detailed information about specific provisions of state MSA programs.

The National Center for Policy Analysis, a think tank based in Dallas, Texas, was another driving force behind MSAs. The organization produced multiple policy briefs on the policy innovation, striving to provide an intellectual justification and rationale for its adoption. These documents describe the advantages of the medical savings accounts and explain why both employees and employers endorse them. They rely on many different private sector examples, some of which have already been mentioned: *Forbes* magazine in New York; Quaker Oats in Illinois; United Mine Workers in Virginia; Golden Rule Insurance Company in Indiana; and Dominion Resources in Virginia (Matthews 1996; National Center for Policy Analysis 1994, 2004). Even though the information in these references is not as detailed as that of the CAHI state synopsis, its national scope is important.

In October 1994, a think tank in Oregon published a policy brief that critiqued the Oregon Health Plan, the state's innovative Medicaid program. The report characterized it as a "central planning fiasco" and proposed a "Power to the People" Plan as its preferred alternative (Ferrara 1994). Medical savings accounts are one of six recommendations included in the proposal, and the report features many of the private sector models that were profiled in other MSA reports. Although the report was published by the Cascade Policy Institute of Portland, it illustrates the reach of national organizations, because its author was a senior fellow at the National Center for Policy Analysis.[35] In other words, national and state-level think tanks relied on the same personnel to produce reports on medical savings accounts. This overlap suggests that the national organizations affected the information generation process at the state level. A subsequent subsection of this chapter will look more directly at this relationship by emphasizing the ties between state officials and these organizations.

TECHNICAL DETAIL AND POLICY MODELS: INDIVIDUAL DEVELOPMENT ACCOUNTS (IDAs)

IDAs attracted less public and media attention than did senior prescription drug programs and medical savings accounts, but national organizations published a number of documents about the policy innovation. These documents are characterized by a careful attention to detail and an impressive geographic reach, both of which suggest their appeal to state lawmakers who want to gather detailed information as efficiently as possible. An NGA issue brief is illustrative. Published in January 1997, it includes a long section on state IDA options that goes into substantial detail. In addition, it features two appendixes that contain specific information about how to design IDA legislation. The first appendix is a chart that examines multiple approaches to matching IDA deposits. It incorporates three headings: approach, description, and example. The examples column lists at least one state that had taken each specific approach. The second appendix examines various ways to structure IDA legislation. Rather than including specific statutory language, it consists of general bullet points and suggestions about how state lawmakers or policy advocates might choose to proceed (Grossman and Friedman 1997).

The NGA issue brief was actually prepared by two individuals affiliated with the Corporation for Enterprise Development (CFED), a private, nonprofit research, policy, and consulting organization in Washington, D.C. CFED has been a major force behind the emergence of IDAs.[36] CFED personnel published many documents on IDAs, such as an article in a Fannie Mae Foundation periodical. That specific document features a brief overview of state-level developments. It divides state action into enacted legislation and administrative rule making and notes that the main distinction among state programs is the source of funds used to match the savings of IDA account holders (Rist 2002). CFED also made policy-relevant information available on its Web site. Many of the documents on the site provide general information about a demonstration project conducted by the organization, the concept of IDAs, and relevant national legislation. They often feature examples from all over the country. One document, for example, reviews national and state IDA policy. The bulk of its discussion centers on national policy, but the document also describes six different ways that states fund their IDA programs and lists states that have used each of these options.[37] These illustrative examples do not provide much detail about individual state programs. For state policymakers interested in programmatic details, the document provides a link to data that had been compiled at the Center for Social Development (CSD) in St. Louis, Missouri.

CSD played a pivotal role in the dissemination of information about

IDAs. It is a unit of the George Warren Brown School of Social Work at Washington University in St. Louis. The founding director of the center, which was established in 1994, is Michael Sherraden, who developed IDAs and authored numerous publications on them (Sherraden 1990, 1991). As a result, CSD played a leading role in designing and carrying out research on the efficacy of IDAs. It was intimately involved in the CFED demonstration project, assisted with IDA programs in many communities, and helped write national and state legislation. Like professional associations, CSD relies on a variety of strategies to disseminate information. Since 2001, the center has hosted an annual IDA state policy conference that provides a forum for state officials to share informational resources as they create and revise IDA legislation. The conferences strive to develop a network that can disseminate general program information in addition to information about political strategies, policy challenges, and funding sources.

In addition, CSD tracks IDA policy initiatives across the country. It profiles IDA-related developments in all fifty states, making this information available on its Web site. CSD updates this information on a bimonthly basis, seeking to assist those interested in advocating state IDA legislation. The national scope and detailed nature of these IDA policy profiles are noteworthy. They indicate whether IDAs have been included in the state welfare reform plan and whether IDA legislation has been passed or is pending, and they supplement this basic information with details about individual state policies. Relevant details frequently include the potential uses of an IDA, program eligibility, monetary limits, and information about the sponsoring organization and administrative agency involved. Some of these profiles include links to the legislation that has been enacted or is being considered. Finally, each profile provides contact information for an individual associated with IDA activity in that particular state.[38] The organization also provides six summary tables (updated on a bimonthly basis) on state IDA policy and initiatives. These tables describe detailed provisions of current state initiatives, including the number of IDA accounts in existence and the match rate for savings.[39]

CSD provides extremely accessible, detailed, and timely information about IDA programs across the country. In this way, the center makes it easy for state policymakers to understand the range of activity being pursued by their colleagues in other states. Officials can acquire detailed information and examples of legislative language through a single source. Furthermore, CSD provides model state legislation to illustrate how IDA legislation might be crafted to include desirable program characteristics. This model bill draws on existing IDA legislation and best-practice program designs, and it also includes explanations and possible alternative wording.[40] Thus, CSD disseminates a combination of detailed policy-relevant information and statutory language that would seem to be of great use to time-pressed state lawmakers who wish to learn about the policy innovation.

In sum, a national network disseminated information about IDAs. Organizations, such as CFED and CSD, worked together on a demonstration project and published many documents on this policy innovation. In addition, the organizations made a wide range of information available on their Web sites. These sources provide background information about IDAs. More important, they paint a detailed portrait of relevant models from around the country. They provide information about policy options, statutory language, and model legislation on which interested state lawmakers can draw. The timeliness, accessibility, and detail of these resources suggest that they would be very useful to time-pressed state officials.

TECHNICAL DETAIL AND POLICY MODELS:
TIME LIMITS AND FAMILY CAPS

During the national debate over welfare reform, various organizations published documents celebrating or lambasting the policy options under discussion. The amount of information produced was staggering. This subsection of this chapter reviews a selection of this advocacy material, but its primary purposes are to examine the extent to which the publications of national organizations referred to existing programs with time limits and family caps and to assess the level of detail in these references. As a result, the documents featured in this subsection provide illustrative examples and should not be considered a representative sample. They nonetheless provide insight into the information generation process and suggest that these types of documents would aid state officials who want to gather information as efficiently as possible.

Many organizations published documents critical of time limits and family caps. The Center for Law and Social Policy (CLASP), for example, is a nonprofit public policy and advocacy organization that tracks national and state policy-making developments and produces comprehensive reports and policy briefs. The organization published numerous reports during the national debate over welfare reform in the 1990s. One policy brief on time limits summarizes a longer report. The policy brief discusses three different types of time limits that had been enacted in the states. It makes frequent reference to the number of states with a policy, but it provides limited specifics (Greenberg, Savner, and Swartz 1996). A general overview of state welfare waivers highlights a wider range of policy reforms. It provides examples that are generally sentence-long summaries of state action (Greenberg 1996). Almost three years after the enactment of national welfare reform legislation, CLASP published an overview of family caps. The report summarizes the evaluative research that had been performed in the first fourteen states to apply for waivers including family cap provisions. It incorporates examples from all over the country, referring frequently to studies of family cap policies in New Jersey and Arkansas (Stark and Levin-Epstein 1999). These reports are national in scope, although they do not provide extremely detailed information about the content of individual state policies.[41]

Professional associations also addressed welfare reform during the early and middle 1990s. The American Public Welfare Association, which includes state agency and local agency members, exemplifies this interest.[42] In November 1992, the organization formed a task force on self-sufficiency that included eleven state human services commissioners plus local directors and program specialists. The task force released a report in January 1994 that recommended major restructuring of the American welfare system. The bulk of the report is devoted to fifteen policy recommendations, and it provides few models and no statutory language. The report makes passing reference to existing state policies in a few contexts and praises multiple interagency collaborations between state human services agencies and other executive branch agencies (American Public Welfare Association 1994). The paucity of state models contained in the report is notable and somewhat surprising.

The National Governors Association devoted more attention to developments across the country, especially in the aftermath of national welfare reform legislation. The professional association's Center for Best Practices published a fifty-state matrix that incorporated multiple dimensions along which welfare reform had proceeded. Consisting mainly of yes-no responses to the question of whether a policy existed in certain states, the matrix does not capture some of the complexities of state welfare policy (National Governors Association 1997, 1999).[43] Despite this lack of specificity, the matrix is a good resource for policymakers who wish to learn about the reach of recent innovations, such as time limits and family caps. Interested officials can also consult an attachment to the matrix that indicates which state agency administers the states' welfare programs and provides governors' welfare reform contacts.

Finally, the U.S. Department of Health and Human Services also tracked state welfare policy changes during the 1990s. The resulting reports provided another source of policy-relevant information for state officials who wished to learn about developments in other jurisdictions. After the passage of PRWORA in 1996, the national agency released a report that examined state welfare waivers. The report provides both an overview of the types of waivers that state officials requested and detailed information on the specific policies they chose. For example, its chart on family caps notes whether state programs include an increased earnings disregard, a child support pass-through, or exemptions for rape and incest, first-time minor parents, disabled children, and contraception failure (U.S. Department of Health and Human Services 1997). Two years later, the agency published a report on changes in state welfare policy between 1992 and 1998. It presents information about these changes in nine distinct tables, one of which focuses on family caps and distinguishes among states that provide no benefit increase for additional children, states that only provide a partial increase for additional children, states that provide the increase in the form of a voucher, and states that pay the increase to a third party (Crouse 1999). These reports do not contain model legislation or present a strong case for or against the policy innovations, but their national scope and level of detail suggest that they would be useful to time-pressed state lawmakers looking to inform themselves as efficiently as possible. These government reports overlap with many of the documents produced by professional associations and think tanks.

STATE OFFICIALS, NATIONAL ORGANIZATIONS, AND INFORMATION ACQUISITION

National organizations, such as professional associations and think tanks, produce materials that frequently describe developments across the country. These descriptions are generally more detailed than the references that appear in other information resources, and this level of detail seems to respond to the objectives of time-pressed state lawmakers. State officials must perform a variety of tasks simultaneously, so they will strive to gather policy-relevant information in an efficient manner. By consulting the materials produced by national organizations, state lawmakers can quickly acquire substantive and political information about recent developments nationwide. They can examine model legislation and existing statutes as they formulate proposals for their own state.

Do state officials gather policy-relevant information from national organizations? Although the preceding discussion suggests that it would make sense for them to do so, it does not demonstrate whether they do. For a variety of reasons, state officials might not consult the documentary resources produced by professional associations and think tanks. At a fundamental level, state officials might not be interested in this sort of information acquisition, if they do not consider developments in other states germane to their decision making. In addition, state officials might not know that national organizations make these resources available through conferences, publications, and other means. However, survey evidence suggests that these concerns are unwarranted. The State Legislative Leaders Foundation surveyed state institutional officials in 1999, asking these leaders about the information resources that professional associations offer. Approximately 70 percent of the respondents ranked conferences as "somewhat" or "very" important, while 63 percent of them characterized publications as either "somewhat" or "very" useful. Policymakers generally described these resources as more useful for policy formulation than for policy adoption (Clark and Little 2002a). Their distinction between formulation and adoption resonates with the process-oriented framework used in this book. More important, the survey results suggest that state officials attach some significance to the resources that professional associations offer. This subsection of this chapter looks more systematically at the connections between national organizations and state officials. Its analysis suggests that the former play a crucial role in generating information about new policy ideas and that state lawmakers are inclined to rely on the resources that these national organizations provide.

Many lawmakers consider NCSL to be a good information resource. For example, one committee chair in Massachusetts characterized its white papers (short summaries of salient political issues) as particularly useful: "I look at them when they come around. In fact, I've used several of them in drafting amendments or in coming up with ideas for bills."[44] Similarly, the executive director of a state health care program in Massachusetts said: "One of the best record-keeping organizations about these issues is the National Conference of State Legislatures. They have a great Web site."[45] NCSL uses many tools to disseminate comparative information to state officials. The preceding comments indicate that these officials are sometimes interested in learning about this sort of comparative information. An NCSL staff member explained, "The demands on us are very great, especially for comparative information like models and assessments of what the states are doing."[46] This interest should reassure scholars of policy diffusion, because it matches their underlying assumption that the existence of a policy innovation in one state influences policy-making elsewhere.

Because national organizations consider information provision to be a key component of their missions, they sometimes survey members about their information needs. These surveys reveal the extent to which state policymakers are interested in comparative policy information and their willingness to rely on professional associations and other national organizations to provide it. In 1996, for example, CSG performed a Survey on State Welfare Reform Activities. One question asked state policymakers: "What areas of welfare reform would your state/agency like to receive more information on? Are there state programs that you would like to learn more about?" The association received thirty-five responses, approximately two-thirds of which asked for information on welfare reform programs in other states. Nebraska and South Carolina requested information on "other state reform efforts." Rhode Island issued a more specific call for data on "proposed national legislation and matrix analysis of state plan choices of other states." Kansas asked for information on "other states' plans for program simplification," while New York requested data on "other states' reforms and specific federal interpretations of reform" (Council of State Governments 1996). Some respondents expressed general interest in other states' welfare reform programs. Other respondents desired information on specific provisions. Their requests overlapped, however, in requesting updates about what their counterparts had done.

Similarly, NGA surveyed governors and their staff about their information needs in May 1994. The survey consisted of seven questions, one of which asked, "What areas of state activity would you like NGA to track and report on over the next year?" NGA used the survey responses to develop its top priorities for the coming year, dividing these priorities into fifteen policy areas. Many items on the list of priorities described national legislation that would be beneficial to the states, but information provision maintained a similarly high profile. NGA noted its intention to track state-level reforms and initiatives in welfare, health, education, crime and juvenile delinquency, workforce preparation, and science and technology/communications. In six cases, this tracking function was the first priority listed. Lawmakers in twenty-seven states completed the survey, and respondents were especially interested in comparative information when they were willing to work on a specific topic. On health care reform, governors who were willing to commit their time, their staff time, or their staff indicated that the issue was of "high priority" or "significant interest" in nineteen states. Twenty-six respondents answered similarly in the context of welfare reform. Not coincidentally, health care and welfare reform received the largest number of responses when NGA asked for policies to track.[47] Public officials seem eager to obtain information about other states when they themselves are willing to work on that particular issue.

While professional associations sometimes survey state policymakers about their information needs, legislators and their staff sometimes approach the organizations with information requests. For example, CSG prepared a welfare reform information packet after receiving a request from the Legislative Reference Center in Virginia. Rather than including a comprehensive report on welfare reform, it compiled dozens of publications from around the country. This compilation provided officials with a national perspective on recent developments in state welfare policy, and the national scope of the publications is notable. A May 1996 article published by the American Public Welfare Association described welfare programs in Ohio, North Carolina, and Texas, three states that had recently received waivers from the U.S. Department of Health and Human Services. The article examined these states' provisions on time limits, benefits, and earnings rules (Odom 1996). The packet also included publications produced by CSG, including an "innovation brief" describing the origins and operation of the Oregon Option welfare reform program (Stuart 1997). It incorporated a recent newsletter from the Illinois Commission on Intergovernmental Cooperation that described a forum on recent national legislation and its state-level impact (Roberts 1997). Finally, the packet included articles from national newspapers, such as the *New York Times,* and from regional media outlets, such as the *Providence (RI) Journal-Bulletin.* The wide-ranging content of this packet suggests that professional associations respond to officials' information requests by providing a national perspective on recent developments.

It is also possible to point to instances in which professional associations provided information that affected specific state actions. ALEC produced model MSA legislation, for example, and a majority of the states drew on this proposal by choosing not to penalize nonmedical withdrawals at the end of the year (Bordonaro 1995). Furthermore, national organizations sometimes maintained connections with influential individuals at the state level. Chapter 3 mentioned Ballot Measure 7, a welfare reform initiative that passed in Oregon in 1990. Ted Abram of Jeld-Wen Inc. was intimately involved in crafting and promoting this initiative and subsequent welfare reform legislation. Importantly, Abram served on ALEC's National Task Force on Empowerment, Opportunity, and Urban Poverty during the early 1990s (Brunelli 1995, 15). This example illustrates how individual members of ALEC and other national organizations facilitate the dissemination of policy-relevant information. An ALEC staff member comments: "We have 2,500 dues-paying members. They are an automatic information distribution system."[48] ALEC and similar organizations create a conservative network that serves as a conduit for policy-relevant information.

In 1996, the Portland-based Cascade Policy Institute organized the Oregon Better Government Competition. The institute selected ten winning reports, one of which was authored by state representative Patti Milne and economist Jim Seagraves. Milne, who was about to begin her third term, had submitted an MSA proposal during the previous legislative session. Seagraves, representing the organization Oregonians for Medical Savings Accounts, testified frequently at legislative hearings on MSAs. Both were important, if not central, figures in the debate over MSAs in Oregon. Their winning report was notable because it referred to existing programs in Montana, Tennessee, and Indiana as possible models for Oregon (Milne and Seagraves 1996). This national frame of reference resonates with many of the resources profiled in this chapter. More important, the content of the report suggests that the authors relied, in part, on national organizations as information sources. The authors cited two different policy reports by the NCPA in their report and thanked a variety of individuals for their help with "references and contacts." These individuals included the health policy director at the NCPA, a fellow of the NCPA, and a staff member at CSG-West.[49] These acknowledgments suggest that national organizations serve as important information sources for officials who want to gather information about a policy innovation.

The surveys, information packet, and other documentary resources profiled in this subsection nicely supplement this chapter's earlier discussion of the information generated by national organizations. That discussion suggested that professional associations and think tanks provide timely, accessible, and relatively detailed information about developments across the country. This information often includes statutory language and model legislation, and its main characteristics imply that it would be useful to state officials. The qualitative evidence in this subsection suggests that state lawmakers do utilize the information produced by national organizations. Such groups as CSG and NGA sometimes administer surveys in an attempt to gauge the kind of information that would be of use to their members. Officials sometimes approach these groups and request information on a topic that is on the state political agenda. Finally, national organizations do not operate in a vacuum. They sometimes possess connections with important officials who serve as conduits for policy-relevant information. Professional associations and think tanks provide references, contacts, and documentary resources that seem to enable time-pressed state policymakers to become informed about innovations in public policy.

National Organizations, Information Generation, and Policy Diffusion

At its core, policy diffusion implies a process of learning, emulation, or imitation during which decision makers look to other jurisdictions as models for their own behavior. The dissemination of policy-relevant information is a crucial component of the process, and it is surprising that most diffusion studies do not address this topic explicitly. It is therefore important to ask about the sources state lawmakers use to acquire information about developments in other locales. This question is especially significant because officials currently operate in an information-rich environment in which they can rely on a multitude of sources to learn about policies that exist elsewhere. The preceding analysis in this chapter examined media reports, legislative testimony, administrative documents, and various documents published by professional associations and national organizations. It suggests that we can draw three tentative conclusions about the information generation process.

First, the preceding analysis suggests that most information resources provide a national or even international perspective on recent developments. When these diverse resources profile existing state programs, their references are generally not constrained by geography. Instead, they describe innovations that exist all over the country and even all over the world. For example, articles in the *Boston Globe* mention time limit programs in Florida, Iowa, and Oregon. Witnesses at legislative hearings attempt to legitimate policy innovations by referring to existing models all over the country. Other resources provide a similar national perspective. These references reflect Jack Walker's suggestion, more than three decades ago, that national information networks had begun to supplant more localized ones (Walker 1969). They also suggest that developments in neighboring states do not have a disproportionately strong impact on the diffusion of policy innovations, at least during the information generation process.

Second, the preceding analysis suggests that professional associations and think tanks provide detailed information more consistently than do the other resources profiled in this chapter. These organizations are more likely to refer to existing policies, and their references are more likely to contain model legislation, statutory information, and other programmatic details. In contrast, newspapers and committee witnesses tend to make passing references to policy innovations that exist elsewhere. Their discussions rarely provide much information about statutory language or programmatic details. It is more common for these resources to refer to the mere existence of a specific program. This distinction is important because it implies that relying on the documents produced by national organizations is the most efficient way to collect policy-relevant information. They provide timely, accessible, and detailed data.

Third, the evidence presented in this chapter suggests that time constraints affect the information generation process. Chapter 1 hypothesized that time-pressed officials rely on information resources that consistently provide relevant information but that do not require a huge time investment. Given their many responsibilities, one would expect state officials to attempt to acquire information as efficiently as possible. Based on our comparison of several potential information sources, professional associations and think tanks appear to fit this profile. Indeed, surveys of state lawmakers suggest that they value the resources produced by national organizations. Furthermore, the survey results imply that state officials are especially eager to obtain information about recent developments in other states when the officials are willing to commit their time or their staff time to those issues. As a result, professional associations and national organizations seem to serve as crucial causal mechanisms during the information generation process.

The preceding analysis suggests several productive avenues for future research on the information generation process. For example, the impact of the documents produced by professional associations and other national organizations certainly merits additional examination. This chapter advanced a general claim that these documents suit the needs of time-pressed state officials. One important task for future research on the information generation process is to extend this analysis by estimating the frequency with which these resources are consulted. Surveys and interviews with state officials and their staff would be one approach to generating such an estimate.

A related task for future research is to identify the political conditions that make officials more or less likely to rely on national organizations as information resources. Characteristics of the state political environment, such as greater party competition and less party strength, have been found to affect the size and strength of nonpartisan research organizations (Hird 2005). They might also affect the dynamics described in this chapter. Similarly, legislative professionalism might affect the relationship between state lawmakers and professional associations, although there is some uncertainty about its impact. One could imagine that legislators in less professional bodies will be especially dependent on national organizations for information, since they do not possess the staff and other resources that facilitate research. However, one could also imagine that these legislators have weak connections to national organizations, since their limited resources may prevent them from attending conferences or purchasing many publications. The relationship between national organizations and officials in highly professional bodies is also open to question. These legislators or their staff may have stronger connections to professional associations, or they may consider those connections unnecessary because they have sufficient research capabilities of their own. Since legislative professionalism is often associated with longer and more frequent sessions, officials in highly professional bodies may face less severe time constraints than other legislators. In short, the uncertain relationship between legislative professionalism and the information generation process poses a particularly intriguing question for future research.

Furthermore, the preceding analysis suggests that interest groups and lobbyists often use existing programs in other states as a rhetorical device to advance their goals. Differences among interest groups might, in turn, foster variation in how well informed they are. For example, organizations that are part of national federations might possess more information about nationwide developments than do their colleagues who are not part of these national networks. Individuals who represent the state chapters of national groups might therefore be more likely to attempt to justify the enactment of an innovative policy by referring to its existence elsewhere.

Many important questions about the information generation process remain open, but the evidence presented in this chapter suggests that national forces play a significant role in this process. State policymakers have access to policy-relevant information about developments across the country. National organizations are especially reliable resources for these types of updates. Combining this insight with this book's earlier discussion of agenda setting suggests that national forces play a very important role during the early stages of policy-making, affecting the models toward which officials are drawn and the resources they consult to gather information about them.

V. *Intrastate Forces and the Politics of Customization*

In the foreword to a book on state-level economic policy during the 1980s, Bill Clinton, then governor of Arkansas, used the "laboratories of democracy" metaphor to describe how officials in the states "learn from one another, borrowing, adapting, and improving on each other's best efforts" (Osborne 1990, xii). This quotation alludes to one of the complexities of policy diffusion, because it implies that lawmakers amend the policy templates that they import. Although officials sometimes copy programs that exist elsewhere, it is more common for them to "adapt" and "improve" these examples. In other words, they customize a policy innovation to "fit" their state in the same way that an individual tailors a suit after buying it off the rack. Policy innovations, as a result, take on various forms in the jurisdictions in which they are enacted. Programs that purport to be the same sometimes vary quite significantly across states.

Consider, for instance, differences across the various family cap programs enacted between 1992 and 1998. When state lawmakers debated family cap legislation, they also had to decide whether to exempt any welfare recipients from this requirement. Table 9 indicates the number of exemptions (out of a possible eight) included in twenty-one state family cap programs (State Policy Demonstration Project 1999).[1] The table indicates that state lawmakers enacted a wide range of exemptions policies. Policymakers in Massachusetts included seven exemptions in their state program, while family cap policies in Arkansas, North Dakota, and Wyoming only included a single exemption. Policymakers exempted children born as a result of rape or incest in eighteen states, but children born as a result of failed contraception were exempt in only California. Thus, family cap exemptions varied significantly across the fifty states, and these programmatic specifics were critically important to the welfare recipients who were affected by them. The policy variation evident in the family caps example is not unusual. Many officials imposed time limits and work requirements as they reformed state welfare programs during the 1990s, and these policy innovations similarly varied along many dimensions, including the individuals to whom they were applied, the length of time before they were imposed, and provisions for extensions and exemptions (Fellowes and Rowe 2004). Most significant for our discussion, such policy variation illustrates the importance of examining program content and the customization process. Simply answering the yes-no question of whether officials chose to adopt the policy overlooks how they may have altered the existing template.

Some politicians view the possibility of customization as one of the main benefits of devolution. They argue that customization is more

TABLE 9.   Family Cap Exemption Policies

State	Date of enactment	Number of exemptions
Arizona	1994	4
Arkansas	1993	1
California	1994	6
Connecticut	1995	4
Delaware	1995	4
Florida	1995	6
Georgia	1993	5
Illinois	1995	3
Indiana	1994	6
Maryland	1994	5
Massachusetts	1995	7
Mississippi	1995	4
Nebraska	1994	5
New Jersey	1992	5
North Carolina	1995	4
North Dakota	1998	1
Oklahoma	1998	4
South Carolina	1995	3
Tennessee	1996	5
Virginia	1994	4
Wyoming	1997	1

democratic and more efficient than imposing a national mandate. It is democratic because, in the words of President George Herbert Walker Bush, it "moves power and decision-making closer to the people."[2] The devolution of authority means that state officials can adjust policy innovations to political conditions within their own jurisdictions. In other words, they can respond to the desires of local constituencies in a way that national officials presumably cannot. In addition, this type of response may also be more efficient than a national mandate. Sometimes, a "one size fits all" policy solution will not be appropriate, and programs will be more effective if they are adapted to conditions in individual states. In sum, devolution advocates argue that customization is desirable for reasons of both responsiveness and efficiency. The preceding quotations from Presidents Clinton and Bush make clear that officials view the possibility of customization as a crucial element of the "laboratories of democracy" metaphor.

Most analyses of policy diffusion focus on the enactment decision and do not examine the content of the policy innovations that gain enactment. Their approach places too much stock in the existence of a specific program.[3] It is just as important to examine the sources of such programmatic differences as those displayed in table 9. Several potential sources might account for variation. Lawmakers might adjust the content of a policy innovation based on early adopters' experiences with it. Alternatively, officials might make technical changes that adapt the policy to objective conditions. For example, some Oregon officials argued that high enrollment in health maintenance organizations (HMOs) in the state would limit the effectiveness of medical savings accounts. Finally, political concerns might dominate the customization process, as officials insert or remove specific provisions in order to generate support or ameliorate opposition.

In overlooking the question of program content, most studies of policy diffusion ignore a crucial component of this phenomenon. This chapter, in contrast, focuses on the customization process and the question of why policy innovations take on different forms in the jurisdictions in which they gain enactment. Its analysis suggests that variation in program content can often be attributed to intrastate forces, such as interest groups. This conclusion is based on two strands of evidence. The first strand assesses the relative balance of in-state and out-of-state forces during the customization process. It draws on campaign finance, lobbying registration, and committee witness data to suggest that customization is driven mainly by intrastate factors. The second strand of evidence revisits the five policy innovations analyzed throughout this book, examining the programs that gained enactment in Massachusetts, Oregon, and Virginia. Developments in these states suggest that policy content often varies due to the diverse identities, strategies, and underlying strengths of the local interest groups involved in these battles.

Reinvention, Customization, and Electoral Considerations

Most research on the spread of innovations emphasizes sameness across adopters. In organizational sociology, this overlap is called *institutional isomorphism*. Scholars in this field attempt to explain homogeneity in organizational forms. In general, they concentrate on mechanisms that encourage organizations to resemble each other. These scholars argue that at a certain point, the adoption of an innovation provides an imprimatur of legitimacy even if its impact on organizational performance is uncertain (DiMaggio and Powell 1983). Other sociologists characterize institutional rules as "myths" that organizations incorporate to enhance their legitimacy, resources, stability, and survival prospects (Meyer and Rowan 1977).[4] Although these two perspectives diverge in their respective explanations of organizational homogeneity, they overlap in emphasizing similarities across adopters.

The notion of isomorphism, however, fails to appreciate how innovations take on varying forms. Differences across adopters characterize technological and various other types of innovations. Since innovations are rarely monolithic and prepackaged, adopters are usually able to modify an innovation or to incorporate some of its components while rejecting others (Rice and Rogers 1980). The enactment of an innovation, in other words, is not an all-or-nothing proposition. Adopters are generally able to make changes if they feel that these changes are warranted. They are not obligated to accept a particular version of the innovation if they wish to modify the underlying template.

Similarly, when lawmakers consider public policy innovations, their choices are not limited to adoption or rejection. Officials can customize a policy to fit their particular jurisdiction. For example, a transportation program called "Dial-a-Ride" diffused across U.S. cities during the 1970s and was characterized by considerable variation. One study concluded that the many programs falling under this heading actually represented a variety of different versions of this innovation (Rice and Rogers 1980). Similarly, state officials coalesced around a general model of using hate crime law to address increases in intergroup violence, but the laws took on a variety of legal forms (Grattet, Jenness, and Curry 1998). Thus, officials might choose to enact the "same" policy innovation, but the specific provisions of these policies might differ so substantially that it is difficult to believe that they fall under the same heading.

Why do policy innovations take on a variety of forms in the jurisdictions in which they gain enactment? Political scientists who examine this question generally attribute variation in program content to a phenomenon known as *reinvention*. Reinvention traces differences across states to the order in which the innovation was enacted. Knowing when officials adopted a policy innovation relative to their peers permits scholars to predict what one state's version of the policy will look like relative to other versions. The timing of enactment, in short, is the most important determinant of program content. The key question for most studies of reinvention is, Do later adopters establish more expansive policies than leaders, do later adopters enact less expansive policies than leaders, or do later adopters practice wholesale borrowing?[5]

Most analyses of reinvention assume that late adopters will enact innovations that are more expansive than the tentative approaches adopted by leading innovators. This dynamic might emerge for one of several reasons. Late adopters might possess more reliable information about the political or administrative feasibility of a policy innovation. A program that was extremely controversial when leaders adopted it might become less contentious by the time late adopters enact it. Less strident opposition might reduce the political pressure to take a minimal approach, facilitating the implementation of more expansive policies (Clark 1985). Alternatively, early adopters' experiences with a policy innovation may provide administrative lessons that also enable late adopters to develop expansive programs. Reinvention might mean that officials are able to develop new approaches for dealing with social problems even if they lag in terms of policy adoption. Studies of state laws concerning living wills (Glick and Hays 1991) and of state regulations on abortion (Mooney and Lee 1995) provide empirical support for the assumption that approaches taken by late adopters will be more expansive than those taken by early adopters. Studies of lobbying regulations and educational accountability measures indicate that late adopters exhibit as much or more of a propensity to adopt broad programs as do leaders, while midrange adopters generally select narrower program options (Allen and Clark 1981; Clark 1985).

Reinvention is a useful idea because it draws attention to differences in program content. It recognizes that officials create substantively different programs even though the policies can be grouped into a broad general category. Despite these advantages, however, reinvention is a problematic concept. Its fundamental weakness is that there is no a priori reason to assume that the content of a policy innovation will inevitably shift in a more expansive direction. The passage of time might encourage officials to take a more restrictive approach. Early adopters' experiences might generate a political backlash that limits the acceptability of an innovation, causing late adopters to take a more cautious approach. Alternatively, the early versions of an innovation might create administrative difficulties that convince late adopters that their peers have overreached. Either dynamic might spur later adopters to enact limited versions of the policy.

In addition, the notion of reinvention does not seem well equipped to explain the patterns in table 9. It is difficult to find a temporal pattern in this table. The three states with the fewest exemptions in their family cap policies (Arkansas, North Dakota, and Wyoming) enacted their policies in 1993, 1998, and 1997, respectively. The state with the largest number of exemptions in its policy (Massachusetts) enacted the policy in 1995. The final family cap policies to gain enactment were those of North Dakota and Oklahoma, both of which were enacted in 1998. These programs created one exemption and four exemptions, respectively. In sum, table 9 reveals no obvious relationship between the breadth of a state's family cap program and the timing of its enactment.[6] While it is important not to overstate the significance of the analysis represented in table 9, the table does suggest the limits of reinvention as an explanation of program content. At the very least, it implies that we should not expect reinvention to occur under all conditions. It may be more likely to occur under specific circumstances that do not always exist.

The most problematic characteristic of the reinvention concept is that it describes a mechanical process in which the order of adoption overrides political factors. Scholars have different expectations for early adopters, midrange adopters, and later adopters. By ascribing variation in policy content to a passive process that leaves little room for state politics, reinvention neglects the dynamic process during which actors and groups frame issues, shape agendas, create coalitions, and attempt to affect public policy (Stonecash 1996). Order of adoption cannot explain program content "in a theoretic sense" (Glick and Hays 1991, 842).

Due to the mechanical connotations of the term *reinvention,* this book refers to the process that affects policy content as *customization*. After being imported into a state, policy templates sometimes undergo an extensive amendment process that considerably alters the original proposal. When the Oregon Senate Committee on Health and Human Services considered omnibus welfare reform legislation in 1995, for example, twenty-three different sets of amendments were proposed. After the committee approved the amended legislation, the chair of the committee thanked "both those who supported and opposed the bill" for their "suggestions and amendments"—"many of which," he added "we've been able to adopt."[7] The amended legislation went to the floor after clearing this hurdle. A floor speech prepared for a supportive representative by a committee staffer closed by noting the "significant amendments" that had been added to the original bill "as the result of public testimony and concern."[8] The welfare reform legislation in question was considerably more complex than the typical proposal, but this example nonetheless showcases how legislation is customized prior to its enactment. Relying on the order of program adoption to explain the content of these changes seems insufficient.

Indeed, there is ample reason to believe that politics affects the specific provisions of policy innovations. The quotations in the preceding paragraph suggest that lawmakers in Oregon amended welfare reform legislation with the intention of generating additional support for the proposal. These types of changes are part and parcel of the policy-making process. Electoral considerations seem to explain why officials are often willing to make these types of changes during the customization process. Elected officials must respond to their constituents if they wish to remain in office. They might therefore amend a policy template when intrastate interest groups or others voice objections to specific provisions. If intrastate groups support or oppose specific provisions of a bill, their stances are likely to be taken into account. During the customization process, lawmakers seeking reelection may be likely to modify policy innovations in ways that resonate with voter preferences or the preferences of groups that mobilize large numbers of voters. Electoral considerations, in sum, may explain why policy innovations take on various forms across the jurisdictions in which they are adopted.

Elected officials are likely to respond to the objections of in-state constituencies because they must face them at the ballot box. As a result, vocal opposition can alter the content of a proposal even when it is insufficient to block its enactment. Advocates for low-income individuals in many states, for example, fought welfare legislation during the early 1990s. Sometimes, their opposition caused policymakers to moderate the strictest provisions of these bills (Winston 2002). These changes will not always convince opponents to endorse the final product, but outright hostility toward opponents can have electoral ramifications. Ignoring the sentiments of a powerful intrastate constituency can potentially mobilize a vocal opposition campaign. Presumably, an elected official who wishes to win reelection would hope to avoid such a campaign. He or she would therefore be especially likely to respond to the entreaties of organizations that represent intrastate constituencies.

The potential relationship between electoral considerations and the customization process cannot be attributed to the electorate's awareness of specific statutory provisions. Most voters are unaware of these details (as chapter 1 discussed), but political activists are attentive to these statutory minutiae. If these activists represent organizations that can mobilize large constituencies, elected officials are likely to heed their entreaties. An elected official who wishes to win reelection is likely to gravitate toward the version of an innovation that has wide support and only modest opposition. Organizations that can mobilize their members are therefore in a good position to influence lawmakers during the customization process. In this manner, electoral considerations might affect specific legislative provisions even though the public at large is inattentive toward these details.

The electoral connection between state policymakers and intrastate constituencies is extremely important. Professional associations (such as those profiled in chapter 4) sometimes recommend specific legislative provisions, but state officials can ignore their recommendations with virtual impunity. The Council of State Governments, for example, cannot try to unseat an incumbent official by activating an in-state constituency. In contrast, the "labor lobby" or "Catholic lobby" in a particular state can undertake such an effort by mobilizing its membership. Politicians must count votes, and they are likely to be particularly sensitive to groups and constituencies that can mobilize large numbers of voters. After lawmakers import a policy template, they may modify it in response to the individuals and organizations that can hold them accountable for their actions. The hypothesis that guides the rest of this chapter is that variation in policy content reflects the impact of intrastate constituencies during the customization process.

Electoral considerations do not inspire all of the changes that are made during the customization process. Customization frequently includes technical changes that make a policy innovation easier to administer. Program administrators, for example, sometimes alert officials to potential conflicts between policy innovations and existing state programs. Amending the provisions of a proposal can eliminate this sort of conflict and explain why the "same" policy varies across the states in which it has been enacted. These technical changes are certainly important, but the analysis in this chapter emphasizes the relationship between electoral considerations and program content.

The Politics of Customization: An Overview

This section provides an overview of the customization process. It compares the impact of groups representing intrastate constituencies to that of groups representing out-of-state constituencies. Assessing this balance requires a systematic examination of the lawmaking process that turns the initial versions of bills into the statutes that ultimately gain enactment. Lobbying and committee work constitute two critical components of this process, because they facilitate the amendment of existing policy templates. After being lobbied on a particular bill or after hearing testimony at a committee hearing, lawmakers can and often do respond by adjusting specific provisions of the measure. Differences in program content can frequently be attributed to the changes that take place in these two settings. Understanding which political actors are most active as lobbyists and committee witnesses can therefore help explain why the same policy innovation takes on a variety of forms. Before undertaking such an analysis, however, it is necessary to take a closer look at the potential impact of electoral considerations.

CAMPAIGN CONTRIBUTIONS AND CUSTOMIZATION

Why would state officials respond to the requests of organizations that lobby and participate in committee hearings? The discussion in the preceding section of this chapter hypothesized that electoral considerations provide officials with an incentive to amend proposals. The possibility of collecting electoral resources—such as endorsements, campaign contributions, and personnel—explains why lawmakers might respond to the entreaties of these groups. Doing so might help them win reelection. This subsection of this chapter investigates the potential strength of this electoral connection by examining campaign finance contributions for state house candidates in Massachusetts, Oregon, and Virginia.[9] It emphasizes the balance between in-state and out-of-state contributions. Elected officials who receive most of their contributions from in-state sources have an especially strong incentive to respond to the lobbying efforts and testimony of intrastate organizations, while those who receive most of their funds from national sources probably feel no such pressure. Table 10 displays contribution information broken down by state, party affiliation, and the outcome of the election.

The data in table 10 suggest that state house candidates, on average, collect the vast majority of their campaign contributions from in-state sources. This pattern exists in Massachusetts, Oregon, and Virginia for successful and unsuccessful candidates, and it is true for members of all political parties. This pattern provides empirical support for the claim (made earlier in this chapter) that an intrastate electoral connection provides officials with an incentive to be receptive to their constituents'

TABLE 10. In-State and Out-of-State Campaign Contributions

State and category	Average amount raised	Average in-state contributions	Average percentage: in-state contributions	Average out-of-state contributions	Average percentage: out-of-state contributions	Contribution source unidentified	Average percentage: unidentified source	Number of observations
Massachusetts								
Average	$37,000	$30,050	76.82	$1,280	3.61	$5,670	19.58	307
Party affiliation								
Democrat	$45,189	$36,886	76.69	$1,577	3.65	$6,925	19.66	206
Green	$17,318	$14,638	71.31	$260	1.10	$2,420	27.59	5
Independent	$19,600	$16,121	79.92	$1,088	6.83	$2,391	13.24	4
Libertarian	$2,015	$1,552	68.37	$8	0.14	$455	31.49	12
Republican	$24,570	$19,938	79.70	$806	4.11	$3,827	16.19	72
Undeclared	$53,360	$48,525	90.94	$2,575	4.83	$2,260	4.24	1
Unenrolled	$4,751	$3,329	63.50	$53	1.01	$1,369	35.49	6
Unknown	$9,990	$7,690	76.98	$1,300	13.01	$1,000	10.01	1
Electoral status								
Won general	$51,568	$41,894	76.24	$1,499	2.42	$8,174	21.34	155
Lost general	$17,509	$14,374	76.89	$663	3.75	$2,473	19.36	77
Lost primary	$27,479	$21,886	77.23	$1,589	6.39	$4,024	16.38	62
Did not run	$25,223	$21,611	80.80	$796	2.83	$2,816	16.37	12
Withdrew	$11,235	$9,835	87.54	$1,400	12.46	$0	0	1
Oregon								
Average	$85,280	$72,240	81.97	$9,134	10.28	$3,906	7.74	115
Party affiliation								
Constitution	$7,723	$7,418	96.05	$305	3.95	$0	0	1

Continued

TABLE 10.—Continued

State and category	Average amount raised	Average in-state contributions	Average percentage: in-state contributions	Average out-of-state contributions	Average percentage: out-of-state contributions	Contribution source unidentified	Average percentage: unidentified source	Number of observations
Democrat	$74,315	$62,328	82.24	$7,948	8.40	$4,039	9.36	63
Libertarian	$8,695	$5,963	68.58	$1,050	12.08	$1,682	19.34	1
Pacific Green	$5,236	$3,900	74.48	$0	0	$1,336	25.52	1
Republican	$106,040	$90,760	82.40	$11,319	12.53	$3,961	5.08	48
Unknown	$13,724	$7,100	51.73	$5,000	36.43	$1,624	11.82	1
Electoral status								
Won general	$124,040	$102,235	82.32	$16,732	12.68	$5,072	5.01	53
Lost general	$65,241	$59,999	83.01	$1,526	3.84	$3,715	13.15	36
Lost primary	$33,200	$27,492	79.52	$4,072	14.49	$1,635	5.98	22
Did not run	$38,505	$31,067	81.64	$4,774	13.42	$2,665	4.94	4
Virginia								
Average	$66,592	$55,457	82.06	$8,460	11.17	$2,675	6.77	219
Party affiliation								
Democrat	$69,659	$57,369	82.57	$8,859	1.16	$3,431	5.83	85
Green	$130	$130	100.00	$0	0	$0	0	1
Independent	$28,881	$23,905	80.89	$819	4.19	$4,157	14.92	15
Libertarian	$2,023	$1,597	75.85	$0	0	$426	24.15	4
Republican	$73,267	$61,328	81.51	$9,866	12.68	$2,074	5.81	110
Unknown	$40,455	$39,372	92.39	$548	0.71	$535	6.90	4
Electoral status								
Won general	$95,007	$80,820	84.75	$11,074	11.84	$3,112	3.41	100
Lost general	$56,883	$46,821	80.83	$6,608	9.81	$3,452	9.36	68
Lost primary	$24,047	$20,026	77.34	$2,054	5.44	$1,967	17.22	13
Did not run	$23,746	$16,284	78.80	$7,084	13.78	$378	7.42	38

requests. Legislators rely on these intrastate constituencies to fund their campaigns, so legislators are likely to try to accommodate these constituencies whenever possible. Modifying the content of an existing legislative proposal is one potential accommodation.[10]

Candidates for the state legislature generally receive more than three-quarters of their campaign contributions from in-state sources. During the 2002 election cycle in the state of Massachusetts, for example, the average state house candidate raised a total of $37,000, of which $30,050 (81.2 percent) came from in-state sources. Table 10 shows that the average state house candidate collected 76.82 percent of his or her contributions from in-state sources and only 3.61 percent from out-of-state sources.[11] This proportion is remarkably consistent across Massachusetts Democrats (76.69 percent) and Republicans (79.70 percent). It is also consistent across victorious candidates (76.24 percent), general election losers (76.89 percent), and primary election losers (77.23 percent). If one makes the rather dubious assumption that all of the unidentified contributions came from out-of-state sources, in-state donations still outnumber out-of-state campaign contributions by more than a three-to-one ratio.

State house candidates in Oregon and Virginia also received the vast majority of their campaign contributions from in-state sources. The average state house candidate in Oregon collected $85,280 in campaign contributions during the 2002 election cycle, and an average of $72,240 (84.71 percent) came from in-state sources. The average candidate collected 81.97 percent of his or her donations from in-state sources and 10.28 percent from out-of-state sources. Once again, the averages for Democrats (82.24 percent) and Republicans (82.40 percent) are strikingly similar. These patterns are also consistent across electoral status, dipping below 80 percent only among candidates who lost primary elections (79.52 percent). The 2001 election cycle in Virginia produced similar patterns. The average state house candidate raised $66,592, of which $55,457 (83.28 percent) came from in-state sources. The average candidate received 82.06 percent of his or her contributions from in-state sources and only 11.17 percent from out-of-state sources. These patterns are consistent across party lines and electoral status. Democrats (82.57 percent), Republicans (81.51 percent), general election winners (84.75 percent), and general election losers (80.83 percent) all received, on average, more than 80 percent of their contributions from in-state sources. The campaign finance data suggest that candidates of all stripes in Massachusetts, Oregon, and Virginia rely heavily on in-state sources to fund their campaigns. This reliance gives them an especially strong incentive to respond to the lobbying campaigns of intrastate individuals and organizations. For this potential influence to translate into an actual impact on program content, however, these intrastate constituencies must urge officials to accept, reject, or amend a proposal. The next step in our analysis of the customization process is therefore to assess the visibility of intrastate organizations as lobbyists and as committee witnesses.

LOBBYING REGISTRATION AND CUSTOMIZATION

When organizations wish to modify the language of a legislative proposal, they often make their case by lobbying elected officials. As a result, analyzing lobbying registration data can provide a reasonably comprehensive perspective on the forces that are active in state politics. By casting a fairly wide net, these data seem likely to include organizations that use diverse strategies to attempt to influence state lawmakers. Certain organizations may be inclined to rely on outsider tactics, such as media appeals and direct mail campaigns (Kollman 1998),[12] while others may be inclined to testify before legislative committees. Because the lobbying registration data incorporates this diversity, it provides a good measure of the range of groups that attempt to persuade state officials to amend, adopt, or reject policy innovations. This subsection examines all lobbying registrations held by health care and welfare organizations in the fifty states between 1997 and 1999,[13] paying special attention to the frequency of multistate registrations. It treats the groups that are registered to lobby in more than one state as "national" organizations and compares the prominence of these national groups to that of groups that are registered to lobby in a single state.

The lobbying registration lists incorporate every organization concerned with either welfare or health care that registered to lobby in any state between 1997 and 1999. The list of welfare organizations consists of 2,088 entries, whereas the list of health care organizations consists of 7,044 entries. This discrepancy suggests that the interest group universe is denser in health care policy than it is in welfare policy. For the specific purposes of this study, examining the extent of multistate registrations required an exhaustive reconciliation of the registration names of various organizations. Such groups as the National Association of Social Workers, for example, were registered under a variety of initials and with the state name sometimes preceding and sometimes following the full title. In keeping with the research of Virginia Gray, David Lowery, and their collaborators, this analysis followed specific guidelines in the categorization of groups as multistate. Most important, state branches of federated organizations are treated as a single organization with multiple state registrations, while the local branches of these federated structures are treated as separate entities (Wolak et al. 2002).[14] After common titles and coding rules have been applied across the states, the main quantity of interest is the number of states in which each organization was registered.

Given the potential effect of electoral considerations on the customization process, we might expect that most of the groups that register to lobby will only register in a single state. The alternative hypothesis is that state interest group communities are highly nationalized and that many organizations will register to lobby in more than one state.[15] Several broad trends seem to have encouraged the nationalization of state interest group communities. Over the last two decades, the locus of public policy control has shifted from the national government to the states. In an era of devolution, businesses and advocacy organizations have a clear incentive to shift their attention to the states and to lobby state officials. At the same time, federal court rulings have promoted heightened spending of national party funds in state elections. These changes in campaign spending might also have stimulated greater lobbying activity. Finally, broader trends in corporate America, including mergers and acquisitions, might have caused corporations to establish a lobbying presence to protect their various lines of business (Wolak et al. 2002, 531–32). All of these trends might lead one to expect multistate lobbying registrations to be a relatively common phenomenon. Such an empirical pattern would suggest that lobbying is largely the province of national organizations, which would contradict the hypothesis that intrastate forces dominate the customization process.

A systematic analysis of lobbying registration data suggests that the composition of state interest group communities remains predominantly local. Table 11 reveals that the visibility of local groups is particularly pronounced in welfare policy. The majority of the 2,088 lobbying registrations (1,443, or 69.1 percent) represent organizations that registered in a single state. On average, welfare-related organizations registered to lobby in 1.33 states. Of the 1,566 unique organizations on the list of welfare lobbyists, only 123 (7.9 percent) were registered in multiple states. It would be an overstatement to characterize most of these 123 organizations as truly national in reach, at least in terms of lobbying activity. Almost two-fifths of them registered in only two states, and three-quar-

TABLE 11.   Multistate Lobbying Registrations in Welfare and Health Care Policy, 1997–99

Number of states in which an organization registered	Welfare policy		Health care policy	
	Number of organizations	Percentage of multi-state registrations	Number of organizations	Percentage of multi-state registrations
2	49	39.84	175	37.55
3	23	18.70	75	16.09
4	12	9.76	39	8.37
5	10	8.13	29	6.22
6	8	6.50	24	5.15
7	7	5.69	18	3.86
8	1	0.81	7	1.50
9	1	0.81	8	1.72
10	1	0.81	6	1.29
11	2	1.63	11	2.36
12	3	2.44	6	1.29
13	1	0.81	2	0.43
14	0	0	6	1.29
15	0	0	4	0.86
16	1	0.81	4	0.86
17	0	0	5	1.07
18	0	0	9	1.93
19	1	0.81	0	0
20	0	0	0	0
21	0	0	3	0.64
22	0	0	5	1.07
23	0	0	1	0.21
24	0	0	1	0.21
25	0	0	1	0.21
26	0	0	1	0.21
27	0	0	0	0
28	0	0	1	0.21

TABLE 11.—*Continued*

Number of states in which an organization registered	Welfare policy		Health care policy	
	Number of organizations	Percentage of multi-state registrations	Number of organizations	Percentage of multi-state registrations
29	0	0	1	0.21
30	0	0	2	0.43
31	0	0	3	0.64
32	1	0.81	1	0.21
33	0	0	1	0.21
34	0	0	1	0.21
35	0	0	2	0.43
36	0	0	2	0.43
37	0	0	0	0
38	0	0	0	0
39	0	0	2	0.43
40	0	0	0	0
41	1	0.81	2	0.43
42	0	0	1	0.21
43	0	0	1	0.21
44	0	0	1	0.21
45	1	0.81	0	0
46	0	0	3	0.64
47	0	0	0	0
48	0	0	2	0.43
Total registrations	2,088		7,044	
Unique organizations	1,566		4,097	
Single state only	1,443		3,631	
Multistate only	123		466	

Note: Single-state and multistate registrations do not add up to the total number of registrations because multistate registrations list the number of organizations registered to lobby in more than one state. The 123 multistate organizations concerned with welfare policy registered to lobby in an average of 4.98 states, with a standard deviation of 6.31. The 466 multistate organizations concerned with health care policy registered to lobby in an average of 6.98 states, with a standard deviation of 8.93.

ters of them registered in five or fewer states. Only three welfare-related organizations registered to lobby in more than thirty states between 1997 and 1999: the National Association of Social Workers registered in forty-five states, AARP in forty-one states, and the Association of Retarded Citizens in thirty-two states. In sum, it was rare for a welfare-related organization to register to lobby in multiple states and even less common for an organization to register in more than a dozen states. The patterns in table 11 suggest that lobbying is largely the purview of local organizations. While the data cannot link these organizations to legislative content, they provide empirical support for the hypothesis that intrastate forces are more influential than national forces during the customization process.

Similarly, patterns of lobbying registration in health care policy suggest that the composition of state interest group communities remains largely local. These patterns are somewhat kinder to the nationalization hypothesis, but they nonetheless imply that most organizations in health care policy registered to lobby in a single state. Table 11 shows that a slight majority of the 7,044 lobbying registrations (3,631, or 51.5 percent) represent organizations that registered in a single state. The average organization in this policy area registered to lobby in 1.72 states. Of the 4,097 unique organizations on this list, only 466 (11.4 percent) were registered in multiple states. These 466 organizations registered to lobby, on average, in 7.32 states. Given the more extensive universe of interest groups in this policy arena, it is not surprising to find that a larger number of health care organizations possess national reach. Five organizations, in fact, registered to lobby in virtually every state: the American Cancer Society and the Nurses Association registered in forty-eight states; and Blue Cross Blue Shield, the Health Insurance Association of America, and the Optometric Association registered in forty-six states. Overall, however, more than three-fifths of these organizations registered in five or fewer states, and more than four-fifths of them registered in ten or fewer states. Table 11, in sum, suggests that lobbying remains an activity that is largely pursued by organizations that are not national in scope. The individuals who lobby on behalf of these groups can therefore make a credible claim that they represent persons to whom elected officials must respond.

In combination, the information in table 11 suggests that the balance between multistate and local registrations varies across policy sectors. Other studies have found that this balance also varies across states, but the overall distribution is skewed toward local organizations (Wolak et al. 2002).[16] This pattern suggests that state lawmakers are especially likely to be lobbied by organizations representing local constituencies. In addition, many of the organizations that are registered to lobby in multiple states represent individuals who live within these states. Such professional associations as the National Association of Social Workers possess intrastate constituencies, as do such advocacy organizations as AARP. It is extremely rare for an organization to fit the caricature of a large "outsider" that is able to manipulate the locals. Organizations registered to lobby in multiple states are more likely to be federations with a membership base within each of the states in which they operate. Many of the organizations characterized as "national" in this subsection of this chapter can argue with some justification that they actually represent intrastate constituencies and concerns.

LEGISLATIVE TESTIMONY AND CUSTOMIZATION

Committee assignments are valuable to state lawmakers because committee work is an extremely significant step of the policy-making process. John McDonaugh, a former legislator in Massachusetts, explains, "Most of the time, floor debate is only the playing out of controversies that have been sorted out and settled in the committee process" (McDonaugh 2000, 12). In Oregon, legislative committees are especially powerful. They can introduce bills with the committee listed as the author; offer substitute bills in place of the original proposal; have committee amendments automatically incorporated into the bill rather than accepted or rejected on the floor; and, by requiring unanimous consent, make it difficult to amend proposals (Hamm and Moncrief 2004, 180). Even though committees in other states do not possess such extensive powers, their activities focused on amending legislative proposals can have an analogous impact on the making of public policy.

Testimony at legislative hearings is therefore a feasible proxy for influence during the customization process. Approaching analysis of testimony in this way cannot establish definitively that the testimony altered the content of a proposal, but it provides a good first cut at assessing the influence of various actors. During legislative hearings, officials gauge a proposal's support and opposition among the constituencies that it would affect. They sometimes respond to testimony by altering proposals in an effort to ameliorate opposition and to generate additional support. As a result, legislative testimony provides an outlet through which it is possible to voice an opinion on pending proposals. Not surprisingly, a recent survey of state lobbyists and state organizations suggests that virtually all interest groups engage in legislative testimony. It found no significant variation across group types in the use of this tactic. "Insider" and "outsider" groups are equally likely to count legislative testimony among their lobbying techniques (Nownes and Freeman 1998).[17]

The subsequent discussion identifies witnesses who testified during hearings on senior prescription drug programs, MSAs, IDAs, and omnibus welfare reform legislation in Oregon. It focuses on Oregon for two reasons. First, as described earlier, committees in Oregon retain substantial power. It stands to reason, then, that testimony before these unusually powerful committees is particularly likely to affect program content. Second, Oregon maintains superior archives, while neither Massachusetts nor Virginia maintains comprehensive records of committee hearings.[18] The purpose of this analysis is to assess the relative visibility of groups representing intrastate and out-of-state constituencies. If the electoral connection is driving the customization process, one would expect most witnesses to represent groups with intrastate constituencies.

Committee witnesses fall into one of five categories. The first category consists of "individual citizens" who do not represent an organization. Their testimony is usually an attempt to personalize an abstract political issue.[19] The second category of witnesses consists of individuals who represent "national organizations" with no presence in a state. Witnesses representing professional associations and think tanks fall under this heading. The third category, "state chapters," consists of witnesses who represent a group located within the state and affiliated with a national organization.[20] State chapters represent federations, hybrid organizations with both a national headquarters and an organizational presence in each of the states.[21] The fourth category of witnesses consists of individuals who represent "intrastate groups," or coalitions that operate exclusively in a single state. Some of these organizations possess national connections, but these links are usually less formal than the federation structure that characterizes state chapters.[22] The fifth and final category, "state and local government," includes testimony by elected officials, executive branch officials, and other individuals who work for local government agencies. These witnesses may voice their political opinions or provide a professional assessment of how a policy innovation will function within the state.

If the customization process is most strongly influenced by intrastate forces, one would expect committee witnesses to fall largely into the final three categories. The vast majority of those testifying, in other words, would represent state chapters, intrastate groups, and state and local government. If witnesses from national organizations testify more frequently than other witnesses do, that would suggest that the customization process is not a product of intrastate forces. This subsection examines, along three dimensions, the balance between witnesses representing intrastate and out-of-state constituencies. The first dimension is a raw count of the number of witnesses that fall into each category, an approach that weighs each appearance equally. The second dimension is the number of witnesses in each category that testify multiple times on a single bill. Bills frequently receive multiple hearings during the legislative process. When witnesses appear at more than one hearing, it may illustrate the importance of the organization that they represent. Occasionally, lawmakers may hear testimony, amend legislation in response, and then ask reappearing witnesses whether they approve of the changes. This dynamic is especially likely to occur during the consideration of omnibus legislation.

The third dimension is the number of witnesses in each category that testify at work sessions. This dimension grows out of the particularities of the legislative process in Oregon. The work of legislative committees takes place in two stages: public hearings and work sessions. Public hearings provide committee members with an opportunity to take the pulse of various constituencies, figuring out where they stand and what it would take to earn their support. Work sessions generally follow public hearings and involve a more careful reading of the proposal. Committee members examine specific provisions and discuss their meaning and administrative feasibility. At the end of a work session on MSA legislation, the committee chair concluded: "This is obviously a pretty complicated thing. I am beginning to get the feeling right now that we are not going to be able to do this or have it in any form that we are going to be ready to move on. I think that we have too many questions and too much to adjust."[23] The chair drew this conclusion after the other members of the committee asked pointed questions about how specific sections of the bill would be implemented. His quotation illustrates the importance of work sessions in shaping program content. Testifying at work sessions therefore seems especially likely to affect the customization process.

An analysis of committee appearances in Oregon reveals three important patterns. First, the representatives of national organizations rarely
testify. Second, representatives of state chapters and intrastate groups
(combined) typically comprise more than half of the committee witnesses. Third, state and local government officials generally comprise
approximately one-third of the committee witnesses. Table 12 classifies
the witnesses who testified on senior prescription drug, MSA, IDA, and
welfare reform legislation. It provides a raw count of the number of witnesses who fall into each category.

The limited number of appearances by witnesses from national organizations is the first noteworthy pattern in table 12. Representatives of
national organizations were most prominent during hearings on medical
savings accounts. They appeared on behalf of the National Federation of
Independent Businesses, the Pharmaceutical Research and Manufacturers
of America, and Kaiser Permanente.[24] The only "national" witness who
testified on welfare reform legislation was a Virginia-based consultant
who specialized in welfare-to-work programs. Despite the nationwide

TABLE 12.   Witnesses at Oregon Committee Hearings

Topic, bill number, and year (in parentheses)	Individual citizens	National organizations	State chapters of national groups	Intrastate groups	State and local government
Senior prescription drug programs					
Senate Bill 9 (2001)	0 (0%)	0 (0%)	2 (40%)	1 (20%)	2 (40%)
Medical savings accounts					
House Bill 2865 (1995)	1 (20%)	1 (20%)	1 (20%)	1 (20%)	1 (20%)
Senate Bill 347/House Bill 2488 (1997)	0 (0%)	2 (22%)	3 (33%)	2 (22%)	2 (22%)
Individual development accounts					
House Bill 3600 (1999)	2 (15%)	0 (0%)	3 (23%)	4 (31%)	4 (31%)
Welfare reform					
House Bill 2459 (1993)	7 (25%)	1 (4%)	7 (25%)	3 (11%)	10 (36%)
Senate Bill 1117 (1995)	0 (0%)	0 (0%)	7 (35%)	5 (25%)	8 (40%)

Note: Cell values are the number of witnesses in each category, with percentages in parentheses. Information about
the identities of these witnesses is available from the author on request.

prominence of welfare reform in the early and middle 1990s, no representatives of national organizations appeared before the committees. None of the witnesses who testified on senior prescription drug legislation or IDA legislation represented a national organization. Overall, the limited number of appearances by the representatives of national organizations suggests that these groups have a relatively minor impact on the customization process.

The second noteworthy pattern in table 12 is that state chapters and intrastate groups (combined) typically provided more than half of the committee witnesses. For the most part, these witnesses could credibly claim that their testimony reflected the views of voters within the state of Oregon. State chapters generally provided between one-fourth and two-fifths of the witnesses who testified. Different kinds of organizations fall under this heading. Some, such as the Oregon Public Employees Union and the Oregon Association of Health Underwriters, are occupationally based. Others, such as Oregon Right to Life and Planned Parenthood Advocates of Oregon, are part of national interest groups that are motivated by a specific political issue. Intrastate groups based exclusively within Oregon usually provided about one-fourth of the witnesses who testified. This category includes individuals from advocacy organizations, such as Oregonians for Medical Savings Accounts, and from businesses, such as Jeld-Wen Inc. These witnesses testified on behalf of groups that represent intrastate constituencies and generally played an advocacy role, stating the positions of the organizations on whose behalf they appeared. As a result, this pattern supports the hypothesis that intrastate forces and electoral considerations play important roles during the customization process.

The prominence of state and local government officials is the third striking pattern in table 12. These officeholders usually represented between one-fourth and two-fifths of all committee witnesses. Sometimes, they appeared as advocates, expressing their support of or opposition to a policy innovation. For example, some legislators testified in support of bills that they themselves had written. State and local government officials, especially those from the executive branch, also provided technical or programmatic expertise about how existing programs functioned or how a policy innovation might have operated if it was implemented. Representatives from the Oregon Department of Revenue and the Oregon State Treasury played this role during hearings on IDAs and MSAs, respectively. This legislative testimony is one of the many ways that executive branch officials keep state policymakers apprised of how programs are working. Legislators often rely on program administrators' technical expertise during the customization process. In sum, witnesses in the category of state and local government were quite prominent and provided a mixture of political and technical information.

If we focus only on witnesses who made multiple appearances before legislative committees in Oregon, similar patterns prevail. All of these witnesses represented state chapters, intrastate groups, or state and local government. Table 13 displays all of the witnesses who made multiple appearances on a single proposal, with the number of appearances in parentheses.[25] No one representing a purely national organization testified multiple times. Witnesses representing state chapters and intrastate groups were more prominent. Witnesses from the Oregon Public Employees Union, for example, appeared twice during the debates over MSA and welfare reform legislation. A witness from Multnomah County Legal Aid Service also testified twice on the 1995 welfare reform measure.[26] Representatives of the Oregon Society of Certified Public Accountants made six appearances on MSA legislation in 1997, illustrating the centrality of this professional association.

Witnesses representing state and local governments made multiple appearances on several bills. Executive branch officials were especially prominent. As lawmakers considered welfare reform legislation in 1993 and 1995, the administrator and assistant administrator of Adult and Family Services testified a total of seven times. In 1993, the director of the Department of Human Resources and a witness representing Clackamas County Social Services testified twice each on omnibus welfare reform legislation. The human services advisor to the governor appeared at two hearings on welfare legislation in 1995. Finally, in 1997, an official from the Department of Revenue testified three times on MSA legislation. Table 13 suggests the significance of intrastate actors during the customization process.

The division between public hearings and work sessions provides a third way to examine the identities of committee witnesses in Oregon.

TABLE 13. Witnesses at Multiple Committee Hearings in Oregon

Topic, bill number, and year (in parentheses)	National organizations	State chapters of national groups	Intrastate groups	State and local government
Senior prescription drug program				
Senate Bill 9 (2001)	None	None	Oregon State University (2)	None
Medical savings accounts				
House Bill 2865 (1995)	None	None	Oregonians for Medical Savings Accounts (2)	None
Senate Bill 347 (1997)/ House Bill 2488 (1997)	None	Oregon Society of Certified Public Accountants (6) Oregon Public Employees Union (2)	None	Department of Revenue (3)
Welfare reform				
House Bill 2459 (1993)	None	None	None	Assistant administrator, Adult and Family Services (4) Director, Department of Human Resources (2) Clackamas County Social Services (2)
Senate Bill 1117 (1995)	None	Oregon Public Employees Union (2)	Multnomah County Legal Aid Service (2)	Administrator, Adult and Family Services (3) Policy advisor to Governor Kitzhaber on Health and Human Resources (2)

Note: No witnesses made multiple appearances on House Bill 3600 (1999), individual development account legislation.

Statutory language is the main topic of work sessions, so witnesses are especially likely to affect program content when they appear at these sessions. Table 14 displays the relevant witnesses.[27] State and local government officials were especially prominent. During welfare reform work sessions, for example, witnesses testified on behalf of Adult and Family Services and the Division of Child Support. In addition, the representatives of influential intrastate interest groups appeared at work sessions. In 1995, representatives of Jeld-Wen Inc. and Multnomah County Legal Aid Service participated in welfare reform work sessions. Relatively few witnesses appeared during work sessions on MSA and IDA legislation, but all that did appear represented an executive agency or an intrastate group. Work sessions often precipitate important changes to proposals, so the dominance of organizations representing intrastate constituencies suggests that these groups have a profound impact on program content.

In sum, patterns of legislative testimony in Oregon suggest that intrastate forces are especially influential during customization. Most witnesses represent organizations that possess intrastate constituencies. These witnesses are more likely to appear before legislative committees, make multiple appearances on a single bill, and testify during the work sessions that focus intently on statutory language. However, one would not want to rely exclusively on this type of evidence. Many groups will not testify on every bill in which they are interested, and legislators might solicit testimony from specific groups or individuals. In addition, modifications to legislation frequently occur in settings outside the hearing room. For that reason, it is important to note that the patterns described in this subsection overlap considerably with those found during the earlier analysis of lobbying registration data. In both settings, the role of intrastate political forces appears to exceed that of national actors.

SUMMARY

This section of this chapter presented data on campaign finance, lobbying registration, and legislative testimony at the state level. This evidence suggests that intrastate forces dominate the customization process. The legislative process provides numerous settings in which interested parties can request that state policymakers support, reject, or amend a proposal. Organizations representing intrastate constituencies seem especially

TABLE 14. Witnesses at Work Sessions in Oregon

Topic, bill number, and year (in parentheses)	National organizations	State chapters of national groups	Intrastate groups	State and local government
Senior prescription drug program				
Senate Bill 9 (2001)	None	Oregon State Pharmacy Association	Oregon State University	None
Medical savings accounts				
Senate Bill 347 (1997) / House Bill 2488 (1997)	None	Oregon Society of Certified Public Accountants	None	Department of Revenue
Individual development accounts				
House Bill 3600 (1997)	None	None	Human Solutions	None
Welfare reform				
House Bill 2459 (1993)	Virginia-Based Consultant on Welfare-to-Work Programs	None	Multnomah County Legal Aid Service	Administrator, Adult and Family Services; Assistant administrator, Adult and Family Services; Director, Department of Human Resources; Clackamas County Social Services
Senate Bill 1117 (1995)	None	Oregon Public Employees Union; Oregon Building and Construction Trades Council; Oregon Catholic Conference	Multnomah County Legal Aid Service; Jeld-Wen Inc.	Administrator, Adult and Family Services; Policy advisor to Governor Kitzhaber on Health and Human Resources; Assistant administrator, Adult and Family Services; Commission for Women; Division of Child Support

likely to take advantage of these opportunities, either during committee hearings or through more general lobbying campaigns. Furthermore, elected officials possess a strong incentive to respond to these requests, because they rely quite heavily on in-state sources for campaign contributions and, of course, for electoral support. Turning from these general patterns to specific programmatic differences across policies in Massachusetts, Oregon, and Virginia will shed additional light on how these intrastate political forces affect specific provisions of policy innovations.

Differences across States in the Politics of Customization

The evidence presented in the preceding section of this chapter suggests that the customization process is fundamentally similar across states. State legislators receive most of their campaign contributions from in-state sources, and various intrastate political actors are especially likely to be active in settings where state officials amend policy proposals. In sum, it seems that internal political factors strongly influence the customization process. Many organizations that register to lobby or testify at committee hearings can argue that they represent the intrastate constituencies to whom elected officials must respond if they want to win reelection. The next step, then, is to turn to individual states and examine the trajectories of specific policy innovations. That is the goal of this section, which focuses on program content in Massachusetts, Oregon, and Virginia. It returns to the five policy innovations analyzed throughout this book and compares the specific provisions of programs that gained enactment in these three states.[28]

An intensive examination of program content suggests two tentative conclusions about the customization process. First, policy innovations are generally backed by a range of interests. Coalition building is important and common at the state level, and the composition of coalitions can vary across states. In some states, a particular group or interest will dominate the customization process, and program content will reflect the interests of that specific constituency. In another state, a different interest may be more influential. Differences in program content can reflect differences in the composition of supporting coalitions.[29] Second, program content can vary across states when an identical coalition of forces supports or opposes a policy innovation in these states. Variation in the strength, size, and strategies pursued by similar coalitions in different states, as well as the political environment in these states, can also create variation in program content.

THE POLITICS OF CUSTOMIZATION:
SENIOR PRESCRIPTION DRUG PROGRAMS

Senior prescription drug programs gained enactment in Massachusetts in 1996 and in Oregon in 2001. The Massachusetts program was created as part of an omnibus measure called the Improved Access to Health Care Act. State policymakers revised it several times before creating a new program called Prescription Advantage during the summer of 2000. Lawmakers in Oregon enacted the Senior Drug Assistance Program in 2001 as part of a statute that also assisted low-income Oregonians with their prescription drug costs. In both states, lawmakers altered the initial proposals that led to the creation of this policy innovation. This customization process had an especially profound impact in Massachusetts in 2000 and in Oregon in 2001.

Massachusetts lawmakers established a senior prescription drug program in 1996. The program was one prong of a larger legislative package designed to improve access to health care, and it proved to be one of the omnibus measure's least controversial elements. Including the senior pharmacy program gave the proposal an "enormous political boost with senior groups and virtually no loss in support from anyone else" (McDonaugh 2000, 273). Among the most important supporters of this provision was the Massachusetts Senior Action Council, an intrastate group that had long supported the creation of such a program. The larger bill underwent major changes during the legislative process, but the senior prescription drug program remained largely intact. Officials removed various employer mandates from the larger bill and excised the Insurance Reimbursement Program, which had originally been proposed by the governor. These modifications were made in an effort to gain the critical support of the state business community. They help explain why the bill was endorsed by several business groups, including the Success by 6 Coalition, Associated Industries of Massachusetts, and the Massachusetts Business Roundtable. A broad array of forces coalesced behind the legislation, and Health Care for All, an intrastate consumer advocacy group, was "at the epicenter" of the lobbying effort (McDonaugh 2000, 273). The creation of a senior prescription drug program in Massachusetts involved a complicated process of negotiation and strategizing that enabled its supporters to achieve their goals.[30] Two intrastate advocacy groups, the Massachusetts Senior Action Council and Health Care for All, led the lobbying effort.

Lawmakers in Massachusetts later amended the Pharmacy Program, which had been created by the omnibus legislation. When it was created, the program provided benefits to Massachusetts seniors who did not have any source of prescription drug coverage and had incomes at or below 133 percent of the federal poverty level. In July 1997, officials raised the income eligibility guidelines to 150 percent of the federal poverty level, and in November of that year, the program's annual benefit was increased to $750. During the summer of 1999, the annual benefit was raised to $1,250, and enrollment was expanded to younger persons. While these relatively modest modifications were important, the most significant changes occurred a year later. During the summer of 2000, policymakers in Massachusetts created a new, more ambitious senior prescription drug program, called Prescription Advantage.

The creation of Prescription Advantage was inspired by a national foundation, but its specific provisions were shaped by intrastate politics. In April 2000, Heinz Family Philanthropies, a foundation with offices in Pittsburgh and Washington, D.C., drew attention to the senior prescription drug issue when it released a report on a proposal called the Heinz Plan to Overcome Prescription Drug Expenses (HOPE).[31] The issue had already emerged as a defining element of the 2000 presidential campaign, but the foundation's proposal put a specific option on the Massachusetts political agenda. Prescription Advantage was modeled in part on the HOPE proposal, but the influence of the foundation receded after it generated an initial burst of publicity. Prescription Advantage is modeled as an insurance program, with plan members who pay monthly premiums, an annual deductible, and copayments at the point of purchase. Although HOPE shared some of these features, Massachusetts policymakers substantially amended the foundation's proposal. One elderly affairs lobbyist attributed the foundation's limited influence to its inability to activate an intrastate constituency. He explained: "What could [Teresa] Heinz do? She has no constituency in the state that she can activate. She can't go back on it. We thought it was great."[32] As a result, the final measure diverged significantly from the program described in the HOPE report.

The creation of the Senior Drug Assistance Program in Oregon also illustrates the importance of the customization process. Ironically, the senior prescription drug program was not part of the original proposal that ultimately led to its enactment. Drafted in 2001, the initial version of Senate Bill 9 created a Patient Prescription Drug Assistance Program through the Oregon State University College of Pharmacy. The purpose of this program is to direct low-income Oregonians without prescription drug coverage to pharmaceutical manufacturers' programs that provide medications for free or low cost to individuals who do not have the resources to purchase prescription drugs.[33] The senior prescription drug program was not a part of Senate Bill 9 when the Senate Health and Human Services Committee held a public hearing in March and a work session in May. A member of the Oregon State Council of Senior Citizens nonetheless expressed the organization's support for the bill at the public hearing. The senior prescription drug program was only added to the legislation in July, when it was appended to a modified version of the bill by the Joint Committee on Ways and Means. The amendment established the basic contours of the Senior Drug Assistance Program. For instance, eligibility was limited to persons whose gross annual income did not exceed 185 percent of the federal poverty level, who did not have over two thousand dollars in liquid assets, and who had not been covered by a private or public prescription drug program in the previous six months. The establishment of the Oregon program illustrates the importance of following a proposal through the legislative process, yet it does not provide as clear an illustration of the impact of intrastate political forces as does the creation of a similar program in Massachusetts.

THE POLITICS OF CUSTOMIZATION: MEDICAL SAVINGS ACCOUNTS

The widely divergent provisions of MSA programs in Oregon and Virginia reflect their diverse intrastate constituencies. Different types of interest groups were involved in the formulation of these two programs. The Oregon legislation grew out of the technical objectives of its main advocate and is consequently limited in scope, while the relatively expansive Virginia program reflects the political ambitions of its primary sponsor. The programmatic differences across the two programs suggest that policy proposals reflect the intentions of their main supporters. If these supporters vary, policy innovations that purport to be similar can actually differ significantly. In keeping with a major theme of this chapter, it is important to emphasize that these programmatic differences grew out of intrastate political dynamics rather than external pressures.

The expansive provisions of the Virginia Medical Savings Account Plan reflect the political ambitions of the Jeffersonian Health Policy Foundation. Established by a group of Virginia physicians, the foundation claimed that MSAs would establish a mutually beneficial relationship between patients and the physician of their choice. Inspired by the national debate over the Health Security Act, the foundation developed model MSA legislation called the American Health Care Plan. In 1995, the Virginia General Assembly unanimously endorsed an MSA bill "based on a health care benefit model developed by the Jeffersonian Health Policy Foundation" (Joint Commission on Health Care 2002, 12).[34] The national government had not yet acted on MSAs, and the Virginia statute was contingent on congressional authorization of this policy innovation. The Virginia program, in other words, would not be operational until Congress passed legislation that defined eligible participants and prescribed criteria for the accounts.

The Virginia statute contains some unusual provisions. It authorizes the use of "direct debit cards" to access the accounts and includes "programs to educate recipients in handling health care services in a cost-effective manner while ensuring that necessary care is obtained." The Virginia plan mandates the "integration of existing coverage," "a system of refundable tax credits," as well as "a system for calculating individual need for health care services in order to ensure that adequate sums are calculated for the care of individuals with great need."[35] The expansiveness of the statute reflects the ambitious policy goals of the foundation that developed the legislation and of other MSA advocates in the state. Compared to both the limited MSA pilot program created by national legislation in 1996 and the Oregon legislation that gained enactment in 1997, the Virginia statute is extremely broad.

The limited provisions of the Oregon MSA program reflect the technical goals of its main sponsor, the Oregon Society of Certified Public Accountants (OSCPA). MSAs achieved agenda status in Oregon in the early and middle 1990s, but no legislation passed until 1997. The creation of a pilot program by the national government in 1996 provided the impetus for the passage of the Oregon statute, which overlaps considerably with the national program.[36] When the state legislature reconvened in 1997, the OSCPA became involved in the MSA debate for the first time. The organization advocated the enactment of MSAs as part of a larger, tax reconnection bill that aligned the Oregon tax code with the national tax code.[37] Its motivation was primarily administrative, and the organization did not view the bill as a political statement about the merits of the accounts. Officials in Oregon showed their traditional deference toward the OSCPA and largely embraced its recommendations.

The Oregon MSA program differed significantly from the bill that was adopted in Virginia. Only three paragraphs of the lengthy reconnection bill mentioned MSAs, and all of them described the Internal Revenue Code as the current and future basis of the law in Oregon. In contrast to the more expansive Virginia legislation, the Oregon bill did not mention debit cards, educational programs, or the integration of existing coverage. The Oregon bill was based almost entirely on national provisions.[38] The adoption of MSAs in Oregon therefore might be described as a "technical" shift. One opponent of the statute, in fact, took umbrage at the political process that produced this bill. He argued that any recognition of the policy innovation "requires a separate policy decision [and] ought to be addressed through separate legislation."[39] Oregon lawmakers were not convinced by this argument, and the tax reconnection bill sailed to enactment.

The MSA provisions that gained enactment in Oregon differed substantially from those adopted in Virginia. In Oregon, OSCPA dominated the customization process and incorporated MSAs within a larger bill linking the state tax code to the Internal Revenue Code. Motivated by administrative concerns rather than by policy goals, the association advocated limited statutory language. By contrast, the Virginia MSA program was stand-alone legislation that reflected the ambitious political objectives of its primary advocate. The Jeffersonian Health Policy Foundation lobbied successfully for a more complex bill. The specific provisions of both MSA statutes can be traced to intrastate political forces. Even though both statutes established state-level MSA programs, their specifics diverged significantly. This divergence suggests that variation in the coalitions that support policy innovations can facilitate variation in program content. Legislative provisions can reflect the goals of the organizations behind their enactment. In addition, juxtaposing these two programs illustrates the hazards of using reinvention to explain variation in program content. The relatively expansive Virginia MSA program preceded the relatively limited Oregon MSA program by two years.[40]

THE POLITICS OF CUSTOMIZATION:
INDIVIDUAL DEVELOPMENT ACCOUNTS

Of the policy innovations profiled in this book, IDAs possessed the lowest public profile and generated the least controversy. Members of both major parties backed the accounts, but the innovation did not generate the intense support or opposition that other policies sparked. IDAs gained enactment in Oregon and Virginia. The programs in these two states overlap in their general provisions and differ in other ways. Interestingly, the customization process did not spark major programmatic changes in either state, and both statutes gained enactment with minimal opposition.

The Virginia Individual Development Accounts Program (VIDA) was established in 1998. To create an IDA demonstration project, the appropriations bill that passed in 1998 set aside five hundred thousand dollars in nongeneral funds from the Temporary Assistance to Needy Families (TANF) block grant. Welfare recipients whose income was 200 percent or less of the federal poverty level could set up and use the money deposited into IDAs for vocational school or college, purchase of a home, or the starting of a business. Account holders receive one dollar from the state for every dollar that they deposit into their accounts and are allowed to deposit up to two thousand dollars over two years. A committee chose five demonstration sites in a competitive application round in 1998, with each site receiving one hundred thousand dollars in state funds to be used for operational costs and program funds. VIDA was created with relatively little fanfare, as a small component of a larger appropriations measure. As a result, the statute did not undergo dramatic changes during the customization process.[41]

The Oregon Individual Development Account Program was established in 1999. It was created by House Bill 3600, a proposal that sailed through the state legislature with minimal opposition and almost no amendments. At a public hearing in April 1999, every witness who appeared before the House Revenue Committee testified in favor of the bill. Discussion centered on the rationale behind the accounts, and the committee made three minor adjustments to the original legislation at its work session five days later. It reduced the income limit for eligible individuals, reduced the percentage of donations that could be claimed as a tax credit, and allowed fiduciary organizations to establish lower thresholds for participants' income and net worth.[42] The Senate Revenue Committee did not make any amendments to the legislation. When the committee held a public hearing and work session in May, its chair urged witnesses to limit their testimony, because no one signed up to testify in opposition to the measure.[43]

House Bill 3600 established the general contours of the Oregon IDA program. It limited account eligibility to households whose income was no greater than 80 percent of the median income for the area and whose net worth was less than twenty thousand dollars.[44] Account holders could use the money deposited in the accounts for higher education, purchase of a home, or the starting of a business. They could contribute up to two thousand dollars per year in the accounts, and fiduciary organizations would contribute not less than one dollar and not more than five dollars for each dollar contributed by the account holder. These provisions were similar to those of the Virginia IDA program. Unlike the Virginia program, however, the Oregon program was funded through tax credits rather than through TANF dollars. Businesses donating to the program were originally entitled to an income tax credit equal to the lesser of twenty-five thousand dollars or 25 percent of the amount donated. In 2001, Oregon lawmakers revisited this provision in House Bill 3391. The original version of House Bill 3391 increased the tax credit limit to the lesser of seventy-five thousand dollars or 75 percent of the amount donated. The House Committee on School Funding and Tax Fairness/Revenue reduced this amount to fifty thousand dollars or

50 percent of the amount donated,[45] but the Senate Committee on Revenue restored the original limit to seventy-five thousand dollars or 75 percent of the amount donated.[46] The final version of House Bill 3391 also amended the 1999 provisions by allowing Indian tribal entities to serve as fiduciary organizations eligible to administer IDAs and by permitting IDAs to be rolled over into Oregon College Savings Plan accounts.

The customization process had a limited impact on IDA programs in Virginia and Oregon. These programs retained the same goals and required account holders to use the deposited moneys for identical objectives, but they differed in important ways. The IDA program created in Virginia relied on TANF funds, whereas the Oregon program utilized tax credits to achieve its objectives. The eligibility criteria of the two programs differed, and the Oregon program permitted more generous matching provisions (albeit funded by private entities, not the state government). IDA advocates faced limited opposition in both states and made only minor adjustments to their original proposals. As a result, the customization process did not have as pronounced an effect on these IDA programs as it did on senior prescription drug programs, MSAs, or welfare reform.

THE POLITICS OF CUSTOMIZATION:
TIME LIMITS AND FAMILY CAPS

When Bill Clinton pledged to "end welfare as we know it" during the 1992 presidential campaign, his promise tapped a general societal unease with Aid to Families with Dependent Children (AFDC). National officials did not reach agreement on welfare reform legislation until 1996. While the national debate continued, officials in many states considered and enacted omnibus welfare reform legislation. State welfare plans diverged considerably. Chapter 3 illustrated that such policy innovations as time limits and family caps were widely considered. However, these innovations did not gain enactment in every state in which they were considered. Furthermore, when time limits and family caps were adopted, the restrictiveness of these programs varied substantially. Officials in some states placed stringent demands on welfare recipients, while others endorsed more flexible policies. This subsection of this chapter examines the political processes that produced this variation. In keeping with one of the major themes of this chapter, it focuses on the lobbying efforts of intrastate groups, particularly the welfare advocacy community. Its analysis suggests that differences in the size, strength, and strategies of these groups profoundly influenced the content of welfare policy in Massachusetts, Oregon, and Virginia.[47] Before tracing the impact of the welfare advocacy community during the customization process, this subsection begins by describing the time limit and family cap provisions in the three states.

In 1995, policymakers in Massachusetts adopted one of the most stringent welfare reform programs in the country. The program imposed a variety of strict requirements on recipients of AFDC, including a work requirement time limit that required nonexempt adults to work at least twenty hours per week after sixty days of independent job search.[48] Recipients who could not find jobs would be placed in community service positions. In the event of noncompliance, welfare grants would be reduced by the proportion attributed to the individual required to work. Continued noncompliance could result in a full family sanction. The family cap provisions of the Massachusetts welfare reform program were similarly stringent. They included two especially strict provisions but did not incorporate certain provisions thought to be favorable to the affected individuals. The Massachusetts family cap required parents to participate in the Job Opportunities and Basic Skills (JOBS) training program when the affected child turned three months of age, a provision known as the "reduced JOBS exemption." It also applied the family cap to children conceived within a year of the family leaving AFDC.[49] In contrast, lawmakers chose not to provide either a partial increase in welfare benefits or vouchers for goods and services in lieu of increased benefits. The Massachusetts policy also did not allow families to keep a larger percentage of their earnings to compensate for the benefits they were denied due to the family cap. The Massachusetts family cap incorporated one generous provision, a child support pass-through allowing families to keep all child support money collected on behalf of the child who was excluded from benefits.[50] Table 9 illustrates how it also incorporated a relatively large number of exemptions. Overall, however, the family cap was most notable for its stringency.

Lawmakers in Oregon endorsed omnibus welfare reform legislation in

1993 and 1995. This legislation incorporated a lenient time limit and did not include a family cap. The state's welfare reform program, known as the JOBS Plus Program, limited AFDC benefit receipt to no more than twenty-four out of eighty-four months for Oregon families with employable parents. This time limit did not apply to caretakers other than parents or to households where the parent was disabled or needed to care for a disabled person. It also exempted individuals who were enrolled in JOBS and welfare recipients who were required to participate in JOBS but had not been offered the chance to enroll or participate in an education, employment, or job training program. This wide range of exemptions, combined with relatively lax sanctions policies, led one analyst to conclude that "welfare recipients [in Oregon] are not subject to the two-year limit at all" (Michaux 2002, 132). Oregon lawmakers held a public hearing on family cap legislation but did not enact that policy innovation.

Lawmakers in Virginia established the Virginia Independence Program (VIP) in 1994. This welfare reform policy incorporated strict time limit and family cap provisions. A strict time limit was a key component of welfare reform in Virginia. The VIP limited benefit receipt to twenty-four cumulative months for cases headed by nonexempt caretakers.[51] It provided hardship exemptions for persons residing in localities where the unemployment rate exceeded 10 percent. It also granted exemptions that would allow an individual to complete a program of employment-related education or training, and it made ninety-day extensions available to individuals who were actively seeking a job but could not find work that would provide income equal to the AFDC cash benefit. While important, these exemptions did not alter the fundamentally strict nature of the Virginia program. Other states provided transitional benefits or limited assistance to a specified number of months within a given period, but VIP imposed a stringent termination time limit at the twenty-four-month mark. VIP also incorporated a strict family cap. It required parents to participate in the JOBS Program after the affected child turned six weeks of age, a particularly strict provision. Virginia lawmakers also extended the family cap to children conceived within six months of the family leaving AFDC. They chose not to include an increased earnings disregard, and the Virginia family cap provided neither a partial increase nor vouchers for goods and services in lieu of increased benefits. Thus, policymakers in Virginia adopted strict family cap provisions and rejected policies that would have softened their impact.

The outcome to be explained, then, is the striking variation across the three states in terms of program content. Policymakers in Massachusetts and Virginia enacted strict time limit and family cap programs, while their colleagues in Oregon put a less stringent time limit in place and did not adopt a family cap. Table 15 describes these outcomes. Other scholars have examined state welfare policy-making in the aftermath of devolution, finding that party politics (Clark and Little 2002b) and state characteristics, such as the racial demographics of the welfare caseload (Soss et al. 2001; Fellowes and Rowe 2004; Gais and Weaver 2002), begin to explain program content. These findings resonate with the general theme of this chapter—namely, that policy variation is largely due to the internal dynamics of state politics.[52] The following discussion focuses explicitly on the impact of intrastate constituencies during the customization

TABLE 15. Time Limit and Family Cap Provisions

Policy innovation	Massachusetts	Oregon	Virginia
Time limit	Enacted in 1995	Enacted in 1995	Enacted in 1994
	Work requirement time limit after sixty days of independent job search	Termination time limit after receiving benefits for twenty-four out of eighty-four months	Termination time limit after twenty-four cumulative months of receiving benefits
	Strict enforcement provisions	Modified enforcement provisions	Strict enforcement provisions
Family cap	Enacted in 1995	Not enacted	Enacted in 1994
	Reduced JOBS exemption		Reduced JOBS exemption
	Applied to children conceived within a year of leaving AFDC		Applied to children conceived within a year of leaving AFDC
	No partial increase or vouchers		No partial increase or vouchers
	No earnings disregard		No earnings disregard
	Child support pass-through		Child support pass-through
	Seven exemptions		Four exemptions

process. It traces the transformation of welfare reform proposals during the legislative process, emphasizing the efforts of the welfare advocacy community to modify their strictest provisions.

Why did stringent time limit and family cap policies gain enactment in a state as liberal as Massachusetts? These outcomes can be traced to many factors, including the strong executive leadership of Republican governor William Weld. Weld was elected on a platform that called for a crackdown on welfare recipients. The strategic choices of the welfare advocacy community in the state were also important. The advocacy community pursued a confrontational strategy that backfired and alienated the very policymakers that it hoped to influence. Excluded from the customization process, these groups could not modify the strict proposals that the governor and other state officials advanced.

A consensus in favor of time limits and family caps emerged in Massachusetts in 1994. In February, the state senate overwhelmingly endorsed a time limit bill proposed by Democrat John O'Brien. The bill constituted a middle ground between a conservative proposal endorsed by Governor Weld and a more liberal house proposal. In March, the Joint Committee on Human Services and Elderly Affairs enraged both Republicans and moderate Democrats by dropping the time limit provision from the measure. The state house responded by passing a more stringent bill that included a time limit and a family cap. KRC Communications Research of Newton conducted a poll that suggested that state residents supported the revised legislation. Seventy percent of the respondents approved of the time limit and family cap provisions contained in the house bill, and less than one-fourth of the respondents voiced opposition.[53] Family caps continued to be controversial, however, as the state senate rejected a family cap bill in June by a vote of twenty-one to eighteen. Family cap provisions also stalled negotiations over a larger budget bill within which they had been embedded. Shortly after the senate vote, the *Boston Globe* argued that negotiators should accept the family cap provisions in order to send "a powerful, if largely symbolic, message that the state advocated personal responsibility."[54] This endorsement by a left-leaning editorial board, in combination with the aforementioned polling results, suggests that a bipartisan consensus had emerged behind time limits and family caps. Legislators and the pub-

lic seemed to agree that these policy innovations were needed to overhaul the state's flawed welfare system.

The welfare advocacy community in Massachusetts vehemently
rejected the emerging consensus on welfare reform. Activists refused to
acknowledge a palpable shift in public opinion, which favored strict welfare reform proposals. Rather than pursuing a consensual lobbying strategy or working through traditional legislative channels, the advocacy
community took a confrontational posture and staged many colorful
protests (Michaux 2002, 77–80). Activists left a bag of manure outside
the office of the Speaker of the House, disrupted floor proceedings by
throwing fake money from the state house balcony, and covered state
house statues with black cloth. They staged a morality play on the state
house steps that included a "legislator" with bloodied hands and a child in
a body bag. Another disorderly protest at the state house resulted in eight
arrests. This adversarial posture alienated the officials that the advocacy
community wanted to influence. With the electorate strongly in favor of
reform, legislators knew that the advocacy community did not pose
much of a threat at the ballot box. The tactics of welfare reform opponents did not guarantee that a stringent reform package would pass, but
this strategic choice proved critical. In Oregon and Virginia, the advocacy community voiced its objections through more conventional political channels and had a larger impact on program content.

Welfare reform surfaced in Oregon in 1990 and was a prominent issue
throughout the early 1990s. The Oregon Full Employment Program, a
ballot initiative that replaced welfare benefits with wages for transitional
jobs leading to regular employment, received 58 percent of the vote in
1990. Its implementation proved immensely controversial, and its supporters filed a lawsuit against the administration of Democratic governor
Barbara Roberts. They argued that the administration had not taken
sufficient steps to obtain the necessary waivers from the U.S. Department of Health and Human Services. Both sides eventually went to the
bargaining table. Negotiations included the sponsors of the ballot initiative, members of the legislature, gubernatorial representatives, and top
officials in the Department of Human Resources.[55] In 1993, these discussions produced House Bill 2459, known as the JOBS Plus Program.
This welfare reform legislation focused on on-the-job training and skill

enhancement and was established as a three-year pilot program. After a contentious debate in 1995, the JOBS Plus Program was expanded statewide.

Welfare reform in Oregon grew out of a complex political process. Over a number of years, state officials adjusted the framework provided by the original ballot measure. The welfare advocacy community played an active role in these discussions. In contrast to their counterparts in Massachusetts, activists in Oregon participated in hearings and in other conventional settings. Two advocates joined a bipartisan, thirteen-member task force formed by two state representatives to deal with the issue of welfare reform. Similarly, a representative of the Multnomah County Legal Aid Service testified at public hearings and work sessions and suggested numerous amendments to the JOBS Plus Program. Some of his suggestions were incorporated into the final measure. In 1993, the assistant administrator for Adult and Family Services explained that a revised bill included new language based on objections voiced by this witness during an earlier hearing.[56] In 1995, Senator Stan Bunn, the chair of the Senate Committee on Health and Human Services, voiced his frustration with the demands of the advocacy community yet at the same time described their effectiveness. Toward the conclusion of a work session, he said: "We have adopted amendment after amendment after amendment to assure that the bill was more compassionate, that it had more of a safety net. I want to say very clearly that we could go on for the next ten years adopting amendments to make it better and better. There is a cutoff point."[57] Clearly, the advocacy community influenced the customization process in Oregon. Officials amended the content of omnibus welfare reform legislation in response to the advocacy community's conventional and consensual tactics.

By pursuing a consensual lobbying strategy, the welfare advocacy community in Oregon was able to eliminate certain provisions of the JOBS Plus Program and to modify others. Its impact did not mean that these lobbyists were satisfied with or enthusiastic about the final legislation. Nor did it imply that lawmakers embraced every amendment they suggested. It was, however, an important reason why JOBS Plus was significantly less stringent than the welfare reform package adopted in Massachusetts. Members of the Oregon advocacy community opposed the statewide expansion of JOBS Plus, but they could not prevent its expansion. The relatively moderate content of the final statute nonetheless reflected their active participation during the customization process. By working through conventional political channels, they affected program content.[58]

In Virginia, the welfare advocacy community faced an uphill battle as it sought to affect the customization process. Virginia is a conservative state, and its political terrain placed the activists in a difficult position. Like its counterpart in Oregon, the welfare advocacy community in Virginia pursued a consensual lobbying strategy. Its utilization of conventional political channels produced an important amendment to the family cap provisions that ultimately gained enactment, but the scope of this change was limited, and its shelf life was short.

Welfare reform figured prominently in Virginia state politics in the early 1990s. It received bipartisan support during the 1993 gubernatorial campaign. In 1994, omnibus welfare reform legislation faced "little opposition" in the Virginia General Assembly.[59] The omnibus measure incorporated the recommendations of the Commission to Stimulate Personal Initiative to Overcome Poverty. It reflected a bipartisan consensus on the need to overhaul the existing welfare program. The welfare advocacy community in Virginia advanced a vision of welfare reform that did not include family caps or time limits. As the omnibus proposal moved through the Virginia General Assembly, the director of Total Action against Poverty contended, "Simply cutting people off will result also in an increased cost in child neglect, foster care, delinquency and crime, and incarceration."[60] Similarly, the director of the Roanoke City Department of Social Services claimed that universal day care and universal health care would be more effective than any of the strict proposals favored by members of both parties.[61] Given the bipartisan consensus behind time limits and family caps, the favored policies of the welfare advocacy community stood virtually no chance of gaining enactment.

The welfare advocacy community nonetheless earned a small victory by working through traditional lobbying channels. The 1994 reform legislation was a three-year pilot program, and its incorporation of a family cap proved particularly controversial. Some legislators' opposition to the reform proposal was based solely on the inclusion of the family cap. The

Black Caucus, women's groups, and the American Civil Liberties Union of Virginia all voiced their opposition to the plan. Attempts to remove this provision failed repeatedly, but policymakers eventually brokered a compromise. The final legislation included a family cap but subjected it to a two-year trial period. Limiting the application of a family cap to the first two years of the pilot program was not the optimal solution for either side, but it was necessary to move the legislation forward. Lieutenant Governor Don Beyer argued that this change would "provide objective data on the impact of the [family cap] limitations."[62] In reality, this concession was made for political reasons. Given the unfavorable position of the welfare advocacy community in Virginia, this alteration was small but significant. Its victory proved fleeting, however. In 1995, Governor George F. Allen proposed—and the Virginia General Assembly adopted—new legislation that made the family cap provisions permanent.

Developments in Massachusetts, Oregon, and Virginia suggest the importance of the lobbying strategies chosen by intrastate interest groups. In Massachusetts, opponents of welfare reform pursued an adversarial, protest-based lobbying strategy that backfired; it effectively excluded the welfare advocacy community from the customization process. A consensual strategy might not have guaranteed a different outcome, but developments in Oregon and Virginia suggest that participating through standard political channels will affect program content. The welfare advocacy community in Oregon utilized consensual lobbying tactics, and officials incorporated many of its suggestions into the JOBS Plus Program. Although these advocates did not get everything they wanted, their consensual tactics were one reason why the Oregon program incorporated weak time limit provisions and no family cap. Similar groups in Virginia operated on less favorable political terrain but were nonetheless able to convince officials to modify the original reform legislation. In combination, developments in these three states suggest that the strategic choices of welfare reform's opponents had an important impact on program content.

The tactics of the advocacy community do not completely explain the content of time limit and family cap programs in the three states. The restrictive provisions of the Massachusetts policies owed a great deal to the active intervention of Governor William Weld and seemed to cohere with state public opinion. The presence of a fundamentally supportive Democratic governor provided the advocacy community in Oregon with more clout than it might have otherwise possessed, as did reformers' emphasis on transitional jobs and job training. The ideological environment in Virginia placed advocacy groups at a disadvantage and limited their impact on program content. Each of these qualifications, however, provides additional support for the hypothesis that variation in policy content reflects the impact of intrastate political forces.

Policy Diffusion and the Customization Process

Policy innovations often take on a variety of forms in the jurisdictions in which they are enacted. Advocates of granting increased policy-making authority to state-level officials argue this is an important advantage of devolution for two related reasons. First, they claim that devolution is efficient because it allows state officials to adjust an existing policy template to social and political conditions within a state when a "one size fits all" solution may not be appropriate. Second, devolution advocates argue that allowing state officials to adjust program content is more democratic than imposing a common policy that must be followed by all fifty states regardless of their residents' opinions. Given the prominence of these arguments, it is surprising that few diffusion studies systematically examine differences across states in terms of policy content. While the notion of policy reinvention draws attention to these differences, it generally attributes them to the timing of policy enactment rather than to internal state politics.

This chapter focused on the customization process through which officials amend a policy template. It began with a general overview suggesting that intrastate actors are likely to be more influential than their out-of-state counterparts. Elected officials have a strong incentive to respond to organizations that represent intrastate constituencies. These groups can mobilize voters to support or to oppose these officials in an upcoming election, and they sometimes provide other valuable electoral resources. The preceding analysis suggests, for example, that state legislators rely very heavily on financial support from in-state sources. More important, the preceding analysis suggests that intrastate political forces are likely to be relatively active in settings that influence program content. National lobbying registration data indicates that most organizations concerned with health care and welfare register to lobby in a single state. Few of the organizations that register to lobby in multiple states possess truly national reach. Furthermore, in comparison to out-of-state organizations, organizations representing intrastate constituencies are more likely to send witnesses to legislative hearings in Oregon. These witnesses are also more likely to make multiple appearances and to testify at work sessions. Important modifications to legislative proposals are likely to be made as a result of general lobbying and committee hearings, so these patterns suggest that intrastate political forces are especially likely to affect program content.

When this chapter turned from its general overview to a closer examination of the customization process in three states, a similar pattern emerged. Intrastate organizations frequently played a critical role. Developments in Massachusetts, Oregon, and Virginia suggest two tentative conclusions. First, policy innovations are generally supported by diverse coalitions. One group or interest may dominate the customization process in one state, while another group or interest may be influential in a different state. Differences in program content can reflect this variation. The divergence of MSA provisions in Oregon and Virginia is a good example. Second, differences in the strength, size, and strategies pursued by similar coalitions in different states can also affect program content. Welfare reform provides a good illustration of this dynamic. The different strategies pursued by the welfare advocacy community in Massachusetts, Oregon, and Virginia helps explain why the stringency of welfare reform varied across these three states.

The preceding analysis suggests several productive avenues for future research on the customization process. Of the policies profiled in this chapter, individual development accounts were subjected to the fewest amendments. Compared to other welfare-related policy innovations, IDAs possessed less visibility and political salience. As a result, one task for future research is to examine whether the limited visibility of this policy begins to explain why minimal changes occurred.[63] In addition to facilitating general changes to a policy template, low visibility might also be conducive to specific types of adjustments. The preceding discussion emphasized changes made for explicitly political reasons and downplayed technical changes made for reasons of "good policy." Technical changes may be more likely to occur when policy innovations are less visible, while a lack of visibility may decrease the likelihood of political changes. Another possibility for future research is to make a finer distinction among the intrastate groups that tend to be especially active during the customization process. A logical next step in this research area is to assess the relative impact of state chapters of national organizations, purely intrastate groups, and program administrators.

Customization sometimes occurs when state officials revisit a policy innovation that has been in existence for a couple of years. Alterations may grow out of the implementation process during which a program is put into operation. Administrative or political difficulties may encourage state officials to limit the scope of a program, and successes may encourage them to expand it. Differences at the enactment stage can be extended by repeals, amendments, and reinstatements (Eyestone 1977). In short, policy expansion may be subject to different dynamics than the initial adoption of an innovation (Boehmke and Witmer 2004). The implementation process lies beyond the scope of this book but merits further examination. It is one of many areas in which the customization process provides potentially rewarding research opportunities.

In conclusion, the preceding analysis helps answer a critical question for policy diffusion research—a question that is often neglected. Why does the same policy innovation take on a variety of different forms in the states in which it is adopted? This question is significant for substantive and theoretical reasons. Differences in program content are important to the individuals who are affected by public policy, and legislative minutiae, such as eligibility requirements and exemptions, can have a profound impact on the lives of average citizens. There are also theoretically compelling reasons to examine variation in program content. Such an examination illuminates the causal mechanisms that affect the diffusion of policy innovations. Intrastate political forces, which seem to have little impact on the processes of agenda setting or information generation, play a more significant role in transforming a policy template during the customization process.

VI. *Conclusion*

THE AMERICAN STATES are sometimes described as "laboratories of democracy" in which it is possible to develop new public policies and to evaluate their effectiveness. In recent years, state officials have enacted a bewildering array of policy innovations across a range of issue areas. These innovations are especially important because they are rarely confined to a single state. The process through which innovative programs spread across the states is known as policy diffusion, and it implies more than an increased number of adoptions. Diffusion implies a process of learning or emulation during which decision makers look to other cities, states, or countries as models to be followed or avoided. In other words, diffusion occurs when the existence of a policy innovation in jurisdiction A significantly affects the likelihood that it will be adopted in jurisdiction B.

Understanding Policy Diffusion

The preceding chapters used a process-oriented analytical framework to examine the diffusion of five recent innovations in health care and welfare policy. This framework divides policy diffusion into four distinct political processes: agenda setting, information generation, customization, and enactment. The process-oriented approach examines more outcomes or dependent variables than are usually incorporated into diffusion research. In most diffusion research, the outcome of interest is where and when an innovation was adopted. In addition to this conventional topic, the process-oriented approach looks at the political processes through which officials become aware of policy innovations, gather information about them, and amend them. Each of these processes is a critical step in the policy-making process and an essential component of policy diffusion. The agenda-setting process determines why state officials consider a specific policy innovation rather than other available alternatives. The information generation process disseminates data about existing policy models, a crucial task since diffusion implies that officials are aware of developments in other jurisdictions. The customization process determines the specific provisions of the innovations that gain enactment, explaining why the very same policy innovation often takes on various forms in the states in which it is enacted. By building on recent diffusion research and examining a wider range of outcomes (Haider-Markel 2001; Mintrom 1997, 2000; Hays and Glick 1997; Hays 1996; Clark 1985), the process-oriented approach enables scholars to focus more intently on the various mechanisms of policy diffusion and on how their impact varies across stages of the policy-making process.

Most research on the diffusion of policy innovations across the American states emphasizes the adoption decision and focuses on the enactment process. Chapter 2 began with a quantitative analysis that assessed several conventional explanations of policy adoption. These factors generally have inconsistent effects and therefore are an unsatisfactory and incomplete explanation of why policy innovations are adopted. The second half of the chapter built on these statistical results and treated enactment as a causal process. Examining the trajectories of five innovations in three states suggests that institutionally critical actors, such as governors and chamber leaders, make the adoption of a policy innovation more or less likely through their active support or opposition. These individuals possess institutional prerogatives that give them considerable power over the enactment process. Furthermore, these leaders distribute many resources that enable their colleagues to win reelection (Clucas 2001).

Chapter 3 systematically examined the agenda-setting process for five recent innovations in health care and welfare policy. Using bill introduction as a proxy for the consideration of a policy, it suggests that the national government has a profound effect on state political agendas. National debates and political controversies, even when they are unresolved, frequently receive substantial media coverage and thereby raise the visibility of specific policy innovations. Rather than shying away from these controversies, state officials seem to respond by submitting legislation to establish salient policies. For example, the debate over President Clinton's health reform plan in the early 1990s raised the political profile of medical savings accounts. Lawmakers in many states introduced MSA legislation in the aftermath of this national controversy. Their reactions suggest that time-pressed state officials are drawn to politically salient and visible innovations. The national government is therefore an important causal mechanism during the agenda-setting stage of policy diffusion.

Chapter 4 compared the content and timing of various information resources. Its analysis suggests that media reports, testimony, and administrative documents do not respond well to the time constraints that state lawmakers face. These resources generally provide a national frame of reference and describe developments across the country, but they rarely provide much information about statutory language or programmatic details. National organizations, such as professional associations and think tanks, provide timelier, more accessible, and more detailed information about policy innovations. For example, the National Conference of State Legislatures (NCSL) tracked state proposals to enact senior prescription drug programs during the 2001–2 legislative session. NCSL publications described these proposals and existing state programs in great detail. They compared benefits and eligibility requirements, provided Web links to state laws, and listed contact telephone numbers. Chapter 4 also presented evidence that state officials use the information resources provided by national organizations and consider them to be important (Clark and Little 2002a). Survey evidence suggests that state officials are especially eager to obtain information about recent developments in other states when they are willing to commit their time to an issue, a finding that is in line with the notion of diffusion. Other evidence suggests that state lawmakers rely on these national organizations for references and contacts about new policies. Thus, professional associations and think tanks are important causal mechanisms during the information generation stage of policy diffusion.

Chapter 5 systematically examined the customization process. Its analysis suggests that intrastate constituencies affect the content of the policy innovations that ultimately gain enactment. Modifications to a proposal frequently grow out of legislative testimony or the general lobbying efforts of particular forces. In both settings, intrastate groups are

far more visible than are organizations representing out-of-state constituencies. Chapter 5 analyzed national lobbying registration data. The
analysis suggests, in line with other research (Wolak et al. 2002), that the
composition of state interest group communities remains predominantly
local. In addition, most committee witnesses in Oregon represent
intrastate organizations, state and local government agencies, and the
state chapters of national groups. In combination, lobbying registration
and committee testimony data suggest that organizations representing
intrastate constituencies are especially influential during the customization process. Chapter 5 also examined the causal processes that produced
differences in program content across three states, identifying two
potential sources of this variation. First, program content can vary
because disparate coalitions support the innovation in different jurisdictions. For example, MSA legislation in Oregon reflected the technical
objectives of its primary sponsor, while the more expansive Virginia
MSA program reflected the political goals of its main supporter. Second,
program content can vary due to the diverse size, strength, and strategies
of largely similar coalitions operating in different states. The strictness of
state time limit and family cap programs diverged in part because of the
strategic choices made by its opponents. In sum, several strands of evidence suggest that intrastate political forces dominate the customization
process. The electoral connection seems to explain variation in policy
content.

The preceding discussion suggests that the diffusion of policy innovations among the American states is a complex and multifaceted process.
It also illustrates one of the main advantages of the process-oriented
approach. Examining a wide range of outcomes suggests that the
influence of several diffusion mechanisms varies across stages of the policy-making process. By focusing exclusively on the enactment of policy
innovations, most diffusion studies underestimate the impact of certain
forces while overestimating the impact of others. The analysis in this
book suggests that a policy innovation generally proceeds along a distinc-
tive trajectory as it diffuses. The program first gains enactment in an individual state or in a handful of states. In keeping with the description of
the fifty states as policy laboratories, all of the innovations profiled in this
book were created or first adopted at the state level. The next stage of

policy diffusion occurs when the policy innovation percolates upward to the national level, at which point national decision makers debate the merits of the innovative program. This is the bottom-up element of the agenda-setting process. National policy debates increase both the visibility and the political salience of a policy innovation, and these controversies frequently prompt lawmakers in state houses across the country to consider the innovation. This is the top-down element of the agenda-setting process. It causes state political agendas to look remarkably similar. Think tanks and national organizations generate policy-relevant information about policy innovations. Their publications, Web sites, and personnel often explain the rationale behind the policy and provide detailed analyses of existing examples. These documents frequently include statutory language or model legislation, and state officials tend to find them particularly useful as they formulate policy proposals.

A policy innovation must navigate the customization and enactment processes after moving onto the political agenda. State lawmakers frequently modify the original proposal during the customization process. They make these changes to generate more support for the proposal or to minimize opposition to it. Most modifications can be traced to the lobbying efforts of organizations that represent and can mobilize intrastate constituencies. As a result, policy innovations take on various forms in the states in which they gain enactment. Innovative programs are most likely to gain enactment when they are actively supported by an institutionally critical actor, such as the governor or a legislative leader. Policy innovations that do not possess this support or that face active opposition from one of these individuals are less likely to navigate the enactment process successfully.

The preceding description of policy diffusion begins to explain why some policy innovations diffuse widely while others remain confined to a smaller number of states. It also provides empirical support for the broader theoretical claims advanced at the outset of this book. Chapter 1 argued that public officials face two important constraints that affect policy diffusion. The first constraint is insufficient time to complete the many tasks for which they are responsible. Time constraints force state officials to prioritize certain activities over others and to neglect certain tasks entirely. The second constraint is the need to retain constituent support in order to win reelection. This electoral connection influences state lawmakers' decisions. In tandem, these two constraints begin to explain the impact of diverse causal mechanisms during the distinct stages of the policy-making process.

Time constraints have an important impact on the diffusion of policy innovations. When confronted with a social problem, state officials do not begin from first principles and analyze every possible policy solution. Instead, time-pressed policymakers are most likely to be drawn to politically salient policy innovations that have achieved a degree of visibility or notoriety. In other words, time constraints affect the agenda-setting process. They encourage lawmakers to consider specific alternatives rather than others. As a result, political forces that are capable of raising the profile of a policy innovation are likely to influence state political agendas. The impact of the national government illustrates this important dynamic and begins to explain the extensive overlap of state political agendas.

Time constraints also affect the dissemination of information, which is a crucial component of policy diffusion. The concept of diffusion implies that late adopters are aware of earlier experiences with a policy innovation. In the current era of instantaneous communications, finding information seems to be less of a challenge than sifting through a glut of information. State lawmakers can receive policy-relevant information from a wide variety of sources, but they do not possess the time to undertake a comprehensive search. Due to time constraints, the timeliness and accessibility of information can be as important as its quality (Sabatier and Whiteman 1985). Time-pressed state policymakers generally begin with the most accessible sources and search sequentially for that which requires more effort (Mooney 1991). They are most likely to utilize information sources that consistently provide the information they need but that do not require a huge time investment. The analysis in chapter 4 suggests that national organizations, including professional associations and think tanks, are highly influential during the information generation process because they fulfill this criterion.

Electoral considerations also have an important impact on the diffusion of policy innovations. Since elected officials must face their constituents at the ballot box, they are usually enthusiastic about addressing voter concerns. Policymakers whose constituents are satisfied with their performance are more likely to win reelection than are lawmakers who take many stands with which their constituents disagree. Acting contrary to voters' preferences can mobilize a vocal opposition campaign and reduce the likelihood that an official will win reelection. As a result, electoral considerations can affect the diffusion of policy innovations in two major ways. First, they can encourage lawmakers to endorse specific versions of an innovation. Policymakers frequently modify a policy template in response to the support or opposition of a particular constituency. This customization process sometimes facilitates major changes. Second, state officials seeking reelection are most likely to endorse policy innovations that are supported by their constituents or by groups that can mobilize these voters. Policy innovations are most likely to survive the customization and enactment processes when they can claim support from the intrastate constituencies to which elected officials must be responsive. Intrastate organizations and institutionally critical actors fulfill this criterion and represent important causal forces during the later stages of policy diffusion.

In sum, this book addressed two primary questions. First, what factors facilitate the diffusion of policy innovations? Second, does the impact of these factors vary across stages of the policy-making process? The book's process-oriented approach suggests that the early stages of policy diffusion are most strongly influenced by political forces that respond to the time constraints that officials must overcome. Time constraints affect both the models toward which officials are drawn and the ways in which they gather information about them. In contrast, electoral considerations are more influential during the later stages of policy diffusion. They affect the enactment of policy innovations as well as the specific provisions of the programs that are adopted.

Directions for Future Research

Using a process-oriented analytical framework to examine a range of outcomes produces an account of policy diffusion that illustrates how various causal mechanisms contribute to the spread of policy innovations across the states. Earlier discussions in this book made several generalizations about policy diffusion, and this study's analyses of individual processes emphasized various similarities across policies and states. National controversies affect state political agendas; national organizations, such as professional associations, generate detailed policy-relevant information; intrastate organizations spark changes in program content; and the active support of institutionally critical actors helps policy innovations gain enactment. It would be a vast overstatement to claim that these generalizations hold without exception. As a result, one fruitful path for future research on policy diffusion is to examine how certain factors affect the generalizations introduced in this study. Changes in the political or institutional context in which state officials operate might affect the processes described in previous chapters. Potential sources of variation include contextual changes and shifts in the type of policy innovation that is diffusing.

Many important questions remain open about all four of the political processes examined in this book. Previous chapters discussed many of these questions in substantial detail, but the questions should also be mentioned in this conclusion. Future research on the enactment process should focus more intently on the different activities of institutionally critical actors, both in combination and separately. Do specific actions have a more profound impact on the adoption of policy innovations? How much energy must critical actors devote to a policy innovation before affecting its likelihood of enactment? Future research on the agenda-setting process can also move in several interesting directions. In addition to the national government, do other forces, such as focusing events and interest groups, have a national impact on state political agendas? Are there particular state attributes that account for resistance to national trends? Is it possible to make a finer distinction among the types of consideration that policy innovations receive and to develop subtler measures of agenda status? Future research on the information generation process should attempt to estimate the frequency with which various information sources are consulted and to identify the conditions that make state officials more or less likely to rely on national organizations. How do party competition and legislative professionalism affect the acquisition of policy-relevant information? Are federated organizations more likely to be well informed about developments in other states than are organizations that operate in a single state or region? Future research on the customization process should make finer distinctions among the types of adjustments that are made. Are certain conditions more conducive to "technical" changes made for policy reasons while others facilitate explicitly political calculations? How does the subsequent expansion, restriction, or repeal of a policy innovation differ from the changes that are made before the program gains enactment? Answering any of the questions in this paragraph will make a valuable contribution to the analytical framework described in this book.

Another task for future research is to extend this study's analysis to other policy areas. This book examined the diffusion of five recent innovations in health care and welfare policy, two policy areas that can be grouped under the broader heading of human services. These five innovations were an appropriate choice for this study because they pursue diverse objectives and vary in terms of the extent and speed with which they diffused across the states. Examining innovations in another policy realm may uncover a different set of causal relationships. Previous research on the intergovernmental sources of innovation, for example, suggests that state executive agencies vary in their reliance and dependence on the national government. Light (1978) finds that state agencies are more likely to take cues from the national government in human services policy than in other areas. This finding has potentially significant implications for this study's analysis of the agenda-setting process, which emphasized the impact of national controversies on state political agendas.

The salience of specific policy innovations may also affect the dynamics of their diffusion. Of the policies examined in this book, individual development accounts (IDAs) were the least visible and the least controversial. Their trajectory suggests that diffusion may operate differently when a policy innovation does not receive a great deal of public attention. The accounts moved onto state political agendas with minimal visibility, and IDA legislation was barely modified during the customization process before it gained enactment in Oregon and Virginia. Recent research suggests that the level of controversy surrounding a policy innovation can affect both its customization (Hays 1996; Mooney and Lee 1999) and its enactment (McNeal et al. 2003). This relationship merits greater scholarly attention. It also points to the general usefulness of extending the present analysis to other policy areas. Examining additional types of policies will test many of the generalizations made in earlier chapters in this book.

Although the substantive focus of this study has been on the diffusion of policy innovations across the American states, the analytical framework of this book may be applicable to other political settings. Policy diffusion occurs in a wide range of environments, from the prefectures of Japan (Ito 2001) to the countries of Latin America (Weyland 2005). Time constraints and electoral considerations, the basic building blocks of the analytical framework described in this book, seem applicable to lawmakers across the globe. Analogues to the causal processes described in this study may exist elsewhere. For example, the Japanese national government might affect prefectures' political agendas in the same way that state officials in the United States seem to take their cues from the national government. There may be a similar relationship between the European Union and its member countries. In terms of information generation, organizations, such as the International Monetary Fund and the World Bank, might disseminate the timeliest, most accessible, and most detailed information about emerging policy innovations. Electoral considerations may influence the customization and enactment processes in these other settings just as they seem to do in the American states. Extending the analysis in this book to other jurisdictions might clarify whether the institutional setting of the American states leads to particularities in how policy diffusion occurs or whether the general dynamics described in this study are also applicable to other parts of the world.

Democratic Laboratories

This book has examined the diffusion of policy innovations among the American states, a complex and multifaceted process. Its analytical framework and findings may be applicable to other political settings, but they are especially significant due to the current role of the states in the American political system. The political forces that affect state lawmaking and the spread of innovative policy ideas are topics of great contemporary significance. The states recently emerged from their worst financial crisis since the Second World War. Constrained by balanced budget requirements that prevented them from running large deficits, state officials responded to this situation in several different ways. Extensive service cuts were one common strategy. Ironically, the scope and magnitude of the cuts testify to the expansive role of state governments. They affected everything from nursing home care and community colleges to homeland security and health care for the poor. It is no exaggeration to claim that state governments reach into almost every corner of American citizens' lives.

In recent years, many officials at the national level have proposed to grant state lawmakers additional policy-making discretion in several areas where the national and state governments currently share responsibility. For example, some of these proposals would provide state governments with lump sum payments to run social programs, such as Head Start and Medicaid. Currently national regulations affect the operation of these programs, but some individuals want state officials to have the power to structure these policies as they see fit. Rather than attaching strings to national grants, they want state policymakers to operate free of any regulations. Proponents of this "devolution revolution" argue that removing these strictures will allow state lawmakers to develop innovative policy ideas and to adapt existing programs to specific conditions within their states. The debate over devolution resonates both with the notion that the fifty states can serve as laboratories of democracy and with some of the major themes of this book.

The discussion in this book provides empirical support for a few of the arguments advanced by supporters of devolution. The five policy innovations profiled in this study were all developed at the state level. In some cases, state officials took action while their colleagues in the nation's capital deadlocked on how to address important policy issues. Devolution advocates claim that the fifty states possess considerable innovative potential, and the episodes profiled in this book suggest that such a claim is not without merit. Advocates also claim that devolution allows state officials to experiment with innovative approaches to public policy and that it is more efficient and more democratic than imposing a single solution across fifty diverse states. This book's examinations of the information generation and customization processes provide general support for these claims. They suggest that state policymakers are well informed about the policy innovations that their colleagues devise elsewhere and are open to new ideas. Finally, policy innovations take on a number of forms in the states in which they gain enactment. All of these dynamics resonate to some degree with arguments that are sometimes made in favor of devolution.

A careful reading of the evidence presented in this book, however, suggests that the diffusion of policy innovations is an inherently political process. Experimentation and institutional learning play a relatively minor role at various stages of the policy-making process, while time constraints and electoral considerations have an especially profound impact. Policy innovations do not necessarily need to illustrate their merits before they diffuse successfully among the states. Instead, the innovations need only respond to the constraints faced by the officials who ultimately decide whether and in what form to endorse the innovations. A convincing account of policy diffusion must acknowledge that it is commonly driven by politics rather than policy effectiveness. The characterization of the fifty states as laboratories of democracy is an appealing image, but it is a standard that is rarely met in practice.

Appendix

Event History Analysis

When scholars examine the enactment of policy innovations, they usually utilize event history analysis (EHA) to assess the impact of internal state attributes, partisanship and political ideology, problem severity, and external pressures. This appendix provides an extremely brief overview of EHA. Several authors provide more detailed treatments (Box-Steffensmeier and Jones 2004; Yamaguchi 1997; Berry and Berry 1990; Buckley and Westerland 2004; Jones and Branton 2005).

EHA models attempt to account for the occurrence of a specific event. Since its introduction a little more than a decade ago, EHA has been the standard method to analyze the one-way transition from not having a policy innovation to enacting it. The unit of analysis is the state year. The dependent variable of interest is the hazard rate, which is defined as the probability that a state will adopt an innovation in a specific year. Hazard rates cannot be directly observed, because they are probabilities. EHA uses a dichotomous dependent variable that indicates whether state officials adopted the policy innovation that year (it is coded "1" if yes and "0" if no). All states are "at risk" once the innovation has been adopted in a single state. After a state enacts the program, it is no longer in the risk set for policy adoption, and there are no more state year observations for that specific state.

To evaluate the determinants of program enactment, the analysis in chapter 2 uses standard logistic regression methods on the culled data set. To test the robustness of the results reported in chapter 2, I examined the fit of two models that make alternative parametric assumptions to those of logistic regression models. The substantive results hold when an exponential model that assumes a flat hazard rate is used. However, a Weibull model, which assumes ever-increasing or ever-decreasing hazard rates, is not appropriate for the analysis in this book.

EHA requires that the probability of enacting the innovation for the remaining nonadopters be constant across time. In other words, the hazard rate must be stabilized, or else the estimated slope for a variable that is correlated with the hazard rate will be biased in the direction of that correlation (Beck, Katz, and Tucker 1998). In keeping with recent work on the diffusion of policy innovations, the analysis in chapter 2 stabilizes the hazard rate by including a nonlinear trend variable that equals the square root of the number of years between an observation and the year during which the hazard rate reached its maximum value. Although this trend variable is not the only way to stabilize the hazard rate, many recent studies use this technique (Haider-Markel 2001; Mooney 2001a; Mooney and Lee 1995).

Table 3 in chapter 2 provides predicted probabilities for program enactment given fixed values of the independent variables. These first differences were derived by manipulating the quantity of interest and by setting all other variables to their means. For dichotomous variables, such as national intervention, the table displays the change in the predicted probability of enactment when the quantity of interest moves from 0 to 1. For other variables, such as personal income, the table displays the change in the predicted probability of enactment when the quantity of interest shifts from one standard deviation below its mean to one standard deviation above its mean. For more on the statistical simulation technique and computer software used in the derivation of these values, see King, Tomz, and Wittenberg 2000. The list on the following page provides detailed information about the measurement and sources of the data included in the analysis in chapter 2. Table A3 in this appendix provides descriptive statistics, and table A4 provides the estimated coefficients from the initial analysis.

Variable Measurement and Data Sources

DEPENDENT VARIABLES

Senior prescription drug programs: dichotomous variable taking the value of "1" for the state year in which the policy innovation gained enactment.
Source: National Conference of State Legislatures, "State Pharmaceutical Assistance Programs (includes seniors, disabled, uninsured, and others)," http://www.ncsl.org/programs/health/drugaid.htm (accessed June 7, 2002).

Medical savings accounts: dichotomous variable taking the value of "1" for the state year in which the policy innovation gained enactment.
Source: Bunce 2001.

Individual development accounts: dichotomous variable taking the value of "1" for the state year in which the policy innovation gained enactment.
Source: Center for Social Development 2001.

Time limits and family caps: dichotomous variable taking the value of "1" for the state year in which the policy innovations gained enactment.

Source: U.S. Department of Health and Human Services 1996, 1997; Stark and Levin-Epstein 1999; Urban Institute, "Welfare Rules Database," available through http://www.urban.org/Content/Research/NewFederalism/AboutANF/AboutANF.htm.

INDEPENDENT VARIABLES

National intervention: dichotomous variable taking the value of "1" for years after the passage of national legislation. In the context of medical savings accounts, the relevant legislation (the Health Insurance Portability and Accountability Act) passed in 1996. In the context of individual development accounts and family caps, the relevant legislation (the Personal Responsibility and Work Opportunity Reconciliation Act) also passed in 1996. This variable was not included in the analysis of senior prescription drug programs or in that of time limits on welfare receipt.

Neighboring states: percentage of neighboring states that have adopted the policy innovation prior to the year of measurement.

Source: Calculated by the author, using the neighboring state pairings in Berry and Berry 1990.

Problem severity for senior prescription drug program: percentage change in expenditures for prescription drugs, 1990 to 1993.

Source: Morgan Quitno Corporation 1998.

Problem severity for medical savings accounts: percentage change in number of uninsured, 1989 to 1991.

Source: Morgan Quitno Corporation 1998.

Problem severity for individual development accounts: number of births in 1992 to females ages fifteen to nineteen per one thousand females in this group.

Source: Annie E. Casey Foundation 1999.

Problem severity for time limits: percentage of welfare caseload receiving benefits for four years or more. Annual values from 1993 to 1996 were averaged to calculate this measure.

Source: Urban Institute, "Assessing the New Federalism State Database," http://www.urban.org/Content/Research/NewFederalism/Data/State Database/StateDatabase.htm (accessed June 15, 2001).

Problem severity for family caps: percentage of welfare caseload consisting of families with four or more children. Annual values from 1993 to 1996 were averaged to calculate this measure.

Source: Urban Institute, "Assessing the New Federalism State Database, http://www.urban.org/Content/Research/NewFederalism/Data/State Database/StateDatabase.htm (accessed June 15, 2001).

Personal income: natural log of state per capita personal income divided by the implicit price deflator.

Source: U.S. Department of Commerce Bureau of Economic Analysis, "Regional Accounts Data," http://www.bea.doc.gov/bea/regional/spi/drill.cfm (accessed June 15, 2001).

Legislative professionalism: measure based on salaries, time in session, and staff.

Source: Squire 1992.

Ideology: state ideology scores (percentage liberal minus percentage conservative).

Source: Erikson, Wright, and McIver 1993, 18. Updated estimates available at http://mypage.iu.edu/~wright1/.

Trend: square root of the number of years between an observation and the year during which the hazard rate reached its maximum value.

Source: Calculated by the author.

TABLE A1. Program Enactments by State and Year

State	Senior prescription drug programs	Medical savings accounts (MSAs)	Individual development accounts (IDAs)	Time limits	Family caps
Alabama	—	—	—	—	—
Alaska	—	—	—	—	—
Arizona	2001	1994	1995	1994	1994
Arkansas	2001	1997	1999	—	1993
California	1999	1996	—	—	1994
Colorado	—	1994	2000	—	—
Connecticut	1986	—	2000	1995	1995
Delaware	1999	—	—	1995	1995
Florida	2000	1997	2001	1993	1995
Georgia	—	—	1998	—	1993
Hawaii	—	—	1999	1996	—
Idaho	—	1994	—	—	1997
Illinois	1985	1994	1998	1995	1995
Indiana	2000	1995	1997	1994	1994
Iowa	—	—	1993	1993	—
Kansas	2000	—	1993	—	—
Kentucky	—	—	1997	—	—
Louisiana	—	1996	—	1995	—
Maine	1975	—	1997	—	—
Maryland	1979	1997	2001	—	1994
Massachusetts	1996	—	—	—	1995
Michigan	1988	1994	1998	—	—
Minnesota	1997	—	1999	—	—
Mississippi	—	1994	—	—	1995
Missouri	2001	1993	—	—	—
Montana	—	1995	2000	—	—
Nebraska	—	1997	—	1994	1994
Nevada	1999	1995	2000	—	—
New Hampshire	—	—	—	—	—
New Jersey	1975	1997	2001	—	1992
New Mexico	—	1995	1996	—	—
New York	1987	—	—	—	—
North Carolina	1999	—	1998	1995	1995
North Dakota	—	—	—	—	1998
Ohio	—	1994	1997	1995	—
Oklahoma	—	1995	1998	—	1998
Oregon	2001	1997	1999	1995	—
Pennsylvania	1984	1996	1997	—	—
Rhode Island	1985	—	1997	—	—
South Carolina	2000	—	2000	1995	1995
South Dakota	—	—	—	—	—
Tennessee	—	—	1996	1996	1996
Texas	2001	—	1999	1995	—

(continues)

TABLE A1.—*Continued*

State	Senior prescription drug programs	Medical savings accounts (MSAs)	Individual development accounts (IDAs)	Time limits	Family caps
Utah	—	1995	1997	—	—
Vermont	1996	—	2000	—	—
Virginia	—	1995	1998	1994	1994
Washington	—	1995	2000	—	—
West Virginia	—	1995	2001	—	—
Wisconsin	2001	1996	1995	1994	1994
Wyoming	1988	1997	—	—	1997

TABLE A2.   Comparison of Massachusetts, Oregon, and Virginia

State characteristic	Massachusetts	Oregon	Virginia
Innovativeness score	0.629 (2nd of 48)	0.544 (8th of 48)	0.451 (21st of 48)
Political ideology	−0.8 (2nd of 48)	−7.9 (10th of 48)	−17.9 (34th of 48)
Party identification	18.3 (10th of 48)	7.4 (22nd of 48)	3.3 (32nd of 48)
Political competition	30.39 (38th of 49)	54.25 (2nd of 49)	40.71 (23rd of 49)
Legislative professionalism	0.614 (3rd of 50)	0.183 (27th of 50)	0.170 (29th of 50)
Population density	809.8 (3rd of 50)	35.6 (39th of 50)	178.8 (14th of 50)
Personal income	$25,952 (3rd of 50)	$20,940 (23rd of 50)	$23,975 (6th of 50)
State population	6,349,097 (13th of 50)	3,421,399 (28th of 50)	7,078,515 (12th of 50)
Percentage high school graduate or higher	84.8 (16th of 50)	85.1 (15th of 50)	81.5 (29th of 50)

Source: Innovativeness score: Walker 1969; Political ideology and party identification: Erikson, Wright, and McIver 1993, tables 2.1 and 2.2; political competition: Holbrook and Van Dunk 1993; legislative professionalism: Squire 1992; population density, personal income, state population, and percentage high school graduate or higher: U.S. Census Bureau 2001.

TABLE A3. **Descriptive Statistics**

Variable	Senior prescription drug programs	Medical savings accounts (MSAs)	Individual development accounts (IDAs)	Time limits	Family caps
National		0.39	0.45		0.39
intervention		(0.49)	(0.50)		(0.49)
Neighboring state	0.10	0.21	0.16	0.10	0.24
effect	(0.20)	(0.29)	(0.23)	(0.18)	(0.26)
Problem severity	29.55	9.87	56.23	23.89	8.45
	(6.97)	(19.01)	(14.51)	(8.53)	(1.92)
Personal income	9.87	10.08	10.08	10.02	10.05
	(0.183)	(0.158)	(0.165)	(0.141)	(0.143)
Professionalism	0.21	0.21	0.22	0.22	0.21
	(0.13)	(0.15)	(0.15)	(0.15)	(0.15)
Ideology	−15.63	−14.74	−14.76	−16.52	−14.81
	(11.35)	(10.93)	(10.65)	(10.33)	(10.05)
Trend	3.52	1.42	1.80	0.87	1.41
	(1.24)	(0.58)	(0.74)	(0.53)	(0.66)

Note: Reported values are variable means. Standard deviations are in parentheses.

TABLE A4.   Nationwide Patterns of Program Enactment

Variable	Senior prescription drug programs	Medical savings accounts (MSAs)	Individual development accounts (IDAs)	Time limits	Family caps
National inter-		−2.21**	1.35*		0.66
vention (+/−)		(0.75)	(0.65)		(0.84)
Neighboring state	−0.68	2.27**	0.71	−1.36	−2.48^
effect (+)	(0.97)	(0.86)	(0.89)	. (1.77)	(1.39)
Problem	−0.059	−0.0094	0.012	−0.017	0.18
severity (+)	(0.037)	(0.0126)	(0.016)	(0.038)	(0.14)
Personal income (+)	2.51	−5.24*	−0.12	4.62^	4.18^
	(2.06)	(2.63)	(1.82)	(2.72)	(2.33)
Professionalism (+)	1.46	3.91*	−1.70	0.031	−0.41
	(1.47)	(1.80)	(1.68)	(2.261)	(1.94)
Ideology (+/−)	0.042^	0.020	0.018	−0.063^	−0.039
	(0.024)	(0.029)	(0.024)	(0.038)	(0.031)
Trend	−0.72**	−1.82**	−0.28	−1.30**	−1.52**
	(0.22)	(0.52)	(0.38)	(0.47)	(0.41)
Constant	−24.65	52.45*	−1.59	−48.10^	−44.64^
	(20.62)	(26.42)	(18.87)	(27.58)	(23.57)
Number of	1,092	273	333	167	339
observations					
Log likelihood	−104.69	−72.61	−96.58	−48.76	−71.16
χ^2	43.75	35.34	26.40	12.37	25.85
Prob. χ^2	0.0000	0.0000	0.0004	0.0543	0.0005
Pseudo R^2	0.1728	0.1957	0.1202	0.1125	0.1537
Percentage correctly predicted	97.53	89.38	89.79	89.82	93.51

Note: Standard errors are in parentheses.

^Significant at the .10 level.

*Significant at the .05 level.

**Significant at the .01 level.

TABLE A5. "State" or "Local" Newspaper Coverage of Five Policy Innovations

Year	Senior prescription drug programs	Medical savings accounts (MSAs)	Individual development accounts (IDAs)	Time limits	Family caps
1990	12	—	0	—	—
1991	6	—	0	1	—
1992	5	0	0	1	—
1993	8	*1*	0	*5*	1
1994	8	3	0	28	79
1995	7	0	0	37	51.5
1996	7	2	*3*	18	4
1997	17	0	1	48	8
1998	17	1	1	53	6
1999	*32*	1	3	32	2
2000	38	2	3	15	4
2001	41	1	10	15	0

Note: Cell values are the number of "state" or "local" articles published on a policy innovation in a given year. Values in italics represent the beginning of the relevant national debate or action. Years preceding the initial appearance of any articles on the policy innovation are indicated by a dash. Although the first "state" or "local" articles on MSAs and IDAs did not appear until 1993 and 1996, respectively, the first "national" articles were published earlier. Consequently, "0" appears in the MSA column for 1992 and in the IDA column for 1990–95. Disaggregated information about the number of articles appearing in individual newspapers is available from the author on request.

Notes

Chapter 1

1. Rogers 1995 provides the most comprehensive review of the many strands of research that examine the diffusion of innovations.

2. Rodgers 1998 provides an especially thorough treatment of how international connections shaped political choices during the Progressive Era. For another historical treatment of international diffusion, see Waltman 1980.

3. This definition of diffusion draws on Weyland 2004, although Weyland's definition limits diffusion to instances in which the existence of an innovation in one jurisdiction increases the likelihood that it will be adopted elsewhere.

4. An emphasis on electoral considerations privileges elected officials over program administrators and other bureaucratic officials who sometimes express technical concerns about policy innovations. Subsequent chapters address the impact of these technocrats in light of their relationships with elected officials.

5. *New State Ice Co. v. Liebmann,* 285 U.S. 262 (1932). In this case, the Supreme Court ruled on the constitutionality of an Oklahoma statute that characterized the manufacture, sale, and distribution of ice as a public business and regulated it accordingly. By a vote of six to two, the Supreme Court ruled the statute unconstitutional.

6. At both the national and state levels, lawmakers frequently create demonstration projects that rely on a similar logic. Demonstration projects typically take place in a limited number of cities or counties or apply to a subset of citizens. After a specified time period, analysts evaluate the demonstration project to assess whether it has achieved its goals. If it meets these objectives, it is extended to a larger group (i.e., the entire state or country).

7. Policymakers might still be hesitant to adopt a policy innovation that is necessary and achieves desirable objectives. Even if they believe that the program achieves its stated objectives, officials might use different policy indicators to gauge programmatic success. Alternatively, they might adjust their levels of aspiration with respect to these indicators (Levitt and March 1988).

8. Informed decision making requires that state officials "demonstrate awareness and consideration of diffused information, of criticisms or research and of application of the diffused information to the adopter's own needs" (Mossberger 2000, 195). Mossberger's study found that officials in the five states possessed varied amounts of diffused information.

9. The wide availability of political information is also a crucial issue for political science research on public opinion and voting behavior (Converse 1990, 371).

10. Lindblom (1959) developed the notion of "muddling through" in a study of bureaucratic decision making, yet it seems equally applicable to the activities of other policymakers.

11. I am grateful to Kurt Weyland for pointing out the applicability of the availability heuristic. Weyland (2005) uses the availability heuristic to explain the geographic clustering of innovation adoption, asserting that nearby examples possess special immediacy. Availability also seems relevant in the context of the American states, but its relationship to geographic propinquity is less clear.

12. For an overview of the availability heuristic and its accompanying biases, see Tversky and Kahneman 2004, 210–14.

13. The issue of the impact of public opinion is further complicated by the fact that voters are sometimes misinformed about broad policy issues and confident in erroneous perceptions. This misinformation can have significant effects on policy attitudes (Kuklinski et al. 1998).

14. The relationship between constituent preferences and policy changes does not preclude the possibility of technical changes based on how effective the innovation has been in other settings. For reasons that have already been discussed, however, assessing programmatic effectiveness is likely to be difficult and highly controversial.

15. This book does not attempt to provide a general perspective on recent developments in state health care and welfare policy, although several such overviews are available (Rom 2004; Barrilleaux 1998; Holahan and Nichols 1996; Deborah Stone 1997b).

16. In addition, some analysts contend that federated organizations possess inherent advantages during the search for policy solutions. These organizations can empower multiple subunits to search for a solution and combine the information discovered by the subunits to come up with even better solutions (Kollman, Miller, and Page 2000).

17. The title of this section of this chapter and the idea of a resurgence of the states is drawn from Bowman and Kearney 1986.

18. Weaver 2000 provides a comprehensive examination of the development of this legislation. Its major provisions reflect an ongoing debate about the

merits of government-provided relief, work, or job training (Skocpol 1995, 237). They also reflect the difficulty of defending "policies that lack clear political and social legitimation as expressions of social compassion and collective solidarity" (Skocpol 1988, 309).

19. Although there has been an overall trend toward increased legislative professionalism, state legislatures are not equally professional. Disparities among state legislatures have increased over time (Squire 1992; King 2000).

20. Although there has been an overall trend toward more formal power for the governor, the extent of these powers varies across the states (Beyle 2004).

21. Table A1 in the appendix lists the complete set of adoptions for each of the policy innovations examined in this book.

22. Variation in programmatic objectives seems likely to affect the influence of various factors—such as state wealth—that previous diffusion research highlights. In the context of expansive innovations that increase governmental prerogatives, state wealth may be essential. When officials consider moralistic or symbolic policy innovations, however, cost will not be an issue. Similarly, the retrenchment of state programs does not require the utilization of state funds. Blanket statements about the importance of wealth might need to be refined. Because initial studies of policy diffusion took place in an era of governmental expansion, they may have overstated the role of specific factors.

23. Skocpol 1997 and Johnson and Broder 1996 provide comprehensive examinations of the politics surrounding the Health Security Act.

24. The concept of a "culture of poverty" is commonly associated with sociologist Oscar Lewis and has been subjected to extensive scholarly analysis. During the welfare reform debates of the mid-1990s, welfare caseload dynamics became an especially heated issue. Policy analysts and scholars examined the balance of long-term and short-term enrollment, the permanence of departures from AFDC, and other elements of welfare receipt.

25. This count includes states in which welfare benefit receipt is terminated, not states in which a work requirement is imposed. It also includes three states (Arizona, Indiana, and Texas) in which only the adult portion of the benefit is terminated.

26. The waiver process demonstrates one way in which the national government constrains policy-making at the state level. As a result, some analysts characterize American federalism as a system of "permissive federalism" (Arsneault 2000).

27. Chapters 2 through 5 in this book focus on the diffusion of time limits among the states between 1993 and 1996, prior to the enactment of national legislation.

28. The twenty-three states with family caps include two states (Idaho and Wisconsin) that offer a flat grant regardless of family size. They do not include

Kansas, where policymakers enacted a family cap but then chose not to implement it.

29. Table A2 in the appendix compares the three states along various socioeconomic and political dimensions. The potential impact of these factors is described in more detail in chapter 2.

30. A second drawback of a "most different systems" research design is that it does not effectively address how antecedent conditions affect the causal relationships it describes. Chapters 2–5 in this book discuss this shortcoming in the context of future research on policy diffusion.

31. All interviews for this analysis were conducted in confidentiality, and the names of interviewees are withheld from this book by mutual agreement.

32. Several authors provide general reviews of the political science literature on the diffusion of innovations across the American states (Berry and Berry 1999; Gray 1994; Berry 1994; Miller 2004).

33. Heightened attention to mechanisms of diffusion resonates with similar developments in comparative politics research. Comparative scholars have recently begun to devote greater attention to the impact of causal mechanisms (McAdam, Tarrow, and Tilly 2001, 3–88).

34. These studies will be discussed in more detail in chapters 3 to 5 in the context of the particular political processes with which they are concerned.

35. This book's process-oriented approach and emphasis on causal mechanisms resonates with what other scholars have characterized as "systematic process analysis" (Hall 2003) or "process tracing" (George and Bennett 2005, 205–32).

36. By focusing on the shifting identities and positions of major actors, the approach taken in chapter 2 resonates with an emerging literature in political science that treats policy-making as an iterative, historical process that cannot be explained by static accounts (Skocpol 1992; Pierson 2004).

37. Mossberger 2000 is one exception to this generalization.

38. The surveys cited in chapter 4 were conducted by interstate professional associations and other political scientists, not by the author.

39. Scholars of comparative public policy frequently focus on distinctions in program content (Esping-Andersen 1990; Bonoli 1997).

40. The emphasis on program adoption in most diffusion research results from the use of event history analysis (EHA). The dependent variable of interest is the hazard rate, defined as the probability that a state will adopt a policy innovation in a specific year. Hazard rates cannot be directly observed, because they are probabilities. Instead, EHA uses a dichotomous dependent variable to indicate whether the policy innovation was adopted that year (coded "1" if yes and "0" if no). While this strategy is useful for analyzing the question of program

enactment, it is not well suited for distinguishing among the programs that have been adopted.

Chapter 2

1. This book's appendix explains how event history analysis was used to examine patterns of program adoption for the five policy innovations incorporated into this chapter. It also describes the data that were used in this particular book as well as their sources. For general treatments of event history analysis, see Box-Steffensmeier and Jones 2004; Yamaguchi 1991.

2. Although EHA is the dominant mode of analysis in diffusion studies, other scholars have used qualitative evidence to examine policy diffusion (Jacob 1988; Mossberger 2000).

3. Table A3 in the appendix provides descriptive statistics. In addition, the present study tested the effects of other variables that might plausibly be linked to the diffusion of policy innovations. These variables included innovativeness, unemployment rates, partisan alignments, and regional effects. After I estimated the five models presented in this chapter, I inserted each of these variables into the models, one at a time. None of them had a statistically significant impact on program enactment.

4. The analysis in this chapter uses a dichotomous independent variable indicating national intervention. This variable receives a value of "1" for any year after the relevant national action, "0" otherwise. Since this variable is only included in cases where national legislation directly addressed the policy innovation under review, it does not appear in this chapter's analysis of time limits and senior prescription drug programs. National welfare reform legislation established time limits as national policy in 1996 and therefore effectively preempted the state-level diffusion of the policy innovation. National officials added a senior prescription drug benefit to Medicare in 2003, after the period examined in this book.

5. Although few state-level studies make an explicit link between geographic distance and communications networks, a study of the spread of fluoridation across American cities assessed the influence of spatial distance between cities "only because distance correlates well with the amount of communication between cities" (Crain 1966, 468).

6. Most studies assume that the neighboring state effect is uniformly positive and that the existence of a policy innovation in a nearby jurisdiction leads officials to mimic the enactment patterns of their neighbors. This assumption is problematic because a program in another state can provide either positive or negative policy or political information. A policy innovation might actually exacerbate the condition it was designed to alleviate, and this failure might

make lawmakers in neighboring states less likely to enact the same policy. Alternatively, an elected official might shepherd an innovation to enactment only to find that it inspires heated opposition during a subsequent campaign. Either development would make lawmakers less willing to follow the same path as their neighbors. The direction of the neighboring state effect therefore depends on the policy under review. This effect is likely to be positive when a successful policy is considered, but the opposite dynamic is likely to occur in the context of an unsuccessful innovation. For more on this theme, see Mooney 2001a.

7. The conventional proxy for measuring the impact of developments in neighboring states is the percentage of a state's neighbors that have adopted the policy innovation prior to the year of measurement. If policymakers in Maryland have not yet enacted a specific policy innovation in 1995, the value of this variable will be the percentage of that state's neighbors (Virginia, West Virginia, Pennsylvania, and Delaware) that enacted the program through 1994.

8. The variables used to assess the impact of problem severity include percentage change in prescription drug expenditures between 1990 and 1993 (senior prescription drug programs), percentage change in the number of uninsured individuals between 1989 and 1991 (medical savings accounts), percentage of state births to teenage women (individual development accounts), percentage of welfare recipients receiving benefits for four years or more (time limits), and percentage of welfare cases with four or more children (family caps).

9. The programmatic structures of IDAs and MSAs differ slightly. In the case of IDAs, state governments do not provide a service or a benefit but instead operate through an intermediary and play a supporting role. MSAs, by contrast, encourage specific behaviors through provisions in the tax code. Battles over these types of tax expenditures have attained greater political significance at the national level (Howard 1997).

10. A similar logic would lead us to expect a weak relationship between slack resources and the enactment of low-cost policy innovations. For example, laws on reporting child abuse gained enactment in every state and the District of Columbia between 1963 and 1967. The symbolic character of this policy innovation and its negligible cost aided its diffusion, and state legislators viewed these laws as an opportunity for low-cost rectitude (Nelson 1984). Similarly, many of the most contentious current issues in state politics, such as abortion and capital punishment, are framed in terms of values or first principles (Mooney 2001b). These programs are only loosely tied to governmental expenditures.

11. Table 3 displays predicted probabilities for program enactment, rather than the coefficients of the initial analysis. These first differences were derived

by manipulating the quantity of interest and setting all other variables to their means. For dichotomous variables, such as national intervention, the table displays the change in the predicted probability of enactment when the quantity of interest moves from 0 to 1. For other variables, such as personal income, the table displays the change in the predicted probability of enactment when the quantity of interest shifts from one standard deviation below its mean to one standard deviation above its mean. These values were derived using the statistical simulation technique and computer software described in King, Tomz, and Wittenberg 2000. Table A4 in the appendix provides estimated coefficients from the initial analysis.

12. Section 402 of the law states that state welfare plans can "[w]aive, pursuant to a determination of good cause, other program requirements such as time limits (for so long as necessary) for individuals receiving assistance, residency requirements, child support cooperation requirements, and family cap provisions," in cases where compliance would negatively affect victims of domestic violence. This statement is the only mention of family caps in the entire piece of legislation. See *Personal Responsibility and Work Opportunity Reconciliation Act,* Public Law 104-193, *U.S. Statues at Large* 110, 104th Cong., 2d sess. (August 22, 1996): 2115.

13. Ten early adopters, states in which a senior prescription drug program was enacted prior to 1996, were excluded from this analysis. If these states are included, the relationship between problem severity and policy adoption is negative ($r = -0.1699$), and the number of low-severity adopters (seven) more than doubles the number of high-severity adopters (three).

14. The relationship between projected increases in total health care payments and the adoption of MSAs is even weaker ($r = 0.0234$). In that case, MSAs gained enactment in seven low-severity states but in only three high-severity states.

15. In the 1990s, top political science journals published twenty-four event history analysis (EHA) models in studies of state policy diffusion. This count and the criteria on which it is based are described in Mooney 2001a. For the twenty-four EHA models, see Berry and Berry 1990, 1992; Mooney and Lee 1995; Mintrom 1997; Hays and Glick 1997; Mintrom and Vergari 1998. Mooney 2001a focuses on the eighteen models that examine the neighboring state effect. The neighboring state effect achieves conventional levels of statistical significance in twelve models, but Mooney argues that five of them assess the consideration, rather than the enactment, of a policy innovation and that five of them are flawed in ways that bias their results toward such a finding. The results of these studies basically match those described in table 3. Per capita income has a significant effect in only four of twelve models. In three cases, this significant effect is negative, thereby contradicting the slack resources hypothesis. Ideol-

ogy has a significant impact in only one of the three models in which it is included. These studies find a stronger relationship between problem severity and enactment, as this relationship is significant in five of the ten models in which it is included.

16. This chapter focuses on the enactment of policy innovations through the legislative process. Innovations can also be adopted through administrative action, but that process is not considered here.

17. Chamber leaders' powers vary across states. For comparative indexes of these prerogatives, see Hamm and Moncrief 2004, 178; Clucas 2001.

18. Many political scientists have examined the relative significance of governors' formal and informal powers and their connection to gubernatorial success (Bernick 1979; Ferguson 2003).

19. Rosenthal 1990 describes the following gubernatorial powers: the power of initiation, the power of rejection, the power of provision, the power of party, the power of experience, the power of unity, the power of publicity, the power of popularity, and the power of persuasion.

20. The Virginia Prescription Drug Payment Assistance Program would have limited the provision of assistance to drugs manufactured by companies that agreed to provide rebates. Another proposal would have assisted Virginia seniors whose incomes did not exceed 200 percent of the federal poverty level, and a third proposal would have created a self-supporting cooperative to provide medically necessary drugs to senior citizen members at the lowest possible prices. See Jeffersonian Area Board for the Aging, "Nursing Homes, Drug Costs on Legislative Agenda," *Silver Linings,* February 2001. The Virginia organization publishes the *Silver Linings* newsletter six times a year.

21. James S. Gilmore III, "United in Purpose, Open to Change," State of the Commonwealth address, Richmond, VA, January 10, 2001, S. Doc. 1.

22. McDonaugh 2000 offers the following description of the selection procedure in the Massachusetts House of Representatives: "In Massachusetts, the choice of committee chairs is made by the Speaker, who sends his nominations to the House Democratic caucus, which duly ratifies his choices in a secret ballot where all ballots are destroyed immediately after voting, sight unseen except for a few of the Speaker's handpicked loyalists. To revolt against this model and fail would guarantee political oblivion, so no one does" (221). Presiding officers can utilize virtually any criterion to make their selections.

23. The powers of legislative committees in Oregon are therefore especially important as a determinant of legislative content. Chapter 5 examines this relationship in greater detail.

24. An unusual episode in Virginia illustrates the importance attached to committee chairs. The Virginia Senate was evenly divided after the 1995 election. Although the Democratic lieutenant governor would have broken this tie,

a maverick Democratic senator broke ranks and insisted on a more equal sharing of committee chairs. The Republicans gained control of four committees as a result (Hamm and Moncrief 1999, 177). The fact that committee chairs were a bargaining chip during this episode illustrates their centrality.

25. Chair Stan Bunn, Senate Committee on Health and Human Services, Work Session on Senate Bill 1117, May 10, 1995, 68th Oregon Legislative Assembly, 1995 Regular Session, Oregon Archives.

26. Leslie Taylor, "Welfare Reform Arrives," *Roanoke (VA) Times,* March 16, 1994.

27. Margaret Edds, "Welfare Reform Toughened," *Roanoke (VA) Times,* June 6, 1995.

28. Terry Scanlon, "Morgan Plans to Put Priorities in Order: Health Care Tops His List," *Newport News (VA) Daily Press,* December 30, 2000. Governor James S. Gilmore III had campaigned on a promise to eliminate the car tax, explaining its relevance to the senior drug debate. The proposal submitted by Delegate Morgan was one of many prescription drug bills defeated during the 2001 legislative session. The Virginia General Assembly appointed the Joint Commission on Prescription Drug Assistance to review these proposals. The panel subsequently recommended that Virginia expand its Pharmacy Connect program statewide. Pharmacy Connect helps seniors apply for free drugs that companies make available to needy people. See Tammie Smith, "Study Panel Favors Prescription Drug Aid," *Richmond (VA) Times-Dispatch,* November 27, 2001.

29. The role of committee chairs is not the only factor that explains these outcomes. This chapter earlier described how gubernatorial activity also had an effect. Governor George F. Allen was an active supporter of welfare reform that provided for time limits and family caps, while Governor James S. Gilmore III opposed the creation of a senior pharmaceutical assistance program.

30. Governor Weld campaigned unsuccessfully for the U.S. Senate in 1996 and left office in the middle of his second term to fight a quixotic battle to become U.S. ambassador to Mexico. Weld's successors, A. Paul Cellucci and Jane Swift, were also Republicans who faced an overwhelmingly Democratic legislature.

31. Doris Sue Wong, "Weld Vetoes Health Bill," *Boston Globe,* July 23, 1996. Weld attempted to claim credit for the health care legislation during his 1996 U.S. Senate campaign against incumbent senator John Kerry. A Weld campaign spokesman claimed that the governor supported the main objectives of the bill but wanted to use different means to achieve them. See Frank Phillips, "Brawling over Health Care: Weld, Kerry, Their Supporters Trade Charges on Who Lied When," *Boston Globe,* October 3, 1996.

32. In his memoirs, former Massachusetts Senate president William M. Bul-

ger characterized the Senate Committee on Ways and Means as the "most potent and most prestigious committee" in the legislative chamber (Bulger 1996, 288).

33. In addition, the Speaker also used his authority to amend the content of the proposal. The initial proposal provided benefits exclusively for poor senior citizens in Massachusetts. Finneran changed the proposal, adopting an insurance model that opened the program to all seniors in the state.

34. Interview with lobbyist for elderly affairs, June 7, 2002.

35. Before Speaker Finneran's resignation in the fall of 2004, an organization calling itself Democracy in the Statehouse was devoted to ending Finneran's "one-man rule" as Speaker. One critic argued that Finneran "[took] arrogance and autocracy to new levels." See Brian Watson, "Democratic Representatives Must Free House, Selves from Finneran's Stranglehold," *Salem (MA) News,* December 4, 2002.

36. In addition, Governor Weld included an MSA program within a Section 1115 waiver seeking federal permission to amend the state Medicaid program. For more on the content of this waiver proposal and its relationship to health care reform in Massachusetts, see McDonough 2000, 237–84.

37. Richard A. Knox, "Two State Health Reform Plans Share Philosophy and Limits," *Boston Globe,* April 13, 1994.

38. The Massachusetts reform program does not impose a conventional welfare time limit. A conventional time limit terminates benefit receipt after a specified period of time, whereas the Massachusetts time limit imposes a work requirement. The statistical analysis presented in this chapter analyzes the enactment of the former but not the latter. Despite this subtle difference, the enactment of welfare reform was seen as a political victory for Governor Weld and others who favored a more stringent approach to welfare policy.

39. Peter J. Howe, "Weld Raises the Stakes on Welfare: Vetoes Initiative, Limits Funds, Threatens to Quit U.S. Program," *Boston Globe,* July 12, 1994.

40. Critics asserted that Governor Weld bamboozled the two state senators, Dianne Wilkerson and Lois Pines, misleading them by making promises that he had no intention of keeping.

41. Michael Mintrom's work on policy entrepreneurs during the diffusion of school choice (Mintrom 1997, 2000) provides a good prototype for this kind of research.

Chapter 3

1. Haider-Markel 2001 and Mintrom 1997 rely on surveys that ask leading authorities in a state whether their officials had considered the program. This is a valid alternative approach to the one taken here, but it raises reliability issues (Mintrom 1997, 748–50).

2. Other landmark events, such as subcommittee approval, can also be used to indicate agenda status. This alternative provides a more subtle measure of agenda status, since state lawmakers might take no action on an introduced bill. However, it suffers two major shortcomings in the context of the American states. First, full committees perform most of the work in state legislatures, and few subcommittees exist. Second, bills that receive committee approval are rarely defeated on the floor. Committee approval therefore approximates passage and is not an effective measure of agenda status.

3. Kathleen Murphy, "Embryonic Stem Cell Debate Bursts onto State Level," *Stateline.org,* August 12, 2004; available at http://www.stateline .org/live/ViewPage.action?siteNodeId=136&languageId=1&cont entID=15736 (accessed May 4, 2006).

4. A study of invention would describe the creative process or the moment at which a new policy idea was first conceived. This type of analysis lies beyond the scope of this book. Invention can occur quickly in response to a pressing political need, or it can take place through an extended process of incubation during which an innovation is refined and adjusted (Polsby 1984, 178).

5. It is important to acknowledge that interest groups and other advocates do not rely exclusively on the legislative process. For example, they sometimes use initiative efforts as part of larger campaigns to shape the national agenda. In recent years, such topics as school choice and the repeal of affirmative action have been placed on the ballot in several different states in an effort to generate this sort of dynamic (Bowler and Donovan 2004, 129–30). A systematic examination of the initiative process lies beyond the scope of this book.

6. Michael Kinsley, "Sympathy for the Times," *Washington Post,* May 23, 2003.

7. The databases cover slightly different time periods—the *Washington Post,* 1977–2001; the *Boston Globe,* 1980–2001; the *Richmond (VA) Times-Dispatch,* 1986–2001; the *Norfolk Virginian-Pilot,* 1990–2001; the *Newport News (VA) Daily Press,* 1989–2001; the *Roanoke (VA) Times,* 1990–2001. Coverage in the *Portland Oregonian* generally looks similar to these other sources, but a lack of data availability over a comparable time period prevents a systematic examination.

8. The following search terms were used to gather the relevant articles: *prescription drug* and *senior citizen* for senior prescription drug programs, *medical savings account* for MSAs, *individual development account* for IDAs, *welfare* and *time limit* for time limits, and *family cap* for family caps. The relatively broad reach of some of these search terms meant that some articles, such as those describing "family caps" on school bus fees, had to be discarded.

9. In a few rare cases, each category received half a point. An article describing both a U.S. Senate race and a gubernatorial campaign, for example, would produce such a result.

10. The number of the articles appearing in table 6 in the next section of this chapter does not add up to 1,938 because it only includes articles classified as "national." Table A5 in the appendix displays the annual number of "state" or "local" articles for each of the five policy innovations examined in this chapter.

11. For an excellent examination of the creation of Medicare, see Derthick 1979, 316–38.

12. Amy Goldstein, "Medicine Costs Spur Battle on Medicare: Issue Set for Talks before Commission," *Washington Post,* March 14, 1999.

13. Howard Kurtz, "DNC Issue Spot Touts Gore's Medicare Plan: Organization Unnamed in 'Party-Building' Ad," *Washington Post,* June 8, 2000.

14. National Conference of State Legislatures, "2001–2002 State Senior Pharmaceutical Subsidy Legislation," http://www.ncsl.org/programs/health/drugaido1.htm (accessed June 10, 2003). This document is "not intended to include all bills affecting senior pharmaceutical programs," so it is possible that proposals emerged in the six other states as well. Lawmakers in New Mexico, for example, considered a senior prescription drug bill in 2000 even though the state was one of six laggards without legislation in 2001. See National Conference of State Legislatures, "State Legislators Moving Ahead to Reduce Costs of Prescription Drugs," news release, May 2, 2000, available at http://www.ncsl.org/programs/press/2000/pr000502.htm (accessed August 8, 2000).

15. State lawmakers introduced a range of proposals that intended to address the issue of rising prescription drug costs. According to one observer, lawmakers in at least forty-three states considered legislation to create or expand state drug discount programs, bulk purchasing plans, negotiated price caps, or direct subsidies. See Lori Montgomery, "Prescription Aid for Md. Seniors: Lawmakers Want to Budget Millions to Help with Costs," *Washington Post,* March 7, 2001.

16. National Conference on State Legislatures, "2001–2002 State Senior Pharmaceutical Subsidy Legislation."

17. This chapter focuses on the impact of national developments on state policy-making and therefore does not provide definitive evidence that the Massachusetts program influenced congressional deliberations. For a systematic examination of the bottom-up element of the agenda-setting process, see Boeckelman 1992.

18. Citizens against Rationing Health included the American Conservative Union, the United Seniors Association, the American Legislative Exchange Council, and Citizens for a Sound Economy.

19. Robert Dole, 103d Cong., 2d sess., *Congressional Record* 140, pt. 1:198.

20. In six states in which MSA programs did not exist, lawmakers had either adopted resolutions calling on Congress to enact MSAs, created a demonstra-

tion project within the state Medicaid program, or considered legislation to create a tax credit for MSA holders (Bordonaro 1995; Bunce 2000).

21. Massachusetts is generally considered to be one of the most liberal states in the Union. According to one index, Massachusetts ranks second in terms of its "policy liberalism" (Klingman and Lammers 1984). Another index ranks the state as the fourth most liberal in terms of citizen ideology (Wright, Erikson, and McIver 1985).

22. Richard A. Knox, "Two State Health Reform Plans Share Philosophy and Limits," *Boston Globe,* April 13, 1994. MSAs were included in a chart outlining "selected highlights" of the competing Republican and Democratic proposals.

23. "The Medical Emergency," editorial, *Boston Globe,* October 19, 1994.

24. "Institute Proposes a System of Medical Savings Accounts," *Portland Oregonian,* February 1, 1995. Cascade Policy Institute belongs to the State Policy Network, a professional service organization for free-market and libertarian think tanks in the United States. The network includes public policy groups from all over the country, providing training and networking opportunities as well as other services.

25. Only nine people attended the conference. See Matt Murray, "Area Doctors Suggest Savings Account as Alternative Approach," *Newport News (VA) Daily Press,* March 6, 1994.

26. The Virginia law was contingent on the enactment of a full national MSA program. Officials in Wisconsin adopted similar legislation in 1996.

27. Although the discussion in this section of this chapter emphasized the early iterations of the national MSA debate, it is important to note that the accounts played an even more prominent role during the consideration of congressional health care legislation in 1996. This later debate, which resulted in the establishment of a national MSA pilot program, had a similar impact on state political agendas. Officials in thirty-one states introduced MSA legislation in 1996, and MSA bills were considered in thirty-four states in 1997 (Herstek 1998).

28. *Personal Responsibility and Work Opportunity Reconciliation Act,* Public Law 104-193, U.S. statutes at large 110, 104th Cong., 2d sess. (August 22, 1996): 2125.

29. Barbara Vobejda, "Interest Grows in Assisted Savings Plans: Popular Anti-Poverty Tool Gets $15 Million Ford Foundation Boost," *Washington Post,* April 25, 1997.

30. Associated Press, "Private Program to Match Savings for the Poor," *Washington Post,* September 25, 1997.

31. In addition to bill introduction, IDA-related activity took on various forms. For example, an IDA task force formed in Nebraska, and an IDA conference was held in West Virginia.

32. IDA programs did not exist in forty-four states as of December 1996. IDA activity had commenced in thirty-two (73 percent) of these states by December 1999 and in forty-one (93 percent) of these states by March 2000. There had not been any IDA activity in Alaska, North Dakota, or Wyoming. See Center for Social Development, "Summary Tables: IDA Policy in the States," http://gwbweb.wustl.edu/csd/policy/StateIDAtable.pdf (accessed July 12, 2000).

33. IDA regulations in Kentucky, for example, used the same language that was included in the national bill. State-by-state policy profiles are available online at Center for Social Development, "State Assets Policy," http://gwb web.wustl.edu/csd/policy/states.htm (accessed October 14, 2000). The narratives in this chapter of events in Massachusetts, Oregon, and Virginia draw on several updated versions of these policy profiles.

34. In sum, IDA activity in Massachusetts began in 1999 with the formation of MIDAS, yet the first bill to establish the innovation was not submitted until two years later. During the preceding discussion of the national trajectory of this program, Massachusetts was included as one of the six states in which an IDA coalition had been formed as of March 2000.

35. House Revenue Committee, Public Hearing on House Bill 3600, April 21, 1999, 70th Oregon Legislative Assembly, 1999 Regular Session, Oregon Archives. Tracy Strickland-Lehto represented Human Solutions, the organization that administered the Portland program site.

36. Representative Jeff Merkley, House Revenue Committee, Work Session on House Bill 3600, April 26, 1999, 70th Oregon Legislative Assembly, 1999 Regular Session, Oregon Archives.

37. William Jefferson Clinton, "Our New Covenant," 1992 Democratic National Convention Acceptance Address, July 16, 1992, New York, available at http://www.americanrhetoric.com/speeches/billclinton1992dnc.htm (accessed May 4, 2006).

38. While he considered launching his own campaign for the presidency, Governor Cuomo critiqued Clinton's proposal on time limits. See Thomas Oliphant, "Cuomo's Foibles," *Boston Globe,* November 15, 1991; Paul Taylor, "Political Left Is Left, Right Is Right, but Perhaps the Twain Shall Meet," *Washington Post,* October 31, 1991.

39. Barbara Vobejda, "Welfare Plan Begins to Emerge: Clinton's Reform Plan May Seek Time Limit and 'Work Support,'" *Washington Post,* May 9, 1993.

40. Rick Santorum, "Faking Reform: Clinton Talks Tough, but Aides Work to Keep Welfare as We Know It," *Washington Post,* December 12, 1993. When this article was published, Santorum was the senior Republican on the welfare subcommittee of the House Ways and Means Committee. For a less partisan

consideration of a similar theme, see William Claiborne, "How Hard a Push on Welfare Reform? Clinton Bill Likely in 1994, but Depth of Commitment Is Uncertain," *Washington Post,* December 27, 1993.

41. Gloria Negri and Anthony Flint, "States Take Hard Line on Dependency: Punitive Actions Gaining Favor," *Boston Globe,* May 16, 1994.

42. "Making Welfare Work," editorial, *Boston Globe,* May 22, 1994. Precisely estimating the number of states in which time limit bills were filed is difficult because the proposals were frequently incorporated into omnibus measures to reform state welfare programs.

43. Barbara Vobejda, "Gauging Welfare's Role in Motherhood: Sociologists Question Whether 'Family Caps' Are a Legitimate Solution," *Washington Post,* June 2, 1994.

44. For more on the formulation of the Clinton administration's welfare reform initiative and congressional Republicans' response, see Weaver 2000, 222–51.

45. Dan Aucoin, "Welfare Plan Is Defended by Weld: New Ideas on Aid Cuts to Mothers Explained," *Boston Globe,* April 8, 1994. A July 1995 newspaper account noted that family caps were pending in Minnesota, North Carolina, and Pennsylvania, three states in which the policy innovation was not adopted. See Margaret Edds, "Analysis Doubts N.J. Efforts to Reduce Babies on Welfare," *Norfolk Virginian-Pilot,* July 18, 1995.

46. Some scholars concluded that the New Jersey family cap reduced births to welfare mothers, while others concluded that it increased the number of abortions among this group. See "Caps on Kids," editorial, *Richmond (VA) Times-Dispatch,* July 25, 1994; Barbara Fitzgerald, "Welfare Cap in N.J. Raised Abortion Rate, Study Finds: State Officials Reject Rutgers Data, Request Revision," *Boston Globe,* June 9, 1998; "Respect for Life: Welfare Failure," editorial, *Norfolk Virginian-Pilot,* June 15, 1998.

47. Leslie Taylor, "Welfare Plan's 'Family Cap' Is Controversial," *Roanoke (VA) Times,* March 26, 1994.

48. Negri and Flint, "States Take Hard Line on Dependency." In Maryland, for example, Governor William Donald Schaefer advanced a family cap proposal that was modeled after the New Jersey plan. See Graciela Sevilla, "Md. NAACP for Welfare Overhaul: Bid to Tighten Rules Gets Surprise Support," *Washington Post,* March 6, 1994.

49. Dan Aucoin, "Mass. Senate Backs Time Limit on Welfare," *Boston Globe,* February 17, 1994; Dan Aucoin, "Welfare Overhaul Loses Two-Year Limit: Panel's Dropping of Key Rule Assailed," *Boston Globe,* March 23, 1994.

50. Anthony Flint, "A Case in Point: Wisconsin," *Boston Globe,* May 17, 1994.

51. Silber did not lose the election simply because he advocated the family cap. A variety of factors were at work in his defeat. The important point is that top politicians in Massachusetts, including the victorious William Weld, treated family caps as a nonstarter during the 1990 gubernatorial campaign. This negative perception gradually evaporated.

52. Victoria Benning, "Welfare-Related Bills Draw Scorn at Hearing," *Boston Globe,* March 23, 1993.

53. Massachusetts lawmakers also considered stand-alone family cap legislation in 1994, but most legislative activity in the state focused on the omnibus measure developed by Governor Weld.

54. A few observers in Massachusetts attributed the governor's dramatic about-face to his national political ambitions. See Flint, "A Case in Point."

55. Chapter 2 describes the political dynamics that ultimately produced the enactment of a rather strict family cap program in Massachusetts. In brief, Democratic legislators attempted to meet the Republican governor halfway by passing a welfare reform bill that included a family cap. Weld rejected this welfare reform package, saying that its family cap provisions contained too many exceptions to be effective. After the 1994 election, which Weld won handily, the legislature revisited the topic and produced legislation that was more in line with the governor's wishes.

56. Representative Charles Starr, House Committee on Children and Families, Public Hearing on House Bill 3154, March 21, 1995, 68th Oregon Legislative Assembly, 1995 Regular Session, Oregon Archives.

57. John F. Harris, "Allen Urges Va. Welfare Restrictions: Plan Would Require Job, Two-Year Cutoff," *Washington Post,* August 17, 1993.

58. Leslie Taylor, "Welfare Reform Plan Unveiled: Project Gives Training, Jobs to Poor," *Roanoke (VA) Times,* March 19, 1994.

59. HIPAA permitted only the self-employed, businesses with fifty or fewer employees, and persons enrolled in high-deductible health insurance plans to purchase MSAs. It capped the total number of tax-advantaged MSAs at 750,000 for the four-year period between January 1, 1997, and December 31, 2000 (Nichols and Blumberg 1998).

60. The five policy innovations examined in this book do not provide the necessary contrast, because all of them involved national intervention. National officials engaged in heated debates over senior prescription drug programs, MSAs, time limits, and family caps. While no such debate occurred in the context of IDAs, national welfare reform legislation affected the state-level emergence of this policy innovation by providing resources to innovate. The statute listed IDAs as an appropriate use of state welfare funds in an action that resonates with a larger scholarly literature on intergovernmental grants (Welch and Thompson 1980; Allen, Pettus, and Haider-Markel 2004; Bingham 1976).

Chapter 4

1. Most research on policy diffusion evaluates the hypothesis that the enactment of a policy innovation in one state is affected by the existence of the policy innovation in neighboring states. Even when this variable has a significant effect on enactment, it does not conclusively establish that officials seek or rely on information about nearby models.

2. Interview with professional association staff member, October 11, 2000.

3. Interview with committee staff member, November 17, 2000.

4. Interview with committee staff member, November 17, 2000.

5. Interview with professional association staff member, November 2, 2000.

6. Chapter 3 describes the set of newspaper articles on which this discussion draws. A lack of data availability over a comparable time period prevents a systematic examination of newspaper coverage in Oregon.

7. Alex Pham, "Battling for Drug Benefits: State House Hearing to Kick Off Debate on Helping Seniors Pay for Pharmacy Costs," *Boston Globe,* March 30, 1999.

8. Michael Crowley, "Officials Target Seniors' Program: Budget Strain Seen as Drug Plan Grows," *Boston Globe,* October 25, 1999.

9. "Medical Savings Mirage," editorial, *Boston Globe,* November 18, 1995; "Indiana Firm Sells Medicare Plan," *Boston Globe,* October 20, 1995.

10. Anthony Flint and Gloria Negri, "Clashing Blueprints Offered for the Road from Welfare to Work," *Boston Globe,* May 15, 1994; Anthony Flint, "Iowa Becomes Partners with Its Jobless," *Boston Globe,* May 16, 1994; Brian McGrory, "Oregon Trying Welfare Funds as Job Subsidies: Experiment Seeks to Create Private-Sector Opportunities Using Welfare Funds," *Boston Globe,* January 22, 1995.

11. Dan Aucoin, "Welfare Plan Is Defended by Weld: New Ideas on Aid Cut to Mothers Explained," *Boston Globe,* April 8, 1994; Gloria Negri and Anthony Flint, "States Take Hard Line on Dependency: Punitive Actions Gaining Favor," *Boston Globe,* May 16, 1994; Anthony Flint, "A Case in Point: Wisconsin," *Boston Globe,* May 17, 1994; "Welfare for Weld?" editorial, *Boston Globe,* August 1, 1995.

12. Christina Nuckols, "Candidates at Forum Court Elderly Voters," *Norfolk Virginian-Pilot,* September 25, 2001.

13. Christopher Connell, "Workers Get Incentives to Forgo Medical Claims," *Roanoke (VA) Times,* May 21, 1995.

14. David Saunders and David Stoesz, "A Booming Economy Eases Welfare's End," *Richmond (VA) Times-Dispatch,* October 26, 1997.

15. "Welfare Reform: Where the Action Is," editorial, *Roanoke (VA) Times,*

February 11, 1996; "Iowa: Welfare As We'll Know It," editorial, *Roanoke (VA) Times,* May 16, 1995.

16. Leslie Taylor, "Welfare Plan's 'Family Cap' Is Controversial," *Roanoke (VA) Times,* March 26, 1994.

17. Stephen B. Soumerai, "Economic and Clinical Effects of Changes in Drug Coverage among Low-Income, Elderly, and Disabled," statement before the Joint Committee on Health Care, March 30, 1999, 178th General Court of the Commonwealth of Massachusetts, 1999 Regular Session, Massachusetts Archives.

18. Testimony of Jim Seagraves of Oregonians for Medical Savings Accounts, House Committee on State and School Finance, Public Hearing on House Bill 2865 and House Bill 3018, April 6, 1995, 68th Oregon Legislative Assembly, 1995 Regular Session, Oregon Archives.

19. Written testimony of Tracy Strickland of Human Solutions, House Revenue Committee, Public Hearing on House Bill 3600, April 21, 1999, 70th Oregon Legislative Assembly, 1999 Regular Session, Oregon Archives.

20. Representative Cynthia Wooten, Exhibit R to House Bill 2459, July 21, 1993, 67th Oregon Legislative Assembly, 1993 Regular Session, Oregon Archives.

21. Representative Frank Shields, Exhibit B to House Bill 2837, March 21, 1995, 68th Oregon Legislative Assembly, 1995 Regular Session, Oregon Archives.

22. A similar reference three pages later noted that "more than half of the states" had developed such programs (Glickman 2002, 1).

23. The Oregon report based its description of these programs on the article "Consumer-First Health Care," *Wall Street Journal,* July 21, 1994.

24. Table 1 in the Oregon MSA report (Gates 1994) compares existing programs in Arizona, Colorado, Idaho, Illinois, Michigan, Mississippi, and Missouri to two congressional bills along seven dimensions: date enacted or signed, effective date, maximum contribution allowed, minimum contribution required, required purchase of catastrophic plan, employer contribution required, and tax status of the account. The report also cites a feasibility study that had been issued by the Minnesota Department of Health in February 1994 and mentions an MSA bill that had been vetoed by the governor of Kansas.

25. The 1994 report by the Oregon Family Support Council covers state agencies that provided services to families caring for a family member with a disability or chronic illness. This population does not consist solely of families receiving welfare benefits, but many such families fall under this heading.

26. In some cases, the time lag between the request for a report and its publication may be intentional. The opponents of a policy innovation may some-

times use administrative reports strategically, as a way to stall legislative progress.

27. National Conference of State Legislatures, "2001–2002 State Senior Pharmaceutical Subsidy Legislation," http://www.ncsl.org/programs/health/drugaido1.htm (accessed June 10, 2003).

28. National Conference of State Legislatures, "State Pharmaceutical Assistance Programs (includes seniors, disabled, uninsured, and others)," http://www.ncsl.org/programs/health/drugaid.htm (accessed June 7, 2002).

29. The June 2000 article in *State Health Notes* quoted Chellie Pingree, majority leader of the Maine Senate. Pingree explained, "We started this effort regionally basically because of logistics, because it's easier to get together." Concerning the possibility that Arizona might want to join Maine in its purchasing effort, Pingree added "[if] it makes sense practically, I'd say, 'Sure.'" Her comment illustrates the geographic pragmatism of state officials.

30. National Conference of State Legislatures, "State Legislators Moving Ahead to Reduce Costs of Prescription Drugs," news release, May 2, 2000, http://www.ncsl.org/programs/press/2000/pr000502.htm (accessed August 8, 2000).

31. Information in the AARP state profiles was grouped under the following headings: year program enacted, minimum eligibility age, other eligible groups, maximum income for eligibility, covered drugs/restrictions, deductible, copayment, ingredient cost reimbursement to pharmacy, pharmacy dispensing fees, administrative agency, telephone number for further information, and number of people enrolled.

32. The documents featured in this section and more generally in this chapter are illustrative rather than exhaustive. Additional organizations tracked these state-level developments. In fact, some NCSL publications mentioned these groups as potential information resources. They included AARP, the National Pharmaceutical Council, the Government Accountability Office, the National Governors Association, the California Senate Office of Research, and the Pharmaceutical Research and Manufacturers of America. Virtually all of these groups are national-level organizations.

33. Unlike the other documents featured in this paragraph, the Urban Institute report expressed serious doubts about the claims of MSA proponents.

34. Council for Affordable Health Insurance, "State MSA Synopsis," http://www.cahi.org/msa/msasyna.asp (accessed February 4, 2001).

35. A similar dynamic existed in Minneapolis, Minnesota. In that city, the Citizens' Council on Health Care supports market-based health care reforms, including MSAs. The organization provides a summary of the policy innovation

on its Web site, relying heavily on Scandlen 1998a. It describes Greg Scandlen as a member of Americans for Free Choice in Medicine who has authored policy briefs for the National Center for Policy Analysis. See Citizens' Council on Health Care, "Medical Savings Accounts," http://www.cchconline.org/privacy/msa.php3 (accessed February 2, 2005).

36. The discussion in this subsection of this chapter describes various documents published by CFED. The organization also affected the emergence of IDAs by conducting a demonstration project to evaluate their effectiveness. The American Dream Demonstration, initiated in September 1997, has program sites in thirteen cities. Its main goal is to test the efficacy of IDAs as an antipoverty strategy.

37. Corporation for Enterprise Development, "Federal and State IDA Policy Overview," http://www.cfed.org/individual_assets/Assets_Policy/fed_state_overview2.html (accessed July 12, 2000).

38. Center for Social Development, "State IDA Policy Profiles," http://gwbweb.wustl.edu/users/csd/ida/stateIDAprofiles2.html (accessed July 12, 2000). The CSD Web site also provides legislative action tips for those seeking information on how to work with state legislators to enact IDA legislation. Policy advocates and interest groups may be more likely to rely on these tips than are state lawmakers.

39. Center for Social Development, "Summary Tables: IDA Policy in the States," http://gwbweb.wustl.edu/csd/policy/StateIDAtable.pdf (accessed February 3, 2005).

40. Center for Social Development, "Model State Legislation for Individual Development Accounts," http://gwbweb.wustl.edu/users/csd/ida/molegis.html (accessed July 12, 2000).

41. After the enactment of national legislation, CLASP provided more detailed policy information through a joint project with the Center on Budget and Policy Priorities, called the State Policy Demonstration Project (SPDP). SPDP tracked policy choices on Temporary Assistance for Needy Families (TANF) and Medicaid in the fifty states and the District of Columbia from 1998 to 2000.

42. The American Public Welfare Association was renamed the American Public Human Services Association in 1997.

43. NGA published the original matrix in 1997 and released an updated version in 1999. The later version made a few minor modifications to the original categories. The columns on time limits and family caps illustrate the matrices' lack of specificity. The matrices indicate whether state time limits are shorter than sixty months but do not indicate their actual length. In terms of family caps, they indicate whether the innovation exists in a given state, but they do not describe programmatic variation, such as exemptions.

44. Interview with state senator, November 15, 2000.

45. Interview with executive branch official, June 21, 2002.

46. Interview with professional association staff member, October 11, 2000.

47. Howard Dean, "Memorandum to All Governors Re: Setting NGA Priorities for 1994–95" (National Governors Association, Washington, DC, July 8, 1994), attachments A and B, Oregon Archives. Governor Dean was vice chairman of NGA when this memorandum was composed. An open-ended question on the survey asked respondents to list the policy areas about which they would like to receive comparative state information. Welfare (with eleven responses) and health care (with eight) received more responses than did any other issue areas.

48. Interview with professional association staff member, November 2, 2000.

49. The two individuals affiliated with the NCPA, Merrill Matthews Jr. and Dr. Brant Mittler, coauthored one of the reports that the authors cited. See Mittler and Matthews 1995.

Chapter 5

1. State Policy Demonstration Project 1999 does not include the two states (Idaho and Wisconsin) that offer a flat grant regardless of family size. It lists eight conditions under which children would be exempt from the family cap: (1) if born less than ten months after the case opened (eighteen states), (2) if the first-born child of a minor (fifteen states), (3) if conceived between TANF spells (eleven states), (4) if the product of rape or incest (eighteen states), (5) if the product of failed contraception (one state), (6) if not living with a biological parent (eleven states), (7) if affected by the family violence option (two states), and (8) other (eleven states).

2. George Herbert Walker Bush, State of the Union address, 1991, 102d Cong., 1st sess., January 29, 1991, House Document 102-1, p. 5.

3. The emphasis on program enactment in most diffusion research results, in part, from its use of event history analysis and a dichotomous dependent variable. This strategy is useful for analyzing the question of program enactment, but it is not well suited for distinguishing among the programs that have been adopted.

4. Meyer and Rowan (1977) argue that there is frequently a harmonization of organizational forms but a divergence in terms of how these organizations actually function. Their distinction raises the question of implementation, which lies beyond the scope of this book.

5. This formulation of the question comes from Clark and French 1984.

6. The number of exemptions was negatively related to the timing of program enactment ($r = -0.3709$), but the relationship between the number of exemptions and political ideology was in the expected direction. In a more conservative state, lawmakers enacted fewer exemptions ($r = -0.4464$). The number of exemptions may not be the best measure of the expansiveness of family cap policies, but these correlations nonetheless illustrate the potential pitfalls of relying on time as an explanation of program content.

7. Chair Stan Bunn, Senate Committee on Health and Human Services, Work Session on Senate Bill 1117, May 15, 1995, 68th Oregon Legislative Assembly, 1995 Regular Session, Oregon Archives.

8. Keith Putman, "Possible Questions, and Answers, for SB 1117," confidential memo to Representative Dennis Luke, June 7, 1995, Oregon Archives.

9. The campaign finance data were compiled using databases maintained by the Institute on Money in State Politics, a nonpartisan organization that is headquartered in Missoula, Montana. These databases are available on the institute's Web site, http://www.followthemoney.org. They contain information for every candidate who ran for the state house, listing his or her party affiliation, the district in which the candidate ran, whether he or she was victorious or defeated in the general or primary election, the total campaign contributions he or she collected, and the amount of contributions the candidate collected from in-state and out-of-state sources. The in-state and out-of-state designations are based on the zip code of the campaign contributor. Table 10 designates as "unidentified" any contributions for which this information is not available. Table 10 does not include information for candidates whose total or in-state contributions were negative, candidates who did not raise any money, candidates for whom no contributions were identified as in-state or out-of-state, or candidates for whom the sum of in-state and out-of-state contributions exceeded the total. Imposing these criteria eliminated nineteen candidates in Massachusetts, fifty-six candidates in Oregon, and six candidates in Virginia.

10. The data in table 10 cannot establish definitively that campaign contributions lead specific provisions to be enacted, but this subsection of this chapter does not make such a claim. Instead, it argues that elected officials have strong incentives to respond to the entreaties of intrastate constituencies during the customization process because they depend on them for reelection. The evidence presented in table 10 provides empirical support for this more general claim by highlighting the extent to which candidates for the state legislature rely on intrastate campaign contributions.

11. The figures used during the campaign finance discussion in this subsection are the average percentage of in-state and out-of-state contributions that

candidates collected. They are not the average dollar figures that fall into each of the categories.

1 2. Kollman (1998) suggests that, at the national level, nationalized interest groups with a federated structure are more likely to engage in outside lobbying tactics.

1 3. I am grateful to Virginia Gray and David Lowery for providing the lobbying registration data, which build on their earlier data set of 1997 lobbying registrations. For a more thorough description of this data set, see Gray and Lowery 2001a, 2001b.

1 4. In practice, this distinction means that such organizations as United Way of California are categorized as part of a national organization, whereas such organizations as United Way of Greater Tucson are not.

1 5. One could argue that by classifying as a "national" group any organization that is registered to lobby in more than one state, the analysis presented in this subsection of this chapter is actually biased toward finding support for this alternative hypothesis.

1 6. Wolak and others (2002) find that unique registrations exceed multiple state registrations in seventeen of twenty-six interest group sectors.

1 7. The virtually universal use of legislative testimony suggests that this proxy for influence during the customization process is not biased in terms of finding specific types of groups to be especially influential. For a variety of reasons, however, one would not want to rely exclusively on this metric. That is why this chapter also examines lobbying registration and campaign finance data, both of which suggest that intrastate organizations are more prominent during the customization process than are national groups.

1 8. The witness list at one hearing in Massachusetts, however, suggests that witnesses representing intrastate constituencies appeared more frequently than did witnesses representing national organizations. The Joint Committee on Health Care heard from twenty-five witnesses when considering senior prescription drug legislation on March 30, 1999. Of the twenty-five witnesses, thirteen represented intrastate groups, and six represented state and local government. Three individual citizens, seniors who testified about the high cost of prescription drugs, also appeared before the committee. Two committee witnesses represented the state chapters of national organizations. The only "national" organization to appear, Harvard Pilgrim Health Care, operated only in Massachusetts, Maine, New Hampshire, and Vermont. Information about the specific organizations represented at this hearing is available from the author on request.

1 9. For example, during a hearing on senior prescription drug legislation, an elderly citizen might describe her struggles to pay for the medicine she needs. Similarly, at a hearing on welfare reform, a witness might testify about

her struggles or her improved self-esteem after leaving welfare and entering the workforce. These witnesses sometimes appear at the behest of an interest group even though they do not work for the organization.

20. The Oregon Medical Association, for example, is a state affiliate of the American Medical Association and qualifies as a "state chapter." Federations have long been an important part of the American political landscape, although their importance has receded in recent years (Skocpol 1999; Putnam 2000, 48–64).

21. Connections between state chapters and national headquarters vary in their intensity. The two usually share policy priorities. For example, when a representative of the Oregon Catholic Conference testified on a welfare reform bill, he submitted a document produced by the United States Catholic Conference to accompany his testimony. See Bob Castagna, Oregon Catholic Conference, Exhibit N to Senate Bill 1117, March 29, 1995, 68th Oregon Legislative Assembly, 1995 Regular Session, Oregon Archives. State chapters usually set their own daily agendas and determine their own strategies, but some federations are highly centralized. AARP is one example of a highly centralized federation.

22. For example, the Oregon Health Action Campaign is part of the Universal Health Care Action Network (UHCAN). UHCAN was formed in 1992 to bring together diverse state groups and activists working for comprehensive health care. It differs from groups categorized as state chapters, because this network exists to connect state groups that are already in place. It is a political campaign rather than an organization per se, and it therefore differs from an interest group or professional association that establishes state chapters to create a presence in all fifty states.

23. Chair John Schoon, House State and School Finance Committee, Work Session on House Bill 2865, April 5, 1995, 68th Oregon Legislative Assembly, 1995 Regular Session, Oregon Archives.

24. The government relations manager of Kaiser Foundation Health Plan of the Northwest submitted written testimony but did not testify before the House Committee on State and School Finance. In addition, the organization lacked truly "national" reach. It operated in only nine states and the District of Columbia.

25. None of the witnesses who appeared at multiple committee hearings or at work sessions fall into the category of "individual citizens." As a result, tables 13 and 14 do not include this category.

26. The witness from Multnomah County Legal Aid Service represented an umbrella organization called the Oregon Human Rights Coalition, a membership organization that represents individuals in the Oregon state welfare system.

27. Table 14 excludes House Bill 2865 (1995) because its work session did not feature any witnesses. It also excludes officials from the Legislative Revenue Office, the Office of Legislative Counsel, and the Senate Democratic Office, because these offices are housed within the legislature and employ individuals who assist legislators in bill drafting.

28. This section of this chapter focuses on programs that gained enactment, because the question that motivates this chapter is why the same policy innovation takes on a variety of forms in the states in which it exists. As a result, this section does not consider episodes during which state officials chose not to adopt a policy innovation.

29. Similarly, Schickler (2001) points to interplay among multiple interests as a source of institutional change in Congress, arguing that coalitions promoting a wide range of member interests drive change. An equally wide range of interests can support policy innovations.

30. The discussion in this subsection of this chapter draws heavily on McDonough 2000, 237–84, which provides a comprehensive examination of the Massachusetts debate.

31. The chairman of Heinz Family Philanthropies, Teresa Heinz, is married to John Kerry, who represents Massachusetts in the U.S. Senate. The organization prepared similar reports for three other states: Maine, Mississippi, and Pennsylvania.

32. Interview with lobbyist for elderly affairs, June 7, 2002.

33. In addition, the program must operate a toll-free hotline, host a Web site with information on its services, and provide information on publicly funded prescription drug programs, such as Medicaid.

34. See also Matt Murray, "Area Doctors Suggest Savings Account as Alternative Approach," *Newport News (VA) Daily Press,* March 6, 1994.

35. *Code of Virginia,* sec. 38.2-5603.

36. Note 59 of chapter 3 describes the provisions of the national pilot program in more detail.

37. Reconnection is defined officially in the following terms: "Oregon generally connects to Federal tax laws to simplify the system for taxpayers and the Department of Revenue. Because of this connection, taxpayers can carry over many calculations on their Federal tax returns to the state return. Oregon then applies its own tax rates and credits. In some cases, however, the Legislature chooses to 'disconnect' from a federal provision either for public policy reasons or because of the revenue impact of connecting. Therefore, in each session the Legislature reviews recent changes to federal tax law and determines which ones Oregon will connect to" (House Committee on Revenue, "Staff Measure Summary: Senate Bill 347," March 19–21, 1997, 69th Oregon Legislative Assembly, 1997 Regular Session, Oregon Archives). The OSCPA argues that

reconnection produces numerous benefits, including "fewer errors in the preparation of Oregon tax returns and the interpretation of Oregon law, greater voluntary taxpayer compliance, and reduced administrative costs of compliance and examination" (Oregon Society of Certified Public Accountants 1997, i).

38. The House Committee on Revenue adopted one "technical amendment" that addressed the "deductibility limit for part-year and non-residents' contributions to medical savings accounts" (House Committee on Revenue, "Staff Measure Summary: Senate Bill 347").

39. Tim Nesbitt, Oregon Public Employees Union, House Revenue Committee, Public Hearing on Senate Bill 347, March 21, 1997, 69th Oregon Legislative Assembly, 1997 Regular Session, Oregon Archives.

40. Although the expansive provisions of the Virginia program are noteworthy, it is important to emphasize that the program is contingent on the approval of national MSA legislation. MSA advocates might view this constraint as more problematic (and less expansive) than the restrictive provisions of the Oregon program.

41. During the 1998 legislative session, Virginia lawmakers also passed Joint Resolution 353. The joint resolution established a subcommittee to study strategies to promote long-term economic self-sufficiency among welfare recipients and the working poor. The legislation instructed the subcommittee to examine "ways to help low-income persons accumulate assets, including the funding of individual development accounts and employer-sponsored savings programs."

42. House Committee on Revenue, "Staff Measure Summary: House Bill 3600," April 21/26, 1999, 70th Oregon Legislative Assembly, 1999 Regular Session, Oregon Archives.

43. Chair Randy Miller, Senate Revenue Committee, Public Hearing and Work Session on House Bill 3600, May 20, 1999, 70th Oregon Legislative Assembly, 1999 Regular Session, Oregon Archives.

44. As was mentioned in the previous paragraph, fiduciary organizations retained the right to establish lower income and net worth thresholds for participants.

45. House Committee on School Funding and Tax Fairness/Revenue, "Staff Measure Summary: House Bill 3391," May 7, 2001, 71st Oregon Legislative Assembly, 2001 Regular Session, Oregon Archives.

46. Senate Committee on Revenue, "Staff Measure Summary: House Bill 3391," June 6, 2001, 71st Oregon Legislative Assembly, 2001 Regular Session, Oregon Archives.

47. In a similar vein, Winston 2002 examines welfare politics in Maryland, Texas, and North Dakota and finds that the welfare advocacy community fre-

quently succeeded in moderating the most stringent elements of the original proposals in those states.

48. A work requirement time limit is qualitatively different from a termination time limit, which eliminates benefits after a prescribed number of months (U.S. Department of Health and Human Services 1997). The quantitative analysis in chapter 2 focuses on termination time limits, excluding work requirement time limits. Incorporating both types of time limits does not affect its main results.

49. Family caps in California, Connecticut, Indiana, Nebraska, Virginia, and Wisconsin incorporated the "reduced JOBS exemption." Family caps in Arizona, Illinois, Mississippi, Nebraska, and Virginia included an extension after families left AFDC.

50. Family caps in Connecticut and Florida provided a partial increase, while those in Maryland, South Carolina, and Indiana provided vouchers in lieu of increased benefits. Family caps in Arizona, Georgia, Illinois, and New Jersey incorporated an increased earnings disregard. Family caps in California, Delaware, Maryland, Mississippi, Nebraska, and Virginia incorporated a child support pass-through.

51. The Virginia Independence Program exempted individuals under age sixteen, individuals between the ages of sixteen and nineteen and enrolled full-time in elementary or secondary schools, individuals incapacitated by a temporary medical condition, individuals receiving benefits from the Supplemental Security Income (SSI) or Social Security Disability (SSD) programs, individuals over age sixty, the sole caregiver of an incapacitated household member, a parent/caretaker of a child under eighteen months, individuals receiving benefits from the AFDC-Foster Care program, families where the primary caretakers are not the adoptive or biological parents of the child, and females in their fourth through ninth month of pregnancy.

52. Although the subsequent discussion in text does not explicitly examine the role of race in the making of welfare policy, its focus on the welfare advocacy community encompasses groups organized around racial identity. Other authors deal more thoroughly with the impact of race on welfare policy (Quadagno 1994).

53. Anthony Flint, "Welfare Reform Wins Big Support: Residents Polled Back Benefits Cuts," *Boston Globe,* May 15, 1994.

54. "Time to Bridge the Budget," editorial, *Boston Globe,* June 18, 1994.

55. Representative Gene Derfler, Exhibit O to House Bill 2459, July 21, 1993, 67th Oregon Legislative Assembly, 1993 Regular Session, Oregon Archives.

56. Jim Neeley, assistant administrator of Adult and Family Services, House Legislative Rules and Reorganization Committee, Work Session on House Bill

2459, May 26, 1993, 67th Oregon Legislative Assembly, 1993 Regular Session, Oregon Archives.

57. Chair Stan Bunn, Senate Committee on Health and Human Services, Work Session on Senate Bill 1117, May 10, 1995, 68th Oregon Legislative Assembly, 1995 Regular Session, Oregon Archives.

58. The consensual lobbying tactics of the welfare advocacy community are only one source of the relatively lenient provisions of Oregon's JOBS Plus Program. Two additional factors merit mention. First, welfare reform supporters were willing to compromise. The coalition that sponsored the ballot measure cared very deeply about its focus on employment and training. It was not as enthusiastic about time limits and family caps. Republicans in the state legislature added a time limit provision to the original ballot initiative but were willing to moderate its provisions. Second, the advocacy community could count on the support of a Democratic governor (Barbara Roberts in 1993 and John Kitzhaber in 1995). The skepticism of these two governors validated efforts to amend the original proposal. When these governors endorsed compromise legislation, however, they effectively made the passage of the omnibus legislation a foregone conclusion.

59. Leslie Taylor, "Welfare Reform Arrives," *Roanoke (VA) Times,* March 16, 1994.

60. Ted Edlich, "Welfare Reform: A Prescription for Real Welfare Reform," *Roanoke (VA) Times,* March 18, 1994. Total Action against Poverty is a welfare advocacy group located in Roanoke, Virginia.

61. Corinne Gott, "Blaming the Poor Is No Way to Reform Welfare," *Roanoke (VA) Times,* July 17, 1994.

62. Don Beyer, "Virginia Independence Program," *Norfolk Virginian-Pilot,* May 3, 1994. For more on the family cap debate, see Leslie Taylor, "Welfare Plan's 'Family Cap' Is Controversial," *Roanoke (VA) Times,* March 26, 1994.

63. The lack of visibility may be related to the noncontroversial nature of IDAs, particularly in comparison to such policy innovations as time limits and family caps. Some studies of reinvention have linked variation in program content to the existence of political controversy (Hays 1996; Mooney and Lee 1999).

References

Allard, Scott W., and Sheldon Danziger. 2000. Welfare Magnets: Myth or Reality? *Journal of Politics* 62:350–68.

Allen, Mahalley D., Carrie Pettus, and Donald P. Haider-Markel. 2004. Making the National Local: Specifying the Conditions for National Government Influence on State Policymaking. *State Politics and Policy Quarterly* 4:318–44.

Allen, Russ, and Jill Clark. 1981. State Policy Adoption and Innovation: Lobbying and Education. *State and Local Government Review* 13:18–25.

American Public Welfare Association. 1994. *Responsibility/Work/Pride: The Values of Welfare Reform.* Washington, DC: American Public Welfare Association.

Annie E. Casey Foundation. 1999. *When Teens Have Sex: Issues and Trends.* Baltimore: Annie E. Casey Foundation.

Arsneault, Shelly. 2000. Welfare Policy Innovation and Diffusion: Section 1115 Waivers and the Federal System. *State and Local Government Review* 32:49–60.

Balla, Steven J. 2001. Interstate Professional Associations and the Diffusion of Policy Innovations. *American Politics Research* 29:221–45.

Barrilleaux, Charles. 1998. The Politics of State Health and Welfare Reforms. In *Governing Partners: State-Local Relations in the United States,* ed. Russell L. Hanson. Boulder, CO: Westview.

Bartels, Larry M. 1996. Uninformed Votes: Information Effects in Presidential Elections. *American Journal of Political Science* 40:193–230.

———. 2003. Is "Popular Rule" Possible? *Brookings Review* 21:12–15.

Baumgartner, Frank R., and Bryan D. Jones. 1993. *Agendas and Instability in American Politics.* Chicago: University of Chicago Press.

Beck, Nathaniel, Jonathan N. Katz, and Richard Tucker. 1998. Taking Time Seriously: Time-Series–Cross-Section Analysis with a Binary Dependent Variable. *American Journal of Political Science* 42:1260–88.

Bernick, E. Lee. 1979. Gubernatorial Tools: Formal vs. Informal. *Journal of Politics* 41:656–64.

Berry, Frances Stokes. 1994. Sizing Up State Policy Innovation Research. *Policy Studies Journal* 22:442–56.

Berry, Frances Stokes, and William D. Berry. 1990. State Lottery Adoptions as Policy Innovations: An Event History Analysis. *American Political Science Review* 84:395–415.

———. 1992. Tax Innovation in the States: Capitalizing on Political Opportunity. *American Journal of Political Science* 36:715–42.

———. 1999. Innovation and Diffusion Models in Policy Research. In *Theories of the Policy Process,* ed. Paul Sabatier. Boulder, CO: Westview.

Berry, William D., and Brady Baybeck. 2005. Using Geographic Information Systems to Study Interstate Competition. *American Political Science Review* 99:505–20.

Berry, William D., Richard C. Fording, and Russell L. Hanson. 2003. Reassessing the "Race to the Bottom" in State Welfare Policy. *Journal of Politics* 65:327–49.

Berry, William D., Evan J. Ringquist, Richard C. Fording, and Russell L. Hanson. 1998. Measuring Citizen and Government Ideology in the American States, 1960–1993. *American Journal of Political Science* 42:327–48.

Beyle, Thad. 2004. The Governors. In *Politics in the American States,* ed. Virginia Gray and Russell L. Hanson. 8th ed. Washington, DC: CQ Press.

Binder, Sarah A. 2003. *Stalemate: Causes and Consequences of Legislative Gridlock.* Washington, DC: Brookings Institution.

Bingham, Richard D. 1976. *The Adoption of Innovation by Local Government.* Lexington, MA: Lexington Books.

Boeckelman, Keith. 1992. The Influence of States on Federal Policy Adoptions. *Policy Studies Journal* 20:365–75.

Boehmke, Frederick J., and Richard Witmer. 2004. Disentangling Diffusion: The Effects of Social Learning and Economic Competition on State Policy Innovation and Expansion. *Political Research Quarterly* 57:39–51.

Bonoli, Giuliano. 1997. Classifying Welfare States: A Two-Dimension Approach. *Journal of Social Policy* 26:351–72.

Bordonaro, Molly Hering. 1995. *Medical Savings Accounts and the States: Growth from the Grassroots.* Dallas: National Center for Policy Analysis.

Bowler, Shaun, and Todd Donovan. 2004. The Initiative Process. In *Politics in the American States,* ed. Virginia Gray and Russell L. Hanson. 8th ed. Washington, DC: CQ Press.

Bowman, Ann O'M., and Richard C. Kearney. 1986. *The Resurgence of the States.* Englewood Cliffs, NJ: Prentice Hall.

Box-Steffensmeier, Janet M., and Bradford S. Jones. 1997. Time Is of the Essence: Event History Models in Political Science. *American Journal of Political Science* 41:1414–61.

————. 2004. *Event History Modeling: A Guide for Social Scientists.* Cambridge: Cambridge University Press.

Brace, Paul, and Aubrey Jewett. 1995. The State of State Politics Research. *Political Research Quarterly* 48:643–81.

Bratton, Kathleen A., and Kerry L. Haynie. 1999. Agenda Setting and Legislative Success in State Legislatures: The Effects of Gender and Race. *Journal of Politics* 61:658–79.

Bridges, Amy. 1997. *Morning Glories: Municipal Reform in the Southwest.* Princeton: Princeton University Press.

Brueckner, Jan K. 2000. Welfare Reform and the Race to the Bottom: Theory and Evidence. *Southern Economic Journal* 66:505–25.

Brunelli, Samuel A., ed. 1995. *Sourcebook of American State Legislation.* Vol. 1. Washington, DC: American Legislative Exchange Council.

Buckley, Jack, and Chad Westerland. 2004. Duration Dependence, Functional Form, and Corrected Standard Errors: Improving EHA Models of State Policy Diffusion. *State Politics and Policy Quarterly* 4:94–113.

Bulger, William M. 1996. *While the Music Lasts: My Life in Politics.* Boston: Houghton Mifflin.

Bunce, Victoria Craig. 1998. The Basics of Medical Savings Accounts. *Association Management* 50:85–90.

————. 2000. Snapshot: What Are Medical Savings Accounts? *CAHI Policy Brief* 4:1–7.

————. 2001. *Medical Savings Accounts: Problems and Progress under HIPAA.* Washington, DC: Cato Institute.

Carter, Larry E., and James T. LaPlant. 1997. Diffusion of Health Care Policy Innovation in the United States. *State and Local Government Review* 29:17–26.

Cauchi, Richard. 1999. Making Medicines Affordable: A Number of States Have for Years Helped Older Americans Buy Needed Prescription Drugs. *State Legislatures* 25:10–11.

————. 2000. New England Tackles High Drug Prices. *State Legislatures* 26:9.

Center for Social Development. 2001. *IDA Policy in the States.* St. Louis: Center for Social Development.

Clark, Jill. 1985. Policy Diffusion and Program Scope: Research Directions. *Publius* 15:61–70.

Clark, Jill, and J. Lawrence French. 1984. Innovation and Program Content in State Tax Policies. *State and Local Government Review* 16:11–16.

Clark, Jill, and Thomas H. Little. 2002a. National Organizations as Sources of Information for State Legislative Leaders. *State and Local Government Review* 34:38–44.

————. 2002b. Party Change and Policy Reform: Welfare Programs in the American States. *American Review of Politics* 23:379–96.

Clemens, Elisabeth S. 1998. *The People's Lobby: Organizational Innovation and the Rise of Interest Group Politics in the United States, 1890–1925.* Chicago: University of Chicago Press.

Clucas, Richard A. 2001. Principal-Agent Theory and the Power of State House Speakers. *Legislative Studies Quarterly* 26:319–38.

Commonwealth of Virginia. 1995. *Virginia Independence Program.* Richmond: Virginia Department of Social Services.

Conlan, Timothy. 1998. *From New Federalism to Devolution: Twenty-Five Years of Intergovernmental Reform.* Washington, DC: Brookings Institution.

Converse, Phillip E. 1990. Popular Representation and the Distribution of Information. In *Information and Democratic Processes,* ed. John A. Ferejohn and James H. Kuklinski. Urbana: University of Illinois Press.

Cook, Fay Lomax, Tom R. Tyler, Edward G. Goetz, Margaret T. Gordon, David Protess, Donna R. Leff, and Harvey Moltoch. 1983. Media and Agenda Setting: Effects on the Public, Interest Group Leaders, Policy Makers, and Policy. *Public Opinion Quarterly* 47:16–35.

Corbett, Thomas. 1991. The Wisconsin Welfare Magnet Debate: What Is an Ordinary Member of the Tribe to Do When the Witch Doctors Disagree? *Focus* 13:19–28.

Council of State Governments. 1950. *The Book of the States, 1950–1951.* Chicago: Council of State Governments.

———. 1996. *Survey on State Welfare Reform Activities.* Lexington, KY: Council of State Governments.

Cox, Gary W., and Mathew D. McCubbins. 1993. *Legislative Leviathan: Party Government in the House.* Berkeley: University of California Press.

Crain, Robert L. 1966. Fluoridation: The Diffusion of an Innovation among Cities. *Social Forces* 44:467–76.

Crouse, Gil. 1999. *State Implementation of Major Changes to Welfare Policies, 1992–1998.* Washington, DC: U.S. Department of Health and Human Services.

Daley, Dorothy M., and James C. Garand. 2005. Horizontal Diffusion, Vertical Diffusion, and Internal Pressure in State Environmental Policymaking, 1989–1998. *American Politics Research* 33:615–44.

Derthick, Martha. 1979. *Policymaking for Social Security.* Washington, DC: Brookings Institution.

DiMaggio, Paul J., and Walter G. Powell. 1983. The Iron Cage Revisited: Institutional Isomorphism and Collective Rationality in Organizational Fields. *American Sociological Review* 48:147–60.

Dye, Thomas R. 1966. *Politics, Economics, and the Public: Policy Outcomes in the American States.* Chicago: Rand McNally.

Elliot, Barbara A. 1993. State "Laboratories" Test Health Reform Solutions. *Minnesota Medicine* 76:14–21.

Erikson, Robert, Gerald C. Wright, and John P. McIver. 1993. *Statehouse Democracy: Public Opinion and Policy in the States.* Cambridge: Cambridge University Press.

Esping-Andersen, Gosta. 1990. *The Three Worlds of Welfare Capitalism.* Princeton: Princeton University Press.

Eyestone, Robert. 1977. Confusion, Diffusion, and Innovation. *American Political Science Review* 71:441–47.

Fellowes, Matthew C., and Gretchen Rowe. 2004. Politics and the New American Welfare States. *American Journal of Political Science* 48:362–73.

Ferguson, Margaret Robertson. 2003. Chief Executive Success in the Legislative Arena. *State Politics and Policy Quarterly* 3:158–82.

Ferrara, Peter J. 1994. *Power to the People: Positive Alternatives to the Oregon Health Plan.* Portland, OR: Cascade Policy Institute.

———. 1995. *More than a Theory: Medical Savings Accounts at Work.* Washington, DC: Cato Institute.

Figlio, David N., Van W. Koplin, and William E. Reid. 2000. Do States Play Welfare Games? *Journal of Urban Economics* 66:505–25.

Foster, John L. 1978. Regionalism and Innovation in the American States. *Journal of Politics* 40:179–87.

Gais, Thomas, and R. Kent Weaver. 2002. *State Policy Choices under Welfare Reform.* Washington, DC: Brookings Institution.

Gates, Vickie. 1994. *Medical Savings Accounts.* Salem, OR: Office of Health Policy, Department of Human Resources.

George, Alexander L., and Andrew Bennett. 2005. *Case Studies and Theory Development in the Social Sciences.* Cambridge, MA: MIT Press.

Gladwell, Malcolm. 2002. *The Tipping Point: How Little Things Can Make a Big Difference.* Boston: Little, Brown.

Glick, Henry R. 1992. *The Right to Die: Policy Innovation and Its Consequences.* New York: Columbia University Press.

Glick, Henry R., and Scott P. Hays. 1991. Innovation and Reinvention in State Policymaking: Theory and the Evolution of Living-Will Laws. *Journal of Politics* 53:835–50.

Glickman, Lillian. 2002. *Report on Prescription Advantage's First Nine Months of Operation.* Boston: Executive Office of Elder Affairs.

Goodman, John C., and Gerald L. Musgrave. 1992. *Patient Power: Solving America's Health Care Crisis.* Washington, DC: Cato Institute.

Grattet, Ryken, Valerie Jenness, and Theodore R. Curry. 1998. The Homogenization and Differentiation of Hate Crime Law in the United States,

1978–1995: Innovation and Diffusion in the Criminalization of Bigotry. *American Sociological Review* 63:286–307.

Gray, Virginia. 1973. Innovation in the States: A Diffusion Study. *American Political Science Review* 67:1174–85.

———. 1994. Competition, Emulation, and Policy Innovation. In *New Perspectives on American Politics,* ed. Lawrence C. Dodd and Calvin Jillson. Washington, DC: CQ Press.

———. 1999. The Socioeconomic and Political Context of States. In *Politics in the States: A Comparative Analysis,* ed. Virginia Gray, Russell L. Hanson, and Herbert Jacob. 7th ed. Washington, DC: CQ Press.

Gray, Virginia, and David Lowery. 2001a. The Expression of Density Dependence in State Communities of Organized Interests. *American Politics Research* 29:374–91.

———. 2001b. The Institutionalization of State Communities of Organized Interests. *Political Research Quarterly* 54:265–84.

Greenberg, Mark. 1996. *Racing to the Bottom? Recent State Welfare Initiatives Present Cause for Concern.* Washington, DC: Center for Law and Social Policy.

Greenberg, Mark, Steve Savner, and Rebecca Swartz. 1996. *Limits on Limits: State and Federal Policies on Welfare Term Limits.* Washington, DC: Center for Law and Social Policy.

Greve, Michael S. 2001. Laboratories of Democracy: Anatomy of a Metaphor. *Federalist Outlook* (American Enterprise Institute) 6, AEI Online (Washington), http://www.aei.org/publications/pubID.12743/pub_detail.asp (accessed October 17, 2001).

Gross, David, and Sharon Bee. 1999. *State Pharmacy Assistance Programs.* Washington, DC: AARP Public Policy Institute.

Grossback, Lawrence J., Sean Nicholson-Crotty, and David A. M. Peterson. 2004. Ideology and Learning in Policy Diffusion. *American Politics Research* 32:521–45.

Grossman, Brian, and Robert G. Friedman. 1997. *Building Assets and Economic Independence through Individual Development Accounts.* Washington, DC: National Governors Association.

Haider-Markel, Donald P. 2001. Policy Diffusion as a Geographical Expansion of the Scope of Political Conflict: Same-Sex Marriage Bans in the 1990s. *State Politics and Policy Quarterly* 1:5–26.

Hall, Peter A. 2003. Aligning Ontology and Methodology in Comparative Research. In *Comparative Historical Analysis in the Social Sciences,* ed. James Mahoney and Dietrich Rueschemeyer. Cambridge: Cambridge University Press.

Hamm, Keith E., and Gary F. Moncrief. 1999. Legislative Politics in the States.

In *Politics in the States: A Comparative Analysis,* ed. Virginia Gray, Russell L. Hanson, and Herbert Jacob. 7th ed. Washington, DC: CQ Press.

―――. 2004. Legislative Politics in the States. In *Politics in the American States,* ed. Virginia Gray and Russell L. Hanson. 8th ed. Washington, DC: CQ Press.

Hays, Scott P. 1996. Influences on Reinvention during the Diffusion of Innovations. *Political Research Quarterly* 49:631–50.

Hays, Scott P., and Henry R. Glick. 1997. The Role of Agenda Setting in Policy Innovation: An Event History Analysis of Living-Will Laws. *American Politics Quarterly* 25:497–516.

Herstek, Jacob. 1998. *Finance: Medical Savings Accounts.* Denver: Health Policy Tracking Service.

Himelfarb, Richard. 1995. *Catastrophic Politics: The Rise and Fall of the Medicare Catastrophic Coverage Act of 1988.* University Park: Pennsylvania State University Press.

Hird, John A. 2005. *Power, Knowledge, and Politics: Policy Analysis in the States.* Washington, DC: Georgetown University Press.

Holahan, John, and Len Nichols. 1996. State Health Policy in the 1990s. In *Health Policy, Federalism, and the American States,* ed. Robert F. Rich and William D. White. Washington, DC: Urban Institute.

Holbrook, Thomas, and Emily Van Dunk. 1993. Electoral Competition in the American States. *American Political Science Review* 87:955–62.

Howard, Christopher. 1997. *The Hidden Welfare State: Tax Expenditures and Social Policy in the United States.* Princeton: Princeton University Press.

Ito, Shuichiro. 2001. Shaping Policy Diffusion: Event History Analyses of Regional Laws in Japanese Prefectures. *Japanese Journal of Political Science* 2:211–35.

Jacob, Herbert. 1988. *Silent Revolution: The Transformation of Divorce Law in the United States.* Chicago: University of Chicago Press.

Jewell, Malcolm. 1982. The Neglected World of State Politics. *Journal of Politics* 44:638–57.

Johnson, Haynes, and David S. Broder. 1996. *The System: The American Way of Politics at the Breaking Point.* Boston: Little, Brown.

Joint Commission on Health Care. 2002. *Virginia's Medical Savings Account Program Study.* Richmond: Joint Commission on Health Care.

Jones, Bradford S., and Regina P. Branton. 2005. Beyond Logit and Probit: Cox Duration Models of Single, Repeating, and Competing Events for State Policy Adoption. *State Politics and Policy Quarterly* 5:420–43.

Jones, Trevor, and Tim Newburn. 2002. Learning from Uncle Sam? Exploring U.S. Influence on British Crime Control Policy. *Governance* 15:97–119.

Jones-Correa, Michael. 2000–2001. The Origins and Diffusion of Racial Restrictive Covenants. *Political Science Quarterly* 115:541–68.

Kaye, Neva. 2002. *Affording Prescription Drugs: State Initiatives to Contain Costs and Improve Access.* Portland, ME: National Academy for State Health Policy.

Kemkovich, Linda. 2000. Northeastern States Seek Cure for a Common Ill: Prescription Drug Costs. *State Health Notes* 21:9.

King, Gary, Michael Tomz, and Jason Wittenberg. 2000. Making the Most of Statistical Analyses: Improving Interpretation and Presentation. *American Journal of Political Science* 44:347–61.

King, James D. 2000. Changes in Professionalism in U.S. State Legislatures. *Legislative Studies Quarterly* 25:327–43.

Kingdon, John W. 1995. *Agendas, Alternatives, and Public Policies.* 2d ed. New York: HarperCollins College.

Klingman, David, and William M. Lammers. 1984. The "General Policy Liberalism Factor" in American State Politics. *American Journal of Political Science* 28:598–610.

Kollman, Ken. 1998. *Outside Lobbying: Public Opinion and Interest Group Strategies.* Princeton: Princeton University Press.

Kollman, Ken, John H. Miller, and Scott E. Page. 2000. Decentralization and the Search for Policy Solutions. *Journal of Law, Economics, and Organization* 16:102–28.

Kopstein, Jeffrey S., and David A. Reilly. 2000. Geographic Diffusion and the Transformation of the Postcommunist World. *World Politics* 53:1–37.

Kousser, Thad. 2005. *Term Limits and the Dismantling of Legislative Professionalism.* Cambridge: Cambridge University Press.

Kuklinski, James H., Paul J. Quirk, David W. Schweider, and Robert F. Rich. 1998. Just the Facts, Ma'am: Political Facts and Public Opinion. *Annals of the American Academy of Political and Social Science* 560:143–54.

Lasswell, Harold D. 1936. *Politics: Who Gets What, When, How.* New York: McGraw-Hill.

Leichter, Howard M. 1997. The States and Health Care Policy: Taking the Lead. In *Health Policy Reform in America: Innovations from the States,* ed. Howard M. Leichter. Armonk, NY: M. E. Sharpe.

Levitt, Barbara, and James G. March. 1988. Organizational Learning. *Annual Review of Sociology* 14:319–40.

Light, Alfred R. 1978. Intergovernmental Sources of Innovation in State Administration. *American Politics Quarterly* 6:147–66.

Lindblom, Charles E. 1959. The Science of "Muddling Through." *Public Administration Review* 19:79–88.

Lindblom, Charles E., and David K. Cohen. 1979. *Usable Knowledge: Social Science and Social Problem Solving.* New Haven: Yale University Press.

Martin, Isaac. 2001. Dawn of the Living Wage: The Diffusion of a Redistributive Municipal Policy. *Urban Affairs Review* 36:470–96.

Matthews, Merrill, Jr. 1996. *Medical Savings Account Legislation: The Good, the Bad, and the Ugly*. Dallas: National Center for Policy Analysis.

Mayhew, David R. 1974. *Congress: The Electoral Connection*. New Haven: Yale University Press.

———. 1991. *Divided We Govern: Party Control, Lawmaking, and Investigations, 1946–1990*. New Haven: Yale University Press.

McAdam, Doug, Sidney Tarrow, and Charles Tilly. 2001. *Dynamics of Contention*. Cambridge: Cambridge University Press.

McDonaugh, John E. 2000. *Experiencing Politics: A Legislator's Stories of Government and Health Care*. Berkeley: University of California Press.

McNeal, Ramona, Caroline J. Tolbert, Karen Mossberger, and Lisa J. Dotterweich. 2003. Innovating in Digital Government in the American States. *Social Science Quarterly* 84:52–70.

McVoy, Edgar C. 1940. Patterns of Diffusion in the United States. *American Sociological Review* 5:219–27.

Menzel, Donald C., and Irwin Feller. 1977. Leadership and Interaction Patterns in the Diffusion of Innovations among the American States. *Western Political Quarterly* 30:528–36.

Meyer, John W., and Brian Rowan. 1977. Institutionalized Organizations: Formal Structure as Myth and Ceremony. *American Journal of Sociology* 83:340–63.

Michaux, Melissa Buis. 2002. Taking States Seriously: Welfare Reform Implementation in Massachusetts and Oregon. PhD diss., Brandeis University.

Miller, Edward Alan. 2004. Advancing Comparative State Policy Research: Toward Conceptual Integration and Methodological Expansion. *State and Local Government Review* 36:35–58.

Milne, Patti, and Jim Seagraves. 1996. *Improving Oregon's Medicaid Program: Why Not Try Means-Tested and Risk-Adjusted Vouchers?* Portland, OR: Cascade Policy Institute.

Mintrom, Michael. 1997. Policy Entrepreneurs and the Diffusion of Innovations. *American Journal of Political Science* 41:738–70.

———. 2000. *Policy Entrepreneurs and School Choice*. Washington, DC: Georgetown University Press.

Mintrom, Michael, and Susan Vergari. 1997. Charter Schools as a State Policy Innovation: Assessing Recent Developments. *State and Local Government Review* 29:43–49.

———. 1998. Policy Networks and Innovation Diffusion: The Case of State Education Reforms. *Journal of Politics* 60:126–48.

Mittler, Brant, and Merrill Matthews Jr. 1995. *Can Managed Care Solve the Medicaid Crisis?* Dallas: National Center for Policy Analysis.

Moncrief, Gary F., and Joel A. Thompson. 2001. On the Outside Looking In: Lobbyists' Perspectives on the Effects of State Legislative Term Limits. *State Politics and Policy Quarterly* 1:394–411.

Moncrief, Gary F., Joel A. Thompson, Michael Haddon, and Robert Hoyer. 1992. For Whom the Bell Tolls: Term Limits and State Legislatures. *Legislative Studies Quarterly* 17:37–47.

Moon, Marilyn, Len M. Nichols, and Susan Wall. 1996. *Medical Savings Accounts: A Policy Analysis.* Washington, DC: Urban Institute.

Mooney, Christopher Z. 1991. Information Sources in Legislative Decision Making. *Legislative Studies Quarterly* 16:445–55.

———. 2001a. Modeling Regional Effects on State Policy Diffusion. *Political Research Quarterly* 54:103–24.

———. 2001b. *The Public Clash of Private Values: The Politics of Morality Policy.* New York: Chatham House.

———. 2001c. *State Politics and Policy Quarterly* and the Study of State Politics: The Editor's Introduction. *State Politics and Policy Quarterly* 1:1–4.

Mooney, Christopher Z., and Mei-Hsien Lee. 1995. Legislative Morality in the American States: The Case of Pre-*Roe* Abortion Reform. *American Journal of Political Science* 39:599–617.

———. 1999. Morality Policy Reinvention: State Death Penalties. *Annals of the American Academy of Political and Social Science* 566:80–92.

Morgan Quitno Corporation. 1998. *Health Care State Rankings.* 6th ed. Lawrence, KS: Morgan Quitno Corporation.

Morone, James. 2000. Introduction to *The New Politics of State Health Policy,* ed. Robert B. Hackey and David A. Rochefort. Lawrence: University of Kansas Press.

Mossberger, Karen. 2000. *The Politics of Ideas and the Spread of Enterprise Zones.* Washington, DC: Georgetown University Press.

Muller, Keith J. 1985. Explaining Variation and Change in Gubernatorial Powers, 1960–1982. *Western Political Quarterly* 38:424–31.

Mutz, Diana C., and Joe Soss. 1997. Reading Public Opinion: The Influence of News Coverage on Perceptions of Public Sentiment. *Public Opinion Quarterly* 61:431–51.

Nathan, Richard P. 2000. *Social Science in Government: The Role of Policy Researchers.* Albany, NY: Rockefeller Institute Press.

National Center for Policy Analysis. 1994. *Medical Savings Accounts: The Private Sector Already Has Them.* Dallas: National Center for Policy Analysis.

———. 2004. *A Brief History of Health Savings Accounts.* Dallas: National Center for Policy Analysis.

National Governors Association. 1997. *Summary of Selected Elements of State Plans for Temporary Assistance for Needy Families*. Washington, DC: National Governors Association.

———. 1999. *Round Two Summary of Selected Elements of State Programs for Temporary Assistance for Needy Families*. Washington, DC: National Governors Association.

Nelson, Barbara J. 1984. *Making an Issue of Child Abuse: Political Agenda Setting for Social Problems*. Chicago: University of Chicago Press.

Nice, David C. 1994. *Policy Innovation in State Government*. Ames: Iowa State University Press.

Nichols, Len M., and Linda J. Blumberg. 1998. A Different Kind of "New Federalism"? The Health Insurance Portability and Accountability Act of 1996. *Health Affairs* 17:25–42.

Nownes, Anthony J., and Patricia Freeman. 1998. Interest Group Activity in the States. *Journal of Politics* 60:86–112.

Odom, Michelle. 1996. The Ohio, North Carolina, and Texas Welfare Waivers. *W-Memo* (American Public Welfare Association) 8:3–6.

Oregon Family Support Council. 1994. *Review of Family Support in Oregon*. Salem: Oregon Family Support Council.

Oregon Society of Certified Public Accountants. 1997. *An Analysis of Changes Resulting from the: Personal Responsibility and Work Opportunity Reconciliation Act, Health Insurance Portability and Accountability Act, and Small Business Job Protection Act*. Beaverton: Oregon Society of Certified Public Accountants.

Oregon Welfare Reform Work Group. 1995. *An Investment Opportunity: Redesigning Oregon's Public Assistance System to Reduce Poverty by Placing More Oregonians in Jobs*. Salem: Oregon Welfare Reform Work Group.

Osborne, David. 1990. *Laboratories of Democracy*. Boston: Harvard Business School Press.

Pavalko, Eliza K. 1989. State Timing of Policy Adoption: Workmen's Compensation in the United States, 1909–1929. *American Journal of Sociology* 95:592–615.

Peterson, Paul E., and Mark C. Rom. 1990. *Welfare Magnets: A New Case for a National Standard*. Washington, DC: Brookings Institution.

Pierson, Paul. 1994. *Dismantling the Welfare State? Reagan, Thatcher, and the Politics of Retrenchment*. Cambridge: Cambridge University Press.

———. 1996. The New Politics of the Welfare State. *World Politics* 48:143–79.

———. 2004. *Politics in Time: History, Institutions, and Social Analysis*. Princeton: Princeton University Press.

Polsby, Nelson W. 1984. *Political Innovation: The Politics of Policy Initiation*. New Haven: Yale University Press.

Przeworski, Adam, and Henry Teune. 1970. *The Logic of Comparative Social Inquiry*. New York: Wiley-Interscience.

Putnam, Robert D. 2000. *Bowling Alone: The Collapse and Revival of American Community*. New York: Simon and Schuster.

Quadagno, Jill. 1994. *The Color of Welfare: How Racism Undermined the War on Poverty*. New York: Oxford University Press.

Rice, Ronald E., and Everett M. Rogers. 1980. Reinvention in the Innovation Process. *Knowledge* 1:499–514.

Rist, Carl. 2002. Self-Sufficiency through Individual Development Accounts (IDAs): What's the Role for State Policy? *Housing Facts and Findings* 4, available at http://www.fanniemaefoundation.org/programs/hff/v4:1-ida.shtml (accessed January 24, 2005).

Roberts, Sandra. 1997. Block Grant Hearing: Welfare Reform Takes Center Stage. *Intergovernmental Issues* 18:1, 6–8.

Rodgers, Daniel T. 1998. *Atlantic Crossings: Social Politics in a Progressive Age*. Cambridge, MA: Harvard University Press.

Rogers, Everett. 1995. *Diffusion of Innovations*. 4th ed. New York: Free Press.

Roh, Jongho, and Donald P. Haider-Markel. 2003. All Politics Is Not Local: National Forces in State Abortion Initiatives. *Social Science Quarterly* 84:15–31.

Rom, Mark Carl. 2004. Transforming State Health and Welfare Programs. In *Politics in the American States,* ed. Virginia Gray and Russell L. Hanson. 8th ed. Washington, DC: CQ Press.

Rom, Mark Carl, Paul E. Peterson, and Kenneth F. Scheve Jr. 1998. Interstate Competition and Welfare Policy. *Publius* 28:17–38.

Rose, Richard. 1993. *Lesson-Drawing in Public Policy: A Guide to Learning across Time and Space*. Chatham, NJ: Chatham House.

Rosenthal, Alan. 1990. *Governors and Legislators: Contending Powers*. Washington, DC: CQ Press.

———. 1993. *The Third House: Lobbyists and Lobbying in the States*. Washington, DC: CQ Press.

Ryan, Bryce, and Neal C. Gross. 1943. The Diffusion of Hybrid Seed Corn in Two Iowa Communities. *Rural Sociology* 8:15–24.

Sabatier, Paul, and David Whiteman. 1985. Legislative Decision Making and Substantive Policy Information: Models of Information Flow. *Legislative Studies Quarterly* 10:395–421.

Saint-Germain, Michelle A. 1989. Does Their Difference Make a Difference? The Impact of Women on Public Policy in the Arizona Legislature. *Social Science Quarterly* 70:956–68.

Sapat, Alka. 2004. Devolution and Innovation: The Adoption of State Environmental Policy Innovations by Administrative Agencies. *Public Administration Review* 64:141–51.

Savage, Robert L. 1985. Diffusion Research Traditions and the Spread of Policy Innovation in a Federal System. *Publius* 15:1–27.

Scandlen, Greg. 1998a. Congress Should Lift Restrictions on MSAs. *Human Events* 54:20.

———. 1998b. *Medical Savings Accounts: Obstacles to Their Growth and Ways to Improve Them.* Dallas: National Center for Policy Analysis.

Schickler, Eric. 2001. *Disjointed Pluralism: Institutional Innovation and the Development of the U.S. Congress.* Princeton: Princeton University Press.

Shaw, Greg M. 2000. The Role of Public Input in State Welfare Policymaking. *Policy Studies Journal* 28:707–20.

Sherraden, Michael. 1990. *Stakeholding: A New Direction in Social Policy.* Washington, DC: Progressive Policy Institute.

———. 1991. *Assets and the Poor: A New American Welfare Policy.* New York: M. E. Sharpe.

Skocpol, Theda. 1988. The Limits of the New Deal System and the Roots of Contemporary Welfare Dilemmas. In *The Politics of Social Policy in the United States,* ed. Margaret Weir, Ann Shola Orloff, and Theda Skocpol. Princeton: Princeton University Press.

———. 1992. *Protecting Soldiers and Mothers: The Political Origins of Social Policy in the United States.* Cambridge, MA: Harvard University Press.

———. 1995. "Brother, Can You Spare a Job?" Work and Welfare in the United States. In *Social Policy in the United States: Future Possibilities in Historical Perspective,* ed. Theda Skocpol. Princeton: Princeton University Press.

———. 1997. *Boomerang: Health Care Reform and the Turn against Government.* New York: W. W. Norton.

———. 1999. Advocates without Members: The Recent Transformation of American Civic Life. In *Civic Engagement in American Democracy,* ed. Theda Skocpol and Morris P. Fiorina. Washington, DC: Brookings Institution.

Soss, Joe, Sanford F. Schram, Thomas P. Vartanian, and Erin O'Brien. 2001. Setting the Terms of Relief: Explaining State Policy Choices in the Devolution Revolution. *American Journal of Political Science* 45:378–95.

Squire, Peverill. 1992. Legislative Professionalization and Membership Diversity in State Legislatures. *Legislative Studies Quarterly* 17:69–79.

Stark, Shelley, and Jodie Levin-Epstein. 1999. *Excluded Children: Family Cap in a New Era.* Washington, DC: Center for Law and Social Policy.

State Policy Demonstration Project. 1999. *Family Cap: Exemptions.* Washington, DC: Center for Law and Social Policy and Center for Budget and Policy Priorities.

Stone, Deborah. 1997a. *Policy Paradox: The Art of Political Decision Making.* New York: W. W. Norton.

―――. 1997b. State Innovation in Health Care Policy. In *Innovation in American Government: Challenges, Opportunities, and Dilemmas,* ed. Alan A. Altshuler and Robert D. Behn. Washington, DC: Brookings Institution.

Stone, Diane. 2000. Non-Governmental Policy Transfer: The Strategies of Independent Policy Institutes. *Governance* 13:45–70.

Stonecash, Jeffrey M. 1996. The State Politics Literature: Moving beyond Covariation and Pursuing Politics. *Polity* 28:559–79.

Strang, David, and Sarah A. Soule. 1998. Diffusion in Organizations and Social Movements: From Hybrid Corn to Poison Pills. *Annual Review of Sociology* 24:265–90.

Stream, Christopher. 1999. Health Reform in the States: A Model of Small Group Health Insurance Market Reforms. *Political Research Quarterly* 52: 499–525.

Stuart, Elaine. 1997. *Oregon Option: Welfare Reform.* Lexington, KY: Council of State Governments.

Thomas, Sue, and Susan Welch. 1991. The Impact of Gender on Activities and Priorities of State Legislators. *Western Political Quarterly* 44:445–56.

Tversky, Amos, and Daniel Kahneman. 1982. Availability: A Heuristic for Judging Frequency and Probability. In *Judgment under Uncertainty: Heuristics and Biases,* ed. Daniel Kahneman, Paul Slovic, and Amos Tversky. Cambridge: Cambridge University Press.

―――. 2004. Judgment under Uncertainty: Heuristics and Biases. In *Preference, Belief, and Similarity: Selected Writings,* ed. Amos Tversky. Cambridge, MA: MIT Press.

Tweedie, Jack. 1994. Resources rather than Needs: A State-Centered Model of Welfare Policymaking. *American Journal of Political Science* 38:651–72.

U.S. Census Bureau. 2001. *Census 2000 Summary File.* Washington, DC. U.S. Department of Commerce, Economics and Statistics Administration, U.S. Census Bureau.

U.S. Department of Health and Human Services. 1996. *State Welfare Demonstrations.* Washington, DC: U.S. Department of Health and Human Services.

―――. 1997. *Setting the Baseline: A Report on State Welfare Waivers.* Washington, DC: U.S. Department of Health and Human Services.

Volden, Craig. 2006. States as Policy Laboratories: Emulating Success in the Children's Health Insurance Program. *American Journal of Political Science* 50:294–312.

Walker, Jack L., Jr. 1969. The Diffusion of Innovations among the American States. *American Political Science Review* 63:880–99.

Waltman, Jerold L. 1980. *Copying Other Nations' Policies: Two American Case Studies*. Cambridge, MA: Schenkman.

Weaver, R. Kent. 2000. *Ending Welfare As We Know It*. Washington, DC: Brookings Institution.

Weissert, Carol S. 1983. The National Governors Association: 1908–1983. *State Government* 56:44–52.

Welch, Susan, and Kay Thompson. 1980. The Impact of Federal Incentives on State Policy Innovation. *American Political Science Review* 24:715–29.

Wellman, Barry, ed. 1999. *Networks in the Global Village: Life in Contemporary Communities*. Boulder, CO: Westview.

Weyland, Kurt. 2004. Theories of Policy Diffusion: An Assessment. Photocopy, Department of Government, University of Texas at Austin.

———. 2005. Theories of Policy Diffusion: Lessons from Latin American Pension Reform. *World Politics* 57:262–95.

Wicks, Elliot K., and Jack A. Meyer. 1998. *The Role of Medical Savings Accounts in Health System Reform*. Washington, DC: Economic and Social Research Institute.

Winston, Pamela. 2002. *Welfare Policymaking in the States: The Devil in Devolution*. Washington, DC: Georgetown University Press.

Winter, James P., and Chaim H. Eyal. 1981. Agenda Setting for the Civil Rights Issue. *Public Opinion Quarterly* 45:376–83.

Wolak, Jennifer, Adam J. Newmark, Todd McNoldy, David Lowery, and Virginia Gray. 2002. Much of Politics Is Still Local: Multi-State Lobbying in State Interest Communities. *Legislative Studies Quarterly* 27:527–55.

Wright, Gerald C., Robert S. Erikson, and John P. McIver. 1985. Measuring State Partisanship and Ideology with Survey Data. *Journal of Politics* 47:469–89.

Yamaguchi, Kazuo. 1991. *Event History Analysis*. Newbury Park, CA: Sage.

Yin, Robert K. 1989. *Case Study Research: Design and Methods*. Newbury Park, CA: Sage.

Index